TEACH BOLDLY!

Studies in the
Postmodern Theory of Education

Joe L. Kincheloe and Shirley R. Steinberg
General Editors

Vol. 356

PETER LANG
New York • Washington, D.C./Baltimore • Bern
Frankfurt am Main • Berlin • Brussels • Vienna • Oxford

TEACH BOLDLY!

Letters to Teachers about Contemporary Issues in Education

EDITED BY **Mary Cain Fehr and Dennis Earl Fehr**

PETER LANG
New York • Washington, D.C./Baltimore • Bern
Frankfurt am Main • Berlin • Brussels • Vienna • Oxford

Library of Congress Cataloging-in-Publication Data

Teach boldly!: letters to teachers about contemporary issues in education /
edited by Mary Cain Fehr, Dennis Earl Fehr.
p. cm. — (Counterpoints, studies in the postmodern theory of education; v. 356)
Includes bibliographical references and index.
1. Creative teaching. 2. Critical pedagogy.
I. Fehr, Dennis Earl. II. Title.
LB1025.3.F44 2010   371.102—dc22   2009026101
ISBN 978-1-4331-0492-3 (hardcover)
ISBN 978-1-4331-0491-6 (paperback)
ISSN 1058-1634

Bibliographic information published by **Die Deutsche Nationalbibliothek**.
Die Deutsche Nationalbibliothek lists this publication in the "Deutsche
Nationalbibliografie"; detailed bibliographic data is available
on the Internet at http://dnb.d-nb.de/.

The paper in this book meets the guidelines for permanence and durability
of the Committee on Production Guidelines for Book Longevity
of the Council of Library Resources.

We lovingly dedicate this book to the memory of
our friend and colleague,
Joe Kincheloe,
a compassionate spirit who taught boldly,

and

to those we hope will ultimately benefit from the information it contains:
children in public schools, including our grandchildren
Jadon, Donovan, Zane, Calvin, Kason, and Olivia
(and those yet to be born) and to the generation that precedes them,
our children Shenoa, Shannon, Amanda, Katie, Lauren, and Austin

Contents

Foreword

Teaching ranks among the most rewarding of jobs, but that doesn't mean it's easy. We are expected to produce students who demonstrate creativity, critical thought, moral character, and world-class knowledge and skills for a new century's job market. And we are to accomplish this while coping with high-stakes testing, scripted curricula, corruption, and school systems that don't understand or honor their students. No wonder new teachers leave the profession. So, woe are we? No. There is much to suggest hope.

On a flight from Madrid to Miami, the two of us talked shop, as professors who are married to each other will do. Dennis had just finished teaching two courses in Seville, and Mary had gone along to experience Spanish culture while working on her writing in our charming faculty apartment. On the flight we discussed education's ills, but we also discussed the wealth of wisdom possessed by people we know. The idea occurred to us to ask some of these people to write letters to teachers and future teachers, describing how to teach with courage and inspiration, in spite of the obstacles, and in fact, *overcoming* the obstacles. We wanted them to describe how to *teach boldly!* When we got home we began contacting these people, asking each of them to write a letter as a chapter for our book.

You hold in your hands the fruition of this idea. The letters, which exceeded our already high expectations, address a range of topics and represent a variety of perspectives. Topics include social justice, assessment, critical pedagogy, censorship, racism, culturally responsive teaching, LGBTQ issues, change facilitation, school leadership, non-violence, and political activism. All of the letters will broaden your thinking and encourage you to do what is right for your students in spite of apparent obstacles. Each author has a unique message to share with you. Collectively the chapters provide a study in contemporary issues in education and a springboard for dialogue and exploration. We hope you will be inspired to hold onto your dreams as an educator and find your own way to *teach boldly!*

Sincerely,
Mary and Dennis

Acknowledgments

Contributing Authors

We wish to extend our gratitude to each contributing author. Their wisdom was our inspiration for creating this book. We feel very fortunate to count them among our colleagues and friends, and we are honored to present their insightful, inspirational letters here.

Illustrations

Dennis Earl Fehr drew the chapter illustrations. Each one represents an aspect of the chapter's content, either literally or metaphorically. Dennis explains the artistic process and the meaning of each drawing in a commentary found at the conclusion of the book. As frequently happens in our marriage and collaborative work, we "fill each other's gaps." While Dennis was busy for months creating this unique artwork, exercising the right side of his brain, Mary was exercising the left side of hers by taking care of logistical and organizational aspects of creating an edited book.

Permissions

Sheng Kuan Chung, photograph by Richard Holt of artwork by Banksy.
Reprinted with permission of the photographer. All rights reserved.

Linda Darling-Hammond, A Marshall Plan: "What It Will Really Take to Leave No Child Behind" (commentary in *Education Week*. 2007).
Reprinted with permission of the author. All rights reserved.

Angela Valenzuela, "Uncovering Internalized Oppression" from *Everyday Antiracism: Getting Real About Race in School*, edited by Mica Pollock. New York: The New Press, 2008.
Reprinted with permission of the publisher. All rights reserved.

Chapter 1

Transgressing Boundaries for Socially Just Teaching

Christine E. Sleeter

Dear Fellow Educators,

   As a student teacher in 1972, I remember hearing about a time in the "dark ages" when teachers were all expected to be on the same page of the same text, at the same time. I was aghast! How stifling that would be! But these days when I go into schools, I feel like I am in a time warp as I see teachers expected to march their students all toward the same page of the same text at the same time, regardless of students' interests. I am told that this approach guards against teaching to low expectations. I see things quite differently, however. I will show how and why by sharing stories about the power of connecting academics with real issues of concern to young people. When done well, such connection not only prompts academic growth, but also enables young people to see themselves as active agents who can appropriate academics for their own purposes.

Teaching Boldly: My Roots

Many of my childhood teachers used creative, student-centered approaches in which they embedded college-preparatory academic skills in interesting projects. I saw my task as a student teacher in the early 1970s as figuring out how to replicate that kind of inspiring, student-centered teaching in an inner-city high school, where I found that teaching meant covering the textbook. As I helped students, I could see that textbook-driven teaching bored them. So, when it came time for me to take the class, I rather spontaneously invited the students to help me organize a unit around a topic of interest to them (they chose "Women's Liberation"), then collaborate with me in planning their learning activities for that unit. Students who had previously slept through class came alive.

At the time, I did not know how to embed academic skills in such teaching, and it took me a couple of years to shed what I later realized were low academic expectations for students from low-income homes. However, through this early experience, I saw clearly the power of engaging students' questions and interests, a lesson that has guided my teaching ever since. About ten years ago, I began to document what academically strong multicultural teaching looks like in practice by following teachers who had completed my multicultural curriculum design course into the classroom. By 2001, this documentation had shifted to focus on how teachers who are committed to such teaching navigate controls over their work in standards-based and test-driven contexts (Sleeter, 2005). Below, I will describe two of the teachers I became acquainted with in California, then a project with a similar focus in Arizona.

Kathy: Teaching Boldly in First Grade

"If I refuse to take a position on something I consider to be harmful
to children, I am contributing to that harm."
(Kathy, in Sleeter, 2005, p. 111)

Kathy had been teaching for over twenty years in California when I met her. Kathy's students were all of Mexican descent, many having recently emigrated; all were from low-income homes. As a bilingual teacher, Kathy taught much of the day in Spanish so her students would have access to grade-level curriculum; she also explicitly taught students English. Kathy is White and had grown up mainly on a farm in Ohio, but had lived several years in Mexico where she became fluent in Spanish. Her current residence was near the school in which she taught. She was involved with the community her students came from, and she welcomed parents into her classroom. Like students' parents, who strongly desired that their children gain a good education in order to have a better future, Kathy's vision for students' learning was ambitious. She wanted them to become "hungry for books. I don't want them to think of reading as using the…text and workbooks. I want them to be able to apply their abilities to analyze, to question, to figure out meanings in text…to be able to draw parallels between nature and their lives, and between one book and another" (Sleeter, 2005, p. 111).

Three features of Kathy's teaching caught my attention: her use of class meetings as a tool for teaching students to work on real problems, her ability to build academic learning on students' everyday knowledge, and her interest in raising their political awareness about social issues. Class meetings regularly provided a space in which student concerns led the agenda, and students took charge of problem solving. Kathy explained, "I figure if kids learn to resolve problems at this level, they're a lot more likely to resolve them later. And I've been amazed at their problem solving abilities and their compassion" (Sleeter, 2005, p. 112). Many problems students brought to class were interpersonal, but some were political. Kathy explained that children regularly hear adults discuss political issues at home and want to know more:

> Last fall when on the ballot there was the tax to keep [the county hospital] open, one of my children brought that up in class and we talked about it…This one little girl said, "Yeah, everybody has to go vote or they're going to close the hospital, and there won't be any place left to go." We talked about that. She's heard her parents, and aunts and uncles discussing it. The war in Iraq. A year ago one of the kids brought in a picture of the soldiers from Salinas that had appeared in the paper, soldiers from Salinas that were serving in Iraq. And so we talked about it. (Sleeter, 2005, p. 113)

Class meetings served as a basis for student-centered teaching Kathy used during the rest of the day, and as a venue for getting to know her students' interests and concerns.

Kathy designed and taught an interdisciplinary thematic unit on Monterey County agriculture, which she mapped carefully against the first grade curriculum standards for reading/language arts, math, and science, and her English Language Development text. She credited her principal for giving her freedom to construct a thematic curriculum as long as it met state standards. She showed me a copy of the first grade standards on which she annotated how various portions of the unit addressed specific standards, so that she would be able to explain the relationship if called on to do so.

Kathy developed this unit because "agriculture directly affects the lives of my students. Out of my twenty students, most have at least one parent who is employed in agriculture or an agriculture-related industry such as vegetable packing. The parents' income and work schedules are determined by the crops and the large companies which grow them" (Sleeter, 2005, p. 112). She wanted the children to learn more about their parents' work, not to become agricultural workers themselves, but to respect the work their parents do. Having grown up on a farm herself, she believed that everyone should know where food comes from and situate that knowledge within a vision of environmentally sustainable farms that ordinary people can afford. She was deeply concerned about "the conflict between what agriculture has become in this country and what it can be." Increasingly, large corporations control agriculture, and thereby also dominate "land use, water use and availability, pesticide use, and economic and political power." She commented, "So many of my students' parents work in agriculture, yet so few can be farmers" (Sleeter, 2005, p. 113).

Kathy creatively connected grade-level academic skills with students' knowledge. For example, the unit addressed several math concepts in the first grade curriculum standards: numbers to 100, the concept more than/less than, units and tens, and graphing. To teach graphing, she had the class construct a bar graph representing how many parents worked with various crops. Across the bottom of the graph were the names and drawings of vegetables indicating crops in which parents worked. Students placed 3 x 3" cards above the vegetable of their parents' work site which, when arranged vertically, became bars. After the graph was made, Kathy engaged students in quantitative reasoning with questions such as: *¿Cuántas personas trabajan en la lechuga?* (How many people work in lettuce?) *¿Trabaja más gente en la casa o en un empaque?* (Do more people work at home or in packing?) As she helped students use the graph to reason numerically, focusing particularly on more than/less than, Kathy prompted students to think in terms of not just isolated numbers, but also what the numbers mean, such as how many students are in the class, and how many of their parents do what kind of work. Linking the abstract concept to what student knew already helped them "get it."

For social studies, Kathy taught critical analysis of the political context in which students' families lived and worked, and a vision anchored in memories and possibilities. Since most of the children's parents worked in agriculture, and since Kathy believed firmly that agribusiness is not the only (or best) way to construct farming systems, she wanted students to explore agricultural economic systems and worker politics. To compare large-scale corporate farms and small family farms, she invited a parent with experience working in agriculture in both the U.S. and Mexico to come and describe the nature of work in both places. Using slides she had taken in rural Mexico, Kathy had students compare the small farm system there with agribusiness students see locally. The class also studied the history and struggles of the United Farm Workers, particularly the work of local organizers, and immigration issues connected with agriculture.

To teach boldly, Kathy identified a rich theme that was significant to the lives of her students and their families, and in which subject matter content could be anchored and then carefully wove the required curriculum standards around this theme. When I asked how her students were doing on the district's tests, Kathy explained that while first graders do not participate in the mandated testing program, they were doing well on benchmark assessments. As long as they did so, Kathy's principal would continue to support her.

Christi: Teaching Boldly in High School

"Are [students] developing in their knowledge of the subject, and also their heart knowledge? Do they have insights?"
(Sleeter, 2005, p. 76).

Christi, a tall blond with blue eyes, had been teaching high school English for seven years. She grew up in a working-class, racially diverse community where she had become very interested in cultural differences. Going through school, she hung out with different groups; she commented to me that, "You could start a conversation with somebody or a friendship with somebody that just changes your whole point of view" (Sleeter, 2005, p. 52). The school in which she was teaching served the community where she grew up, as well as an adjacent affluent, White community.

What caught my attention was Christi's efforts, as a White teacher, to engage a diverse class of students in probing issues related to racism, ethnocentrism, and exclusion in the context of standards-based English. She told

me that she "couldn't tolerate the racism" she found in the White community, and was concerned about its impact on young people. Since California
is experiencing large waves of immigration, Christi cared passionately that
her students develop empathy rather than hostility toward newcomers as well
as people who are already here, commenting that her "passion is contagious"
(Sleeter, 2005, p. 146).

Christi designed and taught a unit on West Coast immigration. Its main
themes included respect for other cultures, understanding of our multicultural
region, historical perspectives of our immigrant nation, family bonds, identity and culture and the American high school experience. I see the entire
unit as a vehicle to assist students in gaining a better grasp of our immigrant
nation, to search for connection and commonalities among immigrants, and
to forge a sense of what makes cultures unique (Sleeter, 2005, p. 53).

As Kathy had done, Christi figured out how to connect the unit with the
state's English Language Arts curriculum standards, which focused largely
on reading comprehension of grade-level text, skill in writing in various gen-
res, and using English-language conventions appropriately. She was equally
interested in both developing students' writing and the substance of what
they wrote about. She explained: "I think that if you ponder and research any
book/topic/lesson long enough you can teach it from a multicultural/activist
perspective" (Sleeter, 2005, p. 51).

Her West Coast immigration unit included three major writing assignments: a narrative written from the point of view of a fictitious adolescent
immigrant, a fictitious diary the immigrant might write about four days of
school, and a poem in which the fictitious immigrant expresses feelings.
Christi had students analyze samples of writing to identify mood and tone,
point of view, and sensory detail and imagery, then practice expanding their
own use of detail words in descriptions. The unit also included a research
project in which small groups of students collaboratively wrote short research papers about West Coast immigrant groups to provide background for
the other writing assignments. As a culminating project, students created a
Web page that synthesized their work. Christi posted her entire unit on the
Internet to make it available to students. There she described its overall rationale, mapped the learning outcomes against state content standards, described the various assignments students would be doing and evaluation
rubrics for each, and posted notes for each day that included handouts,
homework, and readings.

Christi drew from her textbook to the extent that it fit the unit, but she also actively sought additional resources. She extensively used short stories and videos, such as *El Norte* (featuring Mexican and Central American immigrants) and *A Dollar a Day, Ten Cents a Dance* (featuring Filipino immigrants). When asked where she found her rich pool of resources, Christi explained that she had become very good at scavenging.

> Sometimes things just drop into my lap, and like, Wow!...I've actually been collecting over the last seven years, because, you know, I've always wanted to do something like this....So, I dedicated myself to just grabbing everything that I could, you know....I ended up with a lot of stuff, a lot of stuff! I mean, (pointing to a corner) these are just some of the huge file cabinets full of things. (Sleeter, 2005, p. 164)

I visited one day when the class was reading "On the Other Side of the War" by Elizabeth Gordon (1990), who was born in Vietnam to a Vietnamese mother and an Anglo American father, then grew up in Tennessee after the Vietnam War. Christi led a discussion about the story that focused on both the author's experiences and bi-racial identity, as well as how she constructed the narrative and used figurative language. Some of the White students were puzzled by Gordon's struggles around a bi-racial identity, asking questions such as why schools have students check a box indicating race. This discussion was followed by a clip from the film *Lakota Woman* that focused on Mary Crow Dog's experiences in a mission school, particularly the school's efforts to strip Indian youth of their identities, and various ways the youth resisted. Students rearranged their chairs so they could see clearly; they seemed very engrossed. The bell rang signaling the end of class before students were able to discuss the video that day, but later Christi commented that narrative stories, and particularly film, drew in students who were struggling with concepts like racism.

To teach boldly, Christi structured a unit around experiences of ethnically and culturally diverse adolescents, then designed various writing and discussion activities to engage students with ideas related to immigration, race, and ethnicity. She carefully connected the entire unit to the grade-level English Language Arts standards to make sure it was as academically sound as it was intellectually and emotionally engaging. Speaking about how one of the White male students reacted to the stories and videos, she remarked, "It seems like it engages them, it pulls them in, even if they don't want to be pulled in. And he doesn't want to be pulled in, and it's still, it sort of grabs him once in a while" (Sleeter, 2005, p. 77).

Critically Compassionate Intellectualism: Teaching Boldly for Social Justice

"It is in our best interest to transform the education of our people so that our blood is no longer used to grease the wheels of global capitalist greed."
(Cammarota & Romero, 2006, p. 23)

In 1996 in Tucson, Arizona, a group of concerned Mexican American citizens petitioned the district's governing board for a Mexican-American studies curriculum. Two years later, the board approved funding for it, and Tucson Unified School District (TUSD) Mexican American/Raza Studies was launched. I became acquainted with the work of the department in 2005, when I was invited to address the annual Raza Studies Summer Institute. What has continued to catch my attention about this program is its unwavering vision of education reform and its powerful impact on students.

The Mexican American/Raza Studies Department works with schools in Tucson to strengthen teaching and learning, using Chicano studies' intellectual frameworks. The Department describes its objective as creating a "truly equitable educational ecology" by offering students "academic rigor, the opportunity to develop a critical consciousness, and social and academic scaffolds to increase student success" (TUSD, 2007). The Department has developed a rich array of curriculum resources for classroom use from kindergarten through high school, which aligns with the state curriculum standards.

In 2003, a Social Justice Education Project (SJEP) was begun in one of the Raza Studies high schools, "launched as a research study investigating if and how students of color experience inequities in the educational process. It quickly evolved into an effective alternative method of teaching 'underperforming' students" (VisionMark, 2005, p. 2). Three Latino educators (a high school teacher, the director of the TUSD Mexican American/Raza Studies Department, and an assistant professor from the University of Arizona) collaborated to develop a four-semester social studies curriculum that met the state's eleventh and twelfth grade social studies standards, "adjusting the content and pedagogy in ways that facilitated the students' critical consciousness around racial inequalities affecting their educational and general life experiences" (Cammarota & Romero, 2006, pp. 17–18). The model these educators developed embodies critically conscious intellectualism, which has three components: (1) critical pedagogy in which students create rather than consume knowledge, (2) authentic caring in which educators demonstrate deep respect for students as full human beings, and (3) social justice content that directly counters racism through intellectual frameworks that connect directly with students' lived experience (Cammarota & Romero, 2006, p. 22).

The curriculum teaches racial and economic inequalities from Chicano perspectives, immersing students in advanced-level curricula in which they read college-level material and studied concepts such as "hegemony" and "social reproduction" (Cammarota, 2007). Critical to the coursework is a community-based research project in which students examine manifestations of racism in their school and community, such as racist patterns in tracking and racial bias in news reporting. Students gather data and use social science theory to analyze why these patterns exist and how they can be challenged. They give formal presentations of results of their research to the community, as well as to academic and youth conferences. Cammarota and Romero (2006) noted that, "the standard educational system treats them as empty slates ready to be carved and etched on by teachers" but this project had offered students "an opportunity to see themselves as knowledgeable Subjects" (p. 20). Students can learn to do advanced level academic work when it directly addresses realities of their lives. As Cammarota (2007) pointed out, remedial work does not engage students because it is not about changing their lives; a challenging, socially relevant curriculum like the one in this project helps students see how to use academics as a tool for changing their lives.

Four cohorts have now completed the Social Justice Education Project, and as Table 1 shows, their graduation rates exceed those of Anglo students in the site(s) where the SJEP is offered (Cammarota & Romero, 2008; Romero, 2008).

Table 1

Graduation Rates Comparison

	Students in Social Justice Education Project	Anglos in same school
2004	94%	81%
2005	96%	83%
2006	97%	82%
2007	99%	84%

Students who participated in the broader array of Mexican American/Raza Studies courses in middle school and high school demonstrate remarkable achievement gains on Arizona's high-stakes high school graduation exam. When comparing the results in reading, writing, and math, Raza Studies students outperform Anglos, African Americans, Pan Asians, Native Americans, and other Latino students who are not involved in the courses, in several cases by large margins (Romero, 2008). Many students credit the Raza Studies project with saving their lives and with showing them how to stand up and fight racism for themselves. Several have gone on to college and credit the project with motivating them to do so (Cammarota, 2007).

Teaching Boldly in Real Classrooms

In over 30 years as an educator, I do not recall meeting a student who truly does not want to learn anything. However, I have met many students who find textbook-driven teaching incredibly boring and irrelevant; when that is all they are offered, they often appear disinterested in and incapable of learning. I have also met many teachers who can think creatively about students' interests and important social issues, but have little idea how to embed demanding intellectual work in a relevant thematic curriculum. As a result, a good number of school administrators these days are highly suspicious of attempts to be "relevant" and "student-centered." Add to this the number of educators who fear opening up examination of racial, ethnic, and social class inequalities—or anything remotely political—and the result is systemic ex-clusion from academics of that which is meaningful to the lives of many young people.

Ironically, when we use student-centered rather than textbook-centered teaching, embed preparation for college in rich thematic units that have meaning to one's own students, and engage students in critically questioning society and learning to act for justice, then students from communities that had not been achieving well in school blossom in ways that show up even on standardized tests. Doesn't this make more sense than the current approach that consists of marching everyone lock-step through the same prepackaged curriculum materials?

In solidarity,

References

Cammarota, J. (2007). A social justice approach to achievement: Guiding Latina/o students toward educational attainment with a challenging, socially-relevant curriculum. *Equity & Excellence in Education, 40*, 87–96.

Cammarota, J. & Romero, A. (2006). A critically compassionate intellectualism for Latina/o students. *Multicultural Education, 14*(2), 16–23.

Cammarota, J. & Romero, A. (2008). The social justice education project: A critically com-passionate intellectualism for Chicana/o students. In W. Ayers, T. Quinn & D. Stovall (Eds.), *Handbook for Social Justice Education* (pp. 465–476). New York: Laurence Erl-baum.

Gordon, E. (1990). On the other side of the war. In Watanabe, S. and Bruchac, C., (Eds.) *Home to stay: Asian American women's fiction* (1st ed., pp. 48–51). Greenfield Center, New York: The Greenfield Review Press.

Romero, A. (2008). Towards a critical compassionate intellectualism model of transformative urban education. Unpublished doctoral dissertation. Tucson: The University of Arizona.

Sleeter, C. E. (2005). *Un-standardizing curriculum: Multicultural teaching in the standards-based classroom*. New York: Teachers College Press.

TUSD (2007). *Mexican American/Raza Studies*. Retrieved January 8, 2008, http://instech.tusd.k12.az.us/Raza/index.asp.

VisionMark (2005). Students speak out on educational inequalities. Retrieved July 28, 2005, from: http://www.visionmark.org/feature.php.

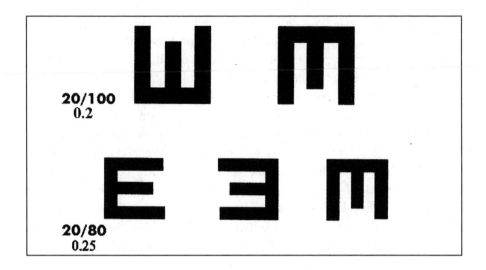

Chapter 2

Excelling Through "E"-Teaching

Mary Frances Agnello

Dear Present and Future Classroom Teachers,

I am writing you to share some of what I have learned over two decades of teaching in public schools, junior colleges, and in four major universities. My educational grounding put me in close contact with *existential* philosophy, and I truly believe that teaching is an existential exercise—we can reinvent ourselves with our students every day and every semester. *What we do determines who we are; we create ourselves through our action in existence.* Here follow some important discoveries that I have made as I did some bad, satisfactory, good, and excellent teaching over the years. As I prepare for a new fall semester, I am writing to share these insights into how I am able to sustain myself as a bold educator. From them, I hope that you will gain some ideas about how to approach your life as a teacher and learner.

Experiences in the classroom can be life changing. They were for me. Many of us can attribute important life or career decisions to teachers in our lives. I became a French major and fell in love with art because of my high school French teacher, Cile Erwin. My Italian professor at the University of Texas, Penny Marcus, was a model for my pursuit of a doctoral degree. Paulo Freire—a teacher I only knew from books—inspired me during my masters work to write my dissertation about critical literacy and teachers. Many other teachers in my background were impassioned about their work as educators. They inspired learning because they were emboldened—yes, they taught boldly. These teachers sent me in new directions, created learning environments that challenged me, and gave of themselves in ways that sent me in search of myself, of self-fulfillment beyond materialism, and of social justice. Their lasting impressions on me coupled with my affinity for things democratic, creative, and critical of injustice led me to my career choice in teacher education. As I reflect on these educators' effects on my life, I contemplate what it means to educate mightily, and I arrive at "e" words (*Experience, Existentialism, Excitement, Energy, Exploration, Environment, Ecology, Economics,* and *Ethics*) that lead me in my quest to be the best teacher I can be, to push my students toward social engagement and creative enterprise, and finally to strive for self-improvement in the ways that we view diversity and "others" around us so that we can improve our society and ultimately the world. It is through becoming and never quite arriving, as Maxine Greene described it (1988), that I strive for international awareness and action through the act of teaching boldly.

Excitement

Learning and applying learning are exciting. The parts of the curriculum that are verbs—doing, achieving, growing, developing, changing—require action. A good teacher might teach information, but a great teacher excites students to do something—to move, to research, to think, to write, to reflect, to act, to sing, to create. When I taught English IV, I found myself to be a bold teacher by moving Shakespeare's *Macbeth* from the students' desks to the stage. My creative writing students wrote and filmed their creations. As I became a better teacher, I listened as students discussed local and world events, redirected students' frustrations and energies, and engaged students in debate and dialogue, as well as activism. The doing of education must be inspired to be done well, and such inspiration usually comes from excitement created by a teacher. The drudgery of school work disappears when enthusiasm is attached to learning. The teacher is enthusiastic, students become excited, and teachers become even more exhilarated about what the students are achieving, which in turn, leads to further student success. Excitement in an educator does not have to be dramatic and overt; teachers express their excitement in different ways—through humor, illustration, modeling, and reinforcement of student talent. The excitement of learning can become an intrinsic motivation in students, but in my experience it was the excitement of teachers that attached purpose to learning, connecting it to the world in ways that propelled me from mental acuity to energized accomplishment.

Energy

Teaching boldly requires energy. The energized teacher communicates excitement about subject matter. Energizing learning takes students far from the toil of drudgery to goals of self and social achievement. When I look back on the classes of my least favorite teachers, I see that nothing energized me to achieve. A lack of energy on a teacher's part leads to lethargy in students. Lethargic teaching is not bold. To the contrary, it is moldy, dusty, and tarnished. A teacher who is energized has high expectations, inspires individuals to push themselves, works smart and hard with students, and collaborates with students in democratic classrooms. Energetic engagement in learning is contagious and empowering. Modeling democratic leadership in classrooms redistributes energy flow from the fount of the teacher's head to the many fountains in students' heads. As the energy of teaching and learning is shared, so is the power. When I have felt energized, I felt empowered. When I empower my students, they direct their enthusiasm to the doing of education—getting it done with self-fulfillment. They are empowered to achieve and excellence becomes attainable. As students gain more confidence, they know they can be successful and excellent. Empowerment of all students to be successful through teacher energy achieves the *doing* of the curriculum so that the product of curriculum inspires more energy, empowerment, and excellence. To have energy, teachers must take care of themselves—eat well, get enough rest, exercise—and balance their home/family lives with their professional lives. A teacher who is a whole person is more stable, strong, and able to exert the energy required to be a great educator.

Exploration

Exploration in teaching boldly first requires self-exploration on the part of a teacher. Maxine Greene encourages her readers to go in search of freedom.

For me, searching for freedom has entailed a long and convoluted effort to become educated about who I am; through my work in education, I have been able to work with students to explore who they are. The exploration of the self helps us to ground our work as educators. As we encourage the success of students, they need to explore many topics, issues, and disciplines. What led me to where I am in my teaching includes serious exploration of difficult topics and issues including race, class, and gender. My research and teaching in literacy and diversity through language arts and social studies has targeted inequities in our society and the world and helped me make sense of international knowledge and the need to share the ecological environment. Because it is so critical that we better educate everyone about these issues, teaching must take into consideration ecological concerns. It is the task of teachers to educate their students about the interdependence of all systems and peoples. My early explorations in culture were centered on France and Italy—language, literature, art, and film from both countries. My recent explorations of Afghanistan through Kahled Hosseini's literature and my friendships with international scholars at Texas Tech University have inspired my interest in the East. Our college is currently working to establish educational connections with Chinese institutions. Along with the Olympic games broadcast from China and our new professional contacts in that part of the world, my interest in Chinese culture is growing. Along with our students, we can expand our understanding of global citizenship through exploration of other cultures and their many relationships to our daily lives.

Also exploration of our local setting is paramount to building pride in individuals about *the place* where they reside. If we explore our local places, understanding their diverse histories, we better appreciate local culture, which enables expansion through exploration of other cultures. A bold teacher is an explorer, unafraid to take chances and able to provide safe environments in which students are motivated to be explorers without fear of failure.

My explorations in education have taught me that many students who fail do so because of economic circumstances beyond their control—therefore *class* is a topic to be studied in a democratic society. Other important lessons I have gained through my explorations have included an ability to connect the importance of what we as educators do with issues of gender and race. My students have not necessarily been happy when they understand the poorest of the poor in this country and in the world are women and children—usually women of color, but not always. Educating about the feminization of teaching and how women earn 70 cents to the dollar made by men does not make me happy, but it makes me more able to understand why I am where I am and how such factors might have influenced my students' lives.

If future educators grasp the many effects of race, class, and gender, they will want to read books by people of color, ascertaining their perspectives on the kinds of cards society and the world have dealt them. Some books that opened my eyes are the *Souls of Black Folk* by W.E.B. Dubois, *The Autobiography of Malcolm X*, and a collection of poetry by Nikki Giovanni, among other works. Willingness to explore the social context in which education occurs leads to more informed teaching. Studying the macro- as well as the microsettings of our teaching helps us to better understand the interconnections between where we are in classrooms and the larger social, political, and economic system. If we fail to explore these issues, it will be easy to be culturally *un*responsive educators. Such failure leads to blaming the students, parents, neighborhood, and often contributes to early burnout in teachers. Exploring and embracing multiple human cultures in social settings, including schools, lead to better human relations in classrooms. Applying principals of democratic classroom practices is more informed when teachers have done the homework of exploring who they are and who their students are. When this knowledge is in place, great teachers understand what they need *to become* together with their students. All of this work requires energy, enthusiasm, and exploration.

Economics, Environment, Ecology

The mission of a great teacher in today's world prepares students for life through academic life, promoting students' critical thought about serious world problems and engaging them in participatory global citizenship. In former times, it was necessary to have money to travel or study abroad to seriously learn about the world. Now, such learning can be done through technology. Although all schools are not equal because educational funding is not equal, there are usually some technological tools available in even remote rural settings. Making the most of computers, students can communicate with students around the world and work at better understanding the relationship between the environment, ecology, and economics. Students can be connected with other schools in other countries or in their own city or town. As recommended by the United Nations, they can consider water as it relates to survival, agriculture, economy, and ecology; they can begin to determine what needs to be done to provide fresh water worldwide. An article by Peter Rogers in the August 2008 issue of *Scientific American* called "Facing the Freshwater Crisis" puts into perspective the annual need of each person for roughly the amount of water required to fill two-fifths of an Olympic-size swimming pool (a thousand cubic meters) to enable drinking, hygiene, and growing food. Rogers informs us in this piece of research (which is accessible for middle to high schoolers) that the world will need to invest one trillion dollars a year on existing and new technologies to sustain life in 2030. Such knowledge is power and can be applied in all disciplines.

Great teachers work with students to calculate, to dialogue, to write about, and to apply, geographically and economically, such knowledge. Despite the pressure for teachers to teach to the test in most states, great teachers know how to teach state and testing standards by applying real world problem solving. This topic of water for instance can be explored in social studies, language arts, speech and debate, drama, science, and mathematics. Great teaching is comprised of such instruction. Student enthusiasm is nurtured when learners can make connections between what they are doing at their desks and the real world. Such economic and ecological reality makes for important global problem solving for tomorrow's leaders in cross-disciplinary teaching and learning. Great teachers instruct about social, economic, and global problems, and students want to learn about these topics. As I teach future teachers the foundations of education, secondary methods, and action research, I must teach about the interconnections among economy, ecology, and the environment. All other subjects become moot when we are not taking care of the mother ship Earth. I believe that it is considered bold by some to do such teaching, but I find it a moral and ethical obligation to do so. Future teachers should understand that it is incumbent on them to teach these "e" words for the same reasons.

Several models help us to achieve a democratic instructional framework or to teach a more just set of values. I will share two. The Parker (1991) social studies democratic framework for five essential learnings includes the democratic ideal, cultural diversity, economic development, global perspective, and participatory citizenship. In the history, geography, and civics curriculum, these five components lend perspective on the various ways that a concept in the *democratic ideal* would take into consideration *cultural diversity*, and account for *economic development* from a *global perspective* assuming *participatory citizenship*. A lesson could start with any of the five concepts and build toward prejudice reduction, equity pedagogy, and transformational teaching and learning.

Another social studies framework that might be more appropriate for the early grades, particularly for understanding local situations from which to advance toward global action, is one developed by Todd and Agnello (2006) as we studied a rural P-12 school in which themes that guide future teachers' study include people, geography, history, primary sources, and citizenship/problem solving. By starting with the available resources of rural populations, establishing connections between schools and the community, and then progressing to more international educational sharing, a topic such as water scarcity can be explored thoroughly. Connecting people to their water sources in the present and past helps explain the development in a given community's location. Other topics could be broached in a similar manner. I believe that ethical teaching includes addressing such important concepts.

Ethics

We hear about ethics, but perhaps we have not considered it in relationship to what we do as classroom teachers. Volumes have been written about ethics, and most recently several scholars in the field of education including Elizabeth Campbell and Douglas Simpson have compiled books on the subject for educators. Web sites offer codes of ethics for educators. Some of the taboos listed for teachers include fraternizing with students, sexual misconduct, and accepting bribes. It is important to read, understand, and abide by these rules. Other ethics are more grounded in moral conscience that individuals must exercise as they educate children. For example, as an English teacher, I taught my students to write and find their voice. That meant that I had a lot of papers to grade. I believe that it is unethical if we do not teach students to understand who they are and to express themselves within the existing curriculum. We must also teach our students ethics through modeling, discussion, and dialogue. Ethics must be exercised. They are not worth much if they do not exist in our behaviors toward each other.

Within the curriculum reside several aspects of ethics. What do we leave in? What do we leave out? Important concepts that could have moral and ethical ramifications include the teacher not helping students make connections to U.S. history beyond the military history presented in many textbooks. When we understand that diverse people make history and build a country, we see that the omission of facts about certain groups of people—those from many parts the world, slaves, and Indigenous people—is unethical. Also of ethical concern is where these groups of people find themselves today. Another group that gets little mention in social studies texts is women. A relatively new film called *Iron Jawed Angels* retells the real story of the women's suffrage movement in this country. When I showed it to students last summer, they were amazed that they did not understand the struggle, violence, and imprisonment that women endured to obtain the right to vote. Works by Nell Noddings explain a feminist perspective on education that helps balance the elitist male perspective that we have learned. Additionally, a book titled *Thinking through Our Mothers: Women's Philosophies of Education* by Connie Titone and Karen Maloney enlightens us about the many contributions of women in education that have gone unacknowledged. Whereas these works would not necessarily be assigned to students, teachers would benefit by utilizing them as teaching tools.

Successful teachers work ethically with their administrators. A host of films presenting ethical dilemmas can be shown, with the principal's permission, about diversity, multiculturalism, immigration, bilingual education, and other issues that are omnipresent in the U.S. It is ethical to guide students' understanding beyond what is narrowly prescribed in state education curricula. Reading books by Howard Zinn about people's history in the U.S. and James Lowen's *Lies My Teacher Told Me: Everything Your American History Textbook Got Wrong* can guide educators in helping students discover important information about who we are and how we came to where we are. Such teaching is ethical.

I will close with another ethical concern: When policies like *No Child Left Behind*, *America 2000*, and *A Nation at Risk* induce fear in teaching, it is important for educators to read and respond ethically to them. When teachers understand that such policies position them as part of a systemic educational problem rather than part of a solution, they must get tough and do the right thing for their students. Working with a strong heart and sense of purpose will go far in helping them achieve success in spite of such policies.

Enough already! And finally *enough is enough.* Sometimes less done well in the classroom is better than more done with little depth. Finding a balance in one's life as an educator also means knowing when to stop, re-fresh, re-invigorate, re-envision, and re-think. Thinking takes time. So do exercising, shopping, eating well, recreating, and other life tasks. If we are going to be effective educators, we must take care of ourselves. Knowing when to take a break and be human goes a long way toward burnout prevention. I have loved teaching in all of its different phases. I have also loved my students. If you believe you are a teacher, go forth boldly! There is no better profession.

Sincerely,

Mary Frances Agnello

References

Greene, M. (1988). *The Dialectic of Freedom*. New York: Teachers College Press.

Parker, W. C. (1991). *Renewing the social studies curriculum*. Alexandria, VA: Association for Supervision and Curriculum Development.

Rogers, P. (2008, August). Running out of water: A six-point plan to avert a global crisis. *Scientific American*, 46–53.

Todd, R. A., & Agnello, M. F. Looking at rural communities in teacher preparation: Insight into a P-12 schoolhouse, *The Social Studies*, 97(4), 178–184.

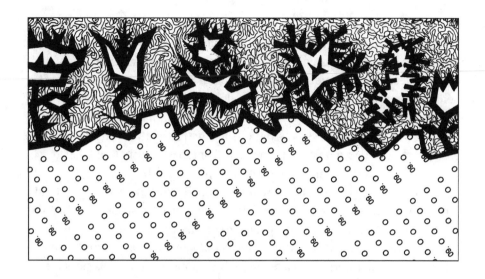

Chapter 3

Many Sizes for All:
A Comprehensive Assessment of Our Students

Pixie Holbrook

Dear Colleagues,

I love our schools. What I love most about them is the diversity of our students and families. I take pride in being part of a national system that commits to teaching ALL children—children who come from different types of homes and who learn in different ways. Yet too often we perpetuate systems that no longer honor this diversity among learners. Every teacher in every school, standing before a classroom of students, learns that one style does not fit all. We also realize that teachers know how to teach and lawmakers do not. This is our profession, and we embrace it with the deepest commitment to protect and educate. Legislators and teachers approach education in distinct ways, and both are necessary and good. We must work together to achieve our common goal of raising for our nation a thoughtful, creative, well-educated, well-socialized citizenry.

In spite of a staggering national influx of dollars for prepackaged curricula, standardized tests, and costly consultants who advise us to bump up the "bubble kids," our children are failing. Because we often ignore the simple fact that learners are unique, children of color and of poverty are left further behind than ever. Powerful people who don't know how children learn legislate instructions for those of us who do. They would have us regard our students as empty, passive vessels to be filled with trivia that enables them to pass one test at one moment in time, and from that snapshot be labeled successes or failures. It's time to think outside of the bubble.

I am forced to compromise my professional ethics every day, and I have felt despair each spring as the dreaded standardized test arrived. But this spring was different. My dread changed to inspiration. Included here is a new design, a multi-faceted assessment that could replace our current pseudo-reform with true reform. It makes the job of improving schools possible by enriching our curriculum and even our communities. Please open your minds to these new ideas. Teachers and legislators have a critical job ahead, and we need each other. Teachers across the state, across the nation, can be the activists our children deserve. Our schools need change today, right now.

I have designed an alternative to our state's standardized test. This alternative is more comprehensive. It acknowledges the need for standards-based education, but it also acknowledges varied learning styles and abilities, places authority back in the hands of local school systems, and better prepares students for post-high school success. My alternative assessment is comprised of eight components.

Component #1

During the sophomore year, a mandatory science fair exhibit will be required of all Massachusetts students. The exhibits will be graded with a state-standard rubric and evaluated by a team of judges from the local area. Students will receive numerical scores, but this science fair does not have place winners. Instead, each student will seek a high score for its own sake rather than as a competition against others.

The projects will be completed during school time to assure that they reflect students' efforts without help from outside of school. This would "equalize the playing field." Also, creating the projects during class enables students to help each other, critiquing and encouraging each other through the process.

A month of school is set aside to create and present the science fair exhibit, though selection of topics would take place prior to that month. During science classes, teachers guide students through the processes of selecting topics, researching and experimenting, gathering required materials, and presenting their findings. The school will provide all lab and presentation materials. During a portion of this month, collaboration will take place with the English department to help students organize and write their presentations.

Evaluation criteria would include quality of research, originality, quality of visual presentation, overall effort, and reflection on their understandings of the Science Frameworks. Students on Individual Education Programs, who represent a wide range of abilities, or those who are not English-dominant speakers, can also participate with staff and peer support. Those in vocational-technical settings can do this also.

In preparation for this, the sixth-grade curriculum will include a less complex science project. It will include presenting for an audience. School staff will form a team of judges and develop a rubric. Ideally, staff will include both certified and non certified personnel, as well as support, secretarial and custodial employees. In this way the school joins together as a complete entity to focus on Science Frameworks and attain a basic standard. Another means of preparing the sixth graders would be for selected tenth graders to share their projects with them. They could serve both as models and mentors, providing a cross-grade experience.

Component #2

During the sophomore year, participation in a debate or speech on a social studies issue will be required. This would be referred to as the Social Studies Presentation (SSP). The debates would be team efforts designed by students. The speeches, to be performed by individual students, will be original and can be read or memorized. They will be judged according to a state-standard rubric and given a numerical score. Criteria will include originality, the quality of the research, the quality of presentation, overall effort and reflection of understandings of Social Studies Frameworks. Again, class time will be set aside to develop the speeches and debate arguments, and the English department can collaborate in substantive ways.

In preparation for this, third- through sixth-grade curricula should include classroom debates, recitations, plays, and persuasive writing assignments.

Component #3

During the senior year, Senior Projects will be required. They must be original and must involve one or more aspects of the Curriculum Frameworks. Examples of original work could include books of poems, one-act plays, musical pieces, research projects, Web pages, original machines, landscape design, cookbooks, photo essays, journals of volunteer work, or children's books. One month will be dedicated to the Senior Projects, but they can be started in earlier grades. All subject area teachers can be involved in these capstone student efforts, which will be judged by rubrics and given a numerical score.

Component #4

Judging teams can consist of college professors, business owners, retirees, community employees, government officials, etc. These opportunities would foster relationships between the schools and community members who would experience first hand the work of their students and teachers.

Component #5

The Iowa Test of Basic Skills, a nationally standardized test, would be given in selected years. Statewide, teachers find this test to be a useful tool to determine students' specific academic strengths and weaknesses. State and local officials would have a standard on which to base growth and compare scores with other districts and states. The test is developmentally appropriate, aligns with grade-level curricula, is reasonably priced, and is far shorter to administer than the MCAS.

Component #6

In grades four, eight, and ten, students will be assessed with a test based specifically on the Massachusetts Frameworks and limited to Literacy and Mathematics. It will be formatted similarly to the current MCAS, with multiple-choice as well as open-ended questions and an essay. It will be titled the Massachusetts Frameworks Assessment (MFA) and will be considered a part of the Massachusetts Comprehensive Assessment System (MCAS). Scores on the MFA will be recorded only numerically. Terms such as Failing or Needs Improvement will not be used, since such terms negatively affect the attitudes of young learners.

Component #7

The scores from the MFA and the Science Fair in 10th grade, the Social Studies Presentation (SSP) in 11th grade, and the Senior Project in 12th grade will be averaged to enable local boards to determine if students meet graduation requirements. This process provides a comprehensive, multidimensional assessment that recognizes the varied learning styles of students. The alternately abled student and the English-language learner can participate on all levels. The vocational student will be fairly assessed. Students who do not demonstrate their full knowledge with paper and pencil tasks have other ways to demonstrate it. For example, if a student does poorly on the MFA, but scores well on the Science Fair and Senior Project, the student's average falls within the expected performance of a high school graduate.

Component #8

Every three years a team will visit each school to evaluate it and report to the state and the local community. This system is already in place for high school accreditation and charter school appraisal. Many who have participated in such assessments have judged them worthwhile.

I offer this proposal in honor of boards of education, who scrutinize and guide the public education system under their jurisdiction while supporting the young people within their schools. I also honor our public school educators and administrators, as well as parents who must be reassured that their children are getting the education they deserve. Combined with smaller class sizes and increased salaries to entice new teachers and compensate veteran teachers, this proposal can restore public schools to their position as among the finest in the world.

Sincerely,

PIXIE J. HOLBROOK

Chapter 4

Ask and Listen with High Expectations

Patty Bode, Nora Elton, and Rachel I. Shuman

Dear Educators,

To reflect teaching boldly when in public schools, I invited two emerging art teachers to share stories from the earliest days of their art-teaching careers. Both teachers are recent alumni from the art education program in which I am a teacher educator, and they provide perceptions about *teaching boldly* from a novice practitioner's daring perspective.

Their stories embody my crucial belief that we need to teach from a multicultural, social justice perspective now. *Teach boldly* with the young people who are in our classrooms today. Do not wait. Do not wait until you have your own classroom or until the new school is built. Do not wait until the principal retires. Do not wait until the contract is ratified. Do not wait until after the department meeting. Do not wait until Derek is expelled or sent to internal suspension. Do not wait until Tatyana's family moves away. Do not wait until the new equipment comes in. Do not wait until the budget is passed. Do not wait until the fundraiser is over. Do not wait until after election day, or after the lunch period. Do not wait until after Thanksgiving break. Do not wait until you feel like you have "enough" experience. Derek, Tatyana, and all their peers will not wait. These two teachers did not wait.

One story, written by Nora Elton, recalls the first art lessons that she designed and implemented as a student teacher in a middle school seventh grade art room. Nora's experience was typical of many student teaching situations; the curriculum was dominated by the mentor teacher's lesson plans and the district's adherence to curriculum standards. Nora's recollections offer inspiration for preservice teachers embarking on their student teaching internships. Her insights offer equally compelling reflection for mentor teachers who take student teachers under their wings.

The other story, by Rachel I. Shuman, recounts a curriculum that Rachel launched in her first three weeks of teaching art in a public school. Rachel was working as an itinerant teacher, bringing art-on-a-cart from classroom to classroom when she embarked on a lesson to conceptually challenge her students with questions that did not have specific answers while encouraging an open door for dialogue. We'll start with Rachel's account as she enters the fifth grade classroom with her art cart while the classroom teachers are looking on. The subsequent section will be Nora's reflection.

Rachel Shuman: Problematizing Peace

OK, here I go. I am about to write the words "Nuclear Disarmament" on the chalkboard of a room that is not my classroom, in front of a group of fifth graders, and their teachers who may or may not be paying attention to my every move, who may or may not have faith in my teaching abilities, and who may or may not even be listening to a word I'm saying. This could go very badly. What if the principal walks in and all she hears is me teaching these children the meaning of nuclear war? I've only been an art teacher here for three weeks. I teach in this school one day a week, so it is my third day of teaching here, and I am defining nuclear war with a group of 10-year olds. I could be seriously questioned here. This is all the result of a student's question though. I am answering their questions. I have done my research. I owe my students that much. I hope this lesson will engage and inform my students, give agency to their views of the world, and make their voices audible.

September 21, the International Day of Peace, falls at the very beginning of the school year.[1] This school celebrates the important event every year, drawing the link between the school's multicultural mission and the need for encouraging peace throughout the world. This year, in keeping with the school's annual tradition, there were peace posters all over the school, and each classroom teacher made "pinwheels for peace"[2] with their students. These activities certainly held meaning as well as some fun activity for the students. However, I was determined to enhance the International Day of Peace events by leading an art lesson that provoked dialogue and questioning based on the concept of "peace".

Peace…a word we, children and adults, hear often. I began the lesson by doing a word association activity for the word "peace." I asked my fifth-grade students, "What does 'peace' mean?" I stood there, marker in hand, ready to write their answers on big chart paper for all to see, but instead silent blank stares returned.

I tried rephrasing my question. "Are there words that you know that relate to the word, or the idea of 'peace'?" I asked. This time there were pauses. Then, the class began to respond: "Quiet," "Not being loud," "Peace sign," "Respect?" "Happiness."

"Peace and quiet" was the only universal link drawn by every one of the students, not only in the fifth grade class, but also in the other grades where I was introducing activities about peace. Peace and quiet? This was truly a sad commentary on the discourse of school culture and the messages conveyed in our broader society. The students in kindergarten through sixth grade associated "peace" with "quiet" but did not grasp the larger meaning of peace, or why the term was used so often in the larger world or in their personal worlds. When the students became more comfortable discussing the concept, they began spontaneously contributing comments, and the big question was revealed: "We don't understand what peace has to do with the world…Oh, wait, I get it—the world needs to be quiet. Right?"

Clearly I had work to do. I planned another activity to develop more conceptual and critical perspectives about the notion of peace.[3] I distributed a slip of paper to each student with the word for peace in a language other than English. Each student walked around the room, and shook each other's hands. They would say, "Hello, nice to meet you, *peace (in the language they were given)*, have a nice day." The students loved this activity; the combination of kinesthetic activity, interaction with all peers, and learning a glimpse of a new language put the students on an equally challenging learning field. While such an activity could appear to be a superficial, empty gesture, it held significance within the context of the art lesson. In addition to sanctioning student voice and dialogue, it also stimulated questions. After the activity we returned to our discussion about the meaning of peace, and students were empowered to speak. They knew I honored their voices and questions. We focused on how peace connected people, and whether peace—or the absence of peace—affected them, their families, and peers on a more personal level. Through this activity, dialogue, and reflection the students were able to draw a connection between individual responsibility and global events. They also contemplated why it was important for every language in the world to have a word for peace.

The discussion uncovered students' concerns about war, the meaning of war, war in general, past wars, and the current U.S. wars in Iraq and Afghanistan. They had inquiries about 9/11 and war-related stories they heard on the news or through their parents' conversations, as well as pictures they had seen in periodicals. The classroom dialogue led to more profound insights about peace as a proactive philosophy, rather than just a lack of noise. They related the philosophy of peace to actions in world events. The idea of war was just as vast as the idea of peace for these students. Although they still could not entirely grasp the enormity either of these concepts (who can?), they began to realize why peace was needed in the world and why so many people were pressing this word on them.

After clarifying a more inclusive meaning of the word peace, the students made a list of questions they had about peace, and we discussed visual culture and visual symbols. One of my students asked, "So, who invented peace?" Another student chimed in, "Who invented the peace sign?"

These questions led to research about the history of the peace sign. It turned out to be an even more expansive question than I would have ever come up with on my own while I was planning this project. In addition to new knowledge, it provided an excellent resource for discussing symbolism and design from artistic perspectives of visual culture. I discovered that the peace sign of popular culture is commonly credited as the invention of Gerald Holtom in England, in 1958 (Kolsbun, 2008).

The design was created by overlapping the semaphore code for the letters *N* and *D* (standing for "nuclear disarmament"). I physically presented this to the class using students and flags to imitate how the arrangement works (more kinesthetic activity). The symbol was adopted in the U.S. and made popular by Bayard Rustin,[4] the civil rights and peace activist. Through his work with Martin Luther King, Jr., the peace sign became prominent in civil rights marches.

Another interesting surprise arose while I was hunting for answers to the students' questions about the image of the dove. The common use of the dove has various roots. One story stems from the Greek myth of Aphrodite, the goddess of love, who kept a dove as a pet. The dove became a symbol for love and eventually became associated with peace and love. Perhaps more commonly known in Western cultures is the dove as a symbol of peace that emerges from the Judeo-Christian tradition in the story of Noah's Ark. The dove returned to the ark with an olive branch in its mouth, signifying the end of the storm. However, as I researched the peace symbol I also learned that Picasso's painting of a dove from a 1949 poster he designed for the World Peace Congress is credited with linking the mainstream use of the dove to represent peace in popular culture—this was a perfect integration of art history and curriculum standards.

This information was interesting, clear, and inspiring for the students. They started to connect the dots among our discussions, activities, and art production. It was that magical point in the curriculum when I was assured that my students had learned, comprehended, and internalized something. I was teaching and learning with them and this project could be successful. I invited the students to create art about peace in a way that held meaning and interest for them. Most students found it comfortable to begin their art making with a peace symbol that we had studied and then transform it, or put it in a context or composition that held meaning for them. During each weekly follow-up art lesson I tried to key into a certain element of design that might facilitate their expression. We discussed design concepts such as composition, including foreground, background, overlapping, and balance. The skill development was authentic because it was embedded in a study of visual culture achieved through viewing examples of artwork and posters expressing themes of peace. This set a context for discussing graphic design and the use of text, logo, and symbolism in art. The students' engagement breathed life into the task of learning these tools and skills.

The fourth week, and the fourth art lesson of the "peace project" took place two weeks after the International Day of Peace had occurred. At the beginning of class, as I was distributing the students' artwork, a student asked, "Why are we still working on our peace project when peace day is over?" It was heartbreaking to hear that question posed so matter-of-factly since I thought we had made it clear through our work in the past three weeks that the concept of peace is actually applicable to my students' everyday lives—and all of our lives. Rather than focus on the heartbreak, however, I took it as a cue that I needed to reiterate and review why we were engaged in the concept of peace and how their projects were personal to them.

The range of skill and comprehension among the students was vast. Nearly half of this class's population was comprised of students enrolled in special education. By challenging myself and my students with such a daring project at the beginning of the year, we all learned how we work successfully by supporting one another's learning in our art-class environment. Holding high expectations for all students cultivated a sense of accomplishment within the classroom culture. All students became successful artists, expressing a deeply conceptual theme.

I owe a great deal of thanks to Charlie, the student who asked about the invention of the peace sign. It was both an obvious question and an ingenious question. It gave me a direction to lead this group of students when I was stuck wondering how a teacher is supposed to begin a profound, conceptual, enriching curriculum. The tensions between my adult expectations of student concepts and student-generated inquiry led me to realize the importance of equipping students with a range of skills and tools as an ongoing process of empowering their voices. They need vocabulary, definitions, connections, technique, prompts, boundaries, guidance, support, and confidence to question and comment, as well as the opportunity to express their interpretations in their own voices.

The peace project turned out to be a success. Each student's piece was unique and had meaning. They wrote their expressions and explanations on accompanying note cards. I am not as nervous about tackling these boundary-pushing concepts in my classes as I was at the beginning of the year. I realize that it requires engaging students in ongoing research, including multiple perspectives, and making room for questioning.

Now when I arrive for my art-on-a-cart lessons, the classroom teachers who witnessed my explanation of "nuclear disarmament" almost always stick around for the introduction to my lessons (in contrast to those who typically leave their rooms for their precious prep-period minutes). They stick around not because they are skeptical of my viewpoint and subject matter or distrustful of my teaching methods, but because, as they have told me, they are interested and impressed by the perspective I present to the students. When I enter the classroom for my fifth-grade art class, Mrs. G. announces, "Your peaceful art teacher is here."

Nora Elton: Achieving Art for Action

The excitement reverberated in my hands and heart while I typed feverously on the computer and my ideas for the lesson cohered. This was going to be it: a lesson that really engaged my students. A lesson that celebrated each student's uniqueness and encouraged him or her to voice opinions, histories, truths, and beliefs. I wanted to hear what they had to say. I wanted to encourage them to use artistic approaches and tools to express their perspectives on important issues in the world. The lesson was titled "Art for Action." It highlighted the work of Romare Bearden, Judy Chicago, and Keith Haring, and explored how some artists use their artwork as a means for inspiring social change. I had been working as a student teacher with my seventh-grade students for two months already, seeing them once a day, but usually I was carrying out the lessons designed by my mentor teacher, so this was the first opportunity to teach my own lesson in her art room at an arts-based middle school. I couldn't wait.

I arrived at school with lesson and examples in hand, and an eager smile on my face, ready to share the lesson with my cooperating teacher, Amanda. I was not scheduled to present the lesson to my classes for a week, but I was required to discuss it with my cooperating teacher in advance. After skimming it with a bit of hesitation, Amanda admitted it would be interesting to see what social issues the students would decide to tackle with the collages that I intended my lesson plan to inspire. While her hesitation might have shown through, my excitement and passion overshadowed it. A week later the students finished the art lesson that Amanda had taught, which meant that the next day I would begin mine.

As I was packing up to leave at the end of the day, Amanda told me she had informed the principal that I was using Keith Haring as an example of an artist who had inspired social change through his artwork. I looked blankly at her. Why did the principal need to know I planned to study Keith Haring? She explained that parents in the district were quite conservative and she felt they might "take issue" with Keith Haring's artwork being used in a lesson because he had been openly homosexual. Furthermore, the principal had contacted the superintendent and the superintendent had said I could not include Keith Haring in the lesson. Amanda explained that she was sorry. My eyes popped. My neck strained. My heart sank. Blood rushed into my head. I felt that there was so much wrong with what she had said I had no idea where to begin.

Keith Haring's identities, including his sexual orientation, were components of his work, but the lesson was not about Keith Haring's homosexuality—not because I thought I should avoid homosexuality, but because the point of the lesson was to study how artists inspire social change. These lesson discussions were more focused on the many organizations Keith Haring had supported, such as UNICEF. It addressed his belief that art should be accessible to all. It highlighted how he used his art to raise money for important issues; it presented an artist who cared about the world and who used his art to better the world. How could anyone "take issue" with these objectives?

I was speechless. Amanda apologized again. I walked to my car with my mind reeling, unwilling to accept this decision. I was disgusted by the discrimination against Keith Haring specifically, and even more so by the blatant homophobia toward the entire gay community. I was saddened by the fear and ignorance that continued to fracture the world; teary-eyed and filled with disappointment, I called my academic advisor. After lots of dialogue, we brainstormed some options: 1) do the lesson by omitting Keith Haring and focusing only on Judy Chicago and Romare Bearden, 2) replace Keith Haring with another artist, or 3) advocate for my lesson to be approved as is. With my advisor's support and suggestions, I chose the final option.

Now I was invigorated. I was going to stand up for the lesson I believed in. Following the plan I had mapped out with my academic advisor, I drafted a letter to the superintendent. The e-mail letter had to be scholarly, firm, professional, and persuasive. It read:

Dear _____,

Attached are the Keith Haring images that I am planning to use in my lesson. I pulled them all from the Keith Haring Education Web site that is designed to be used in K–8 schools. Here is the link to the Web site: www.haringkids.com.

As you know, I am using the Wiggins and McTighe "Backwards Design" model to create my lesson plans. Here are the Enduring Understandings, Essential Questions, Learning Objectives and Massachusetts State Frameworks that are covered in my lesson.

The Enduring Understandings for this lesson are:

Art can be used as a tool for social action.

Art can create change.

Artists create art in response to experience and environment.

The Essential Questions for the lesson are:

How do artists use art to create awareness?

How can art be used as a tool to incite change?

How can one's experience and environment inspire one's artwork?

How can I express my beliefs through art?

What issues do I care about and how can I create art that will bring awareness to an issue?

The Learning Objectives for this lesson are:

Students will acquire knowledge about the different ways artists have used art to bring awareness to social issues.

Students will examine how art has incited change.

Students will identify how artists' experiences and environments have influenced their artwork.

The students will research different social issues that are important to them.

The students will express their beliefs on an issue through collage.

The Massachusetts Framework Learning Standards this lesson will address are:

[quoted directly from Massachusetts Department of Education Web site at http://www.doe.mass.edu/frameworks/current.html]

"3. Observation, Abstraction, Invention, and Expression. Students will demonstrate their powers of observation, abstraction, invention, and expression in a variety of media, materials, and techniques.

6. The purpose of art. Students will describe the purpose for which works of dance, music, theatre, visual arts, and architecture were and are created, and when appropriate, interpret their meanings.

7. Roles of artists in communities. Students will describe the roles of artists, patrons, cultural organizations, and arts institutions in societies of the past and present."

Keith Haring was a talented artist who organized with museum education departments, anti-drug organizations, peace activists, and organizations such as UNICEF to create artwork that would promote positivity, progress, peace, awareness and action. His contribution to AIDS research has been integral in the world's fight against this deadly disease and for that, we all owe him gratitude. I hope that your administration will see the educational value and artistic value of my lesson.

Sincerely,

Nora Elton

It was bold; it was direct; and I felt that it was necessary. I closed my eyes, took a deep breath and pressed SEND. I found myself waiting nervously for a reply. I read the letter over and over; I paced around my house; and I smiled hopefully. I felt that I was making a difference, and I hoped I was fostering acceptance.

I knew that it was necessary to present the lesson as clearly as possible in my letter. I wanted the superintendent to know what I was planning to do and how I was hoping to empower my students. I also wanted to exhibit my academic research and artistic dedication. The more transparent I was with my lesson plan, I reasoned, the less the superintendent could take issue with it. I continued to wait, eagerly checking my in-box every minute.

About an hour later I received a phone call from Amanda. The superintendent had read the e-mail and decide to allow me teach the lesson! I was elated and proud.

I entered the school the following day feeling as if I were on a mission. In the first period class I showed images of the artwork of Romare Bearden, Judy Chicago, and Keith Haring. I asked the students what they thought about them. There was a pause, and I realized that being encouraged to state opinions was a new experience for the students. As they realized that there were no right or wrong answers to the questions, as they realized I was asking for *their* opinions, the classroom became a sea of raised hands. I asked the students questions about what they felt, witnessed, experienced and knew. What meaning do you see in the artwork of Keith Haring, Judy Chicago and Romare Bearden? What symbols do you recognize in Keith Haring's work? Who would you want to honor if you were going to create a place-setting for Judy Chicago's *Dinner Party*? What are your impressions of Romare Bearden's depictions of an urban environment? These artworks illustrated environments to which my students felt connections. These artists used symbols they knew how to read. The content focused on people standing up for and honoring themselves and others; they revealed worlds in need of change and understanding. I was asking for their voices, and they realized I cared about what they had to say.

The final pieces of artwork from this lesson were powerful and ringing with truth. There is so much to process and confront at the age of 13, and I was proud to see how eloquently my students expressed their opinions, fears, questions, and concerns. Their artwork expressed statements about important issues such as peace, war, teen pregnancy, child abuse and neglect, the environment, unity, violence, discrimination, acceptance, immigration, and hope.

One student who had learning disabilities that affected his fine motor skills, who had struggled with previous art projects, achieved great success with his collage about ending the war in Iraq and bringing the American soldiers home. He cut out an image of a soldier's boots and wrote around the boots, "Bring these feet home." He set this photograph with his text in a sea of black and red. He cut out more images and added them to the collage, with his commentary. It was moving to see this student overcome the frustration he had previously felt in art class, to reach success. It was inspiring to see how much he had to say and how effectively and intelligently he was able to say it.

At the end of the year these collages were exhibited in a show. At the opening reception, various adults came up to me and asked me how I had motivated the students to be so expressive of their concerns and the injustices they observe in the world. My response was, "I asked."

Patty Bode: Commentary

Rachel's story holds many implications for *teaching boldly*. While she planned a well-organized lesson plan with big ideas and clear objectives rooted in visual culture, she did not start her lesson with a linear focus on a destination. She had questions for her students, but she did not have firm answers. Her students' questions led her classroom community to more deeply research her initial question to them: What does peace mean? To her surprise her students were not accustomed to being invited into open dialogue. It took some coaxing, support, and kinesthetic activities, as well as novice teachers' high expectations in students' intellectual and creative prowess to uncover her students' confidence in their voices. Nora Elton reports a similar experience when she launches a classroom discussion about "Art for Action."

With those two words, "I asked," Nora succinctly sums up the nucleus and heart of *teaching boldly* that both she and Rachel demonstrate. This is the message that I hope you take with you from our stories: Ask your students. Nora and Rachel ask students what they know, what they don't know, what they see, what they speculate, what they hope to know, what they question, what they wonder, what they hear from one another, what they need to learn, and what they want to say.

Their students echo what I heard in my research with students in urban art rooms in public schools (Bode, 2005). When I asked students what they believe art teachers need to know to address students' realities of the current era, some major motifs emerged that I shaped into collages from hundreds of students' voices. In one of these four collages that I call "Curriculum and Representation: Ask me who I am" students consistently expressed the necessity for teachers to include student voice and student perspective in the curriculum, which often translated into classroom practice that addressed multiple identities and social and political relevance.

The students' call for curriculum that is relevant to their sociopolitical contexts was closely tied to another collage in my research, that is likewise illustrated by Nora and Rachel's pedagogy: the desire of students to be held to high expectations. When students stared blankly at open-ended questions, Nora and Rachel did not assume that "these kids" lacked knowledge; they realized the need for a new framework on classroom discourse and their responsibility in setting up a dialectical classroom. They took on the challenge by re-framing questions, providing compelling visual media, and restructuring classroom events. In essence, they helped students redefine what counts as knowledge.

In these art classroom communities students volunteered several strategies for teachers to integrate culturally relevant content into the curriculum. However, this was not a simplistic quest to do whatever they wanted in art class. Accompanying the pleas for choices within the curriculum was the desire to develop their skills.[5]

Ask and Listen with High Expectations

Asserting student voice in education is not a simple matter of asking students for their ideas (although many curricula would be enhanced by that first step). Three specific strategies emerge in Nora's and Rachel's stories. To ask students to voice their ideas and to present high expectations, these three pedagogical frames may serve as guideposts for *teaching boldly* for many educators. For preservice teachers, for seasoned teachers who are mentoring student teachers, and for teacher educators, the practices that undergirded Nora's and Rachel's affirmations of student voices urge us to:

1. Understand that a multicultural art curriculum can be standards based but *not* standards driven.[6]
2. Create a web of critical support.
3. Meet resistance with research and hope.

Understand That a Multicultural Art Curriculum Can Be Standards Based but *Not* Standards Driven

Curriculum development in public schools is increasingly directed by sources outside the learners' lived worlds, and art education is no exception. Moreover, the art curriculum is being reduced and eradicated in many schools as budgets and priorities turn resources toward preparation for and compliance with standardized tests. If art education programs survive budget cuts, state and federal mandates often focus the art education program on checklists of skills and irrelevant concepts. In this standards-frenzied climate, it is critical that art educators consider the political implications and pressures that weigh on administrators to comply with state mandates. Yet revolutionary educators can simultaneously engage in critical pedagogy. Nora and Rachel found standards within the state frameworks that supported their multicultural, social justice goals. By referring to the standards, and consciously weaving student voice into their practice, they were able to defend the integrity of their curriculum goals in a language that was valuable to administrators. They did not allow the standards to *drive* their curriculum; rather, they found support for their multicultural goals by mining the standards for parallel concepts. In many cases, the practice of referencing standards in curriculum documents, on bulletin boards and in lesson plans can preempt public resistance to revolutionary curriculum content. A critical stance on standards maintains that student voice can drive curriculum.

Create a Web of Critical Support

While asking students for their ideas, these teachers found that they were questioning themselves or were questioned by others. So they sought out critical friends[7] with whom to connect. Nora called her academic advisor and Rachel established relationships with the classroom teachers. Popular culture is fraught with images and stories of lone, heroic teachers who fight the odds, the system, and the administration to make the world a better place for their students. Neither teachers nor students are served by this unrealistic narrative. To cultivate a lasting, effective life in teaching that leaves enduring, positive influences on our students, we need to open our minds and our classroom doors and ask for help. Engaging in the rejuvenating dialogue of inquiry with colleagues and mentors emphasizes that teaching is not a task of isolation. *Teaching boldly* is an ongoing learning process filled with daily routines, puzzling dilemmas, exciting epiphanies, heartbreaking stumbles, exhausting tasks, and glorious achievements. Creating communities of critical dialogue guides us in self-reflection, engages us in current research, encourages new practices, and reveals our strengths.

Meet Resistance with Research and Hope

Active scholarship plays a critical role in *teaching boldly* while asking and listening with high expectations. Rachel and Nora engaged in research to make their students' voices more audible. Their research supported their determination to provide their students with meaningful reflection and outspoken art production. In addition to their preliminary research about the curricular themes, their classroom communities responded to student inquiry. Rachel's response to Charlie's question about the origin of the peace sign engaged the classroom community in lively scholarship and purposeful art production. Nora's clarity of scholarship was central in her letter to the superintendent. Since it is likely that we will be met with resistance when we center student voice, it is essential that our curriculum be rooted in rigorous intellectual growth and robust artistic expressions. Research can contextualize our practices by citing educational scholarship, referring to contemporary artists, quoting social theorists, drawing from traditional art communities and investigating art historians. We can meet resistance with the fierce hopefulness required to teach boldly.

Rachel and Nora's examples of understanding that a multicultural art curriculum can be "standards-based and not standards driven" (Sleeter, 2005), creating a web of critical support, and meeting resistance with research and hope demonstrate that listening to our students' voices with high expectations can bring about tangible, recognizable curricular change among art education communities. Whether you are starting your student teaching, or starting your final year before retirement, mentoring a preservice intern or teaching in the college classroom, consider these strategies to affirm your students' voices. We urge you: Don't wait.

Best wishes,

Patricia Bode   *Nora Elton*   *Rachel Shuman*

Notes

1. The International Day of Peace, established by a United Nations resolution in 1981, was inaugurated in 1982. In 2002, the UN General Assembly set 21 September as the now permanent date for this observance. See http://www.internationaldayofpeace.org.

2. "Pinwheels for Peace" is an art installation project started in 2005 by two art teachers, Ann Ayers and Ellen McMillan, in Coconut Creek, Florida, as a way for students to express their feelings about what's going on in the world and in their lives. The project has been embraced by millions of art teachers, teachers, parents, children and adults who desire peace in our world. See http://www.pinwheelsforpeace.com.

3. This activity is drawn from the Web site of the peaceCENTER, P.O. Box 36, San Antonio, Texas, 78291 See www.salsa.net/peace/teach/teach7.html.

4. For a closer study of Bayard Rustin's life for upper elementary students, see *We Are All One: The Story of Bayard Rustin* by Larry Dane Brimmer from Calkins Creek Books (October 2007) - reading level approximately age 9–12. Available from www.teaching forchange.org.

5. Some excerpts of this analysis about "Curriculum and Representation: Ask me who I am" first appeared in Bode, Patricia. (2005). *Multicultural art education: Voices of art teachers and students in the postmodern era.* Unpublished doctoral dissertation, University of Massachusetts, Amherst.

6. Christine Sleeter provides an inspirational treatment of how to address the hegemonic devices of the standards movement in her book *Un-Standardizing Curriculum: Multicultural Teaching in a Standards-Based Classroom* (2005: Teachers College Press).

7. Arthur Costa and Bena Kallick (1993) advanced this definition of "critical friend": Every student and educator needs a trusted person to ask provocative questions and offer helpful critiques....Critical friendships begin through building trust; critical friends must listen well, offer value judgments on the learner's request, respond honestly, and promote the work's success

References

Ayers, A. & McMillan, E. *Pinwheels for Peace.* Retrieved August 10, 2008, from http://www. pinwheelsforpeace.com/.

Bode, P. (2005). *Multicultural art education: Voices of art teachers and students in the postmodern era.* Unpublished doctoral dissertation, University of Massachusetts, Amherst.

Brimmer, L. D. (2003). *We Are All One: The Story of Bayard Rustin.* Honesdale, PA: Calkins Creek Books.

Costa, A.L. & Kallick, B. (1993, October). Through the lens of a critical friend. *Educational Leadership, 51*(2), 50.

Kolsbun, K. (2008). *Peace: The Biography of a Symbol.* Washington, DC: National Geographic.

Massachusetts Department of Education. Retrieved August 10, 2008,from http://www.doe.mass.edu/frameworks.current.html.

Pathways to Peace, Inc. *International Day of Peace.* Retrieved August 10, 2008, from http://www.internationaldayofpeace.org/

PeaceCENTER, peace tools for teachers. *A New Language of Peace.* Retrieved August 10, 2008. from http://www.salsa.net/peace/teach/teach7.html.

Sleeter, C. (2005). *Un-Standardizing Curriculum: Multicultural Teaching in a Standards-Based Classroom.* New York: Teachers College Press.

Resources for Teaching about Peace Symbolism

Mann, J. (2004). *Peace: The Anti-war Movement.* Illustrated. Zurich: Edition Olms.

Santino, J. (2001). *Signs of War and Peace: Social Conflict and the Use of Public Symbols in Northern Ireland.* New York: Palgrave.

Sontag, S., Moore, M., Roy, A., Chomsky, N., et al. (2003). *2/15: The Day the World Said NO to War.* Oakland: UK Press/ Hello NYC.

Chapter 5

Teaching Authentically

Geneva Gay

Dear Teachers,

Teaching is at its best when teachers act in ways that are congruent with and amplify its inherent qualities. But it is not always easy for some individuals to recognize these or be courageous enough to act in accordance with them in the face of pressures and influences that lead in other directions. A lot of what is done in the name of teaching is actually manipulating controlling, and constraining students. At its best genuine teaching is about empowering, honoring, and cultivating the potential of students (and teachers) to be more than they currently are and are capable of imagining. Many existing conceptions distort the nature of teaching so much that even teachers with good intentions find it difficult to separate fact from fiction. They try to appease all of the conflicting and unnatural demands placed upon them by engaging in false impressions of teaching even though they know these are not the real deal.

Teaching authentically means actualizing the inherent character of the process as it exists prior to being politicized by various interest and pressure groups. Before this actualization can occur, teachers need to become more critically reflective of the various ideological claims underlying the practices, programs, policies, and expectations imposed upon them, by whom, and how these perpetuate distortions. Once this is accomplished they can begin to resurrect and reclaim the true character of teaching, implant it in the forefront of their minds, and activate it in designing and implementing learning experiences for students. In hopes of contributing to these reclamations I will discuss first some illusions and then some realities of teaching. The underlying messages of these thoughts are: (1) teaching grounded in reality is always better than that based on wishes and dreams; (2) understanding underlying beliefs is essential to changing instructional behaviors; and (3) teaching cannot be revitalized without a thorough analysis of how the process is affected by a wide variety of contextual factors.

*Teaching is not...*Much fiction and folklore surround teaching. Some make learning a requisite, arguing that teachers haven't taught if students haven't learned. There is no question in my mind that teaching and learning are interconnected, but to make one totally dependent upon the other is a bit problematic to say the least. To do so ignores the critical part that the individuals who inhabit these roles play in these processes. Students contribute a great deal to the learning process that is beyond the control of teachers regardless of how committed and competent they may be. Furthermore, teachers frequently are conduits for the transmission of other people's ideas, beliefs, and preferred actions.

Another claim commonly made today is teachers are completely powerless; they are pawns of policies and pressures beyond their control. Consequently, they have to function in highly constricted ideological, creative, and pedagogical spaces; they are forced into reactive modalities where they have to do as they are told, and they are stripped of opportunities to be innovative and imaginative. Prescriptive curricula, limited funding, legislative mandates, high-stakes testing, conservative policies, punitive sanctions, and hostile and alienated students are among the specific causes cited for powerlessness among teachers.

A third frequently heard folkloric idea is that teaching is either a scientific or technical act that can be predetermined with exactitude, and perfectly replicated across time, setting, and population, that it is immune to the complex contextual realities involving who is teaching, what, where, why, and to whom. Among some people, much attention is given to searching for best practices applicable to all students, teachers, and subjects, standardized curricula, and empirical-based evidence of effectiveness. These efforts seem to be trying to remove the 'person and personal' from teaching and learning.

Yet another feature of the fiction and folklore surrounding teaching is the belief that the best results can be obtained through emphasizing content knowledge. There is no doubt that teachers need to have a deep knowledge of the subjects they teach. The fault lies in assumptions that teaching is exclusively about conveying knowledge to students. These assumptions generate emphases in professional preparation that are counter-productive in the long run, such as creating false senses of security, intractability, and inflexibility. They lead to overly generalized ideas or highly prescribed mandates. When these strategies, with their implicit notions of permanence, fail to produce desired results in practice, teachers become frustrated, disenchanted, dependent, and helpless. Many soon realize that mastery of disciplinary knowledge is no guarantee that they can teach it to students. Since they have not been professionally socialized for self-determined pedagogical adaptability and flexibility, these teachers do not know how to convert general principles into actual practices for the realities of their particular classrooms. For example, what does having high-performance expectations and providing academically rigorous and relevant curriculum content (two often cited 'best practices') mean for teaching U. S. History or Algebra to poor and middle class students; to males and females; to students in urban, suburban, and rural schools; to high and low achievers; to mainstream and marginalized African, Asian, Latino, European, and Native Americans; to native speakers, and English-language learners?

*Teaching is...*Teaching is a complex, dynamic, and organic phenomenon that involves much more than mastery of disciplinary knowledge and pedagogical skills. As William Ayers (2004) explains, "teaching is alive and ...spectacularly unlimited" (p. 119). The desire to make it less so may be part of the human impulse for order, stability, and certainty in important processes in life that otherwise appear to be chaotic, unstructured, unpredictable, and overwhelming. Teaching certainly is a critical, recurrent, and sometimes illusive function in our lives, whether it occurs within or outside the formalities of schooling. This makes it even more susceptible to efforts to direct it, to anoint it with certainty, predictability, and replicability. These needs seem to grow exponentially as the pressures in our social, personal, and civic lives become more and more demanding.

Unfortunately, as we try to make better sense of a somewhat mystifying process and simplify its complexities, we tend to do injustice to or distort its inherent nature, and add more and more layers of fiction, fantasy, and folklore. Teaching effectively requires stripping away these layers of distortion and reasserting its most fundamental essence. To do so constitutes a courageous (and sometimes unpopular) act of going against the grain of prevailing practices. But acts of moral righteousness and social justices (as teaching is!) often are not popular undertakings. Nor are they for the weak minded and softhearted. However, the benefits accrued are worth the investments made for all the stakeholders, teachers, students, and society at large.

Authentic teaching is more than a single act or attitude; it is a habit of mind, a way of being, a disposition that involves being clear and confident in one's pedagogical beliefs; having the strength to resist pressures to conform to notions of teaching that contradict its inherent nature; and the will to act according to one's beliefs even at the risk of displeasing various stakeholders in the educational enterprise. Authentic teachers exemplify the characteristics of teaching in its more naturalistic state. It is grounded more in ethics than politics because it is about doing what is right with respect to what constitutes inherent essence, not what is expedient, popular, or imposed. The results are higher achievement for students, and better job satisfaction for teachers.

Authentic teaching is a composite of many different behavioral attributes. To begin, it is a process in continuous progress. However good any particular act of teaching is, or competent a teacher may be in any given time, place, or circumstance, the success is transitory and somewhat fleeting, although noteworthy. It is virtually impossible for teaching acts to be replicated exactly because they are contextually bound. Once the context changes, the teaching act has to be reconstructed. Factors that shape teaching contexts are numerous and constantly changing, too. Sometimes they are major events and readily apparent, while at other times they may appear to be miniscule, and unconscious but still contribute significantly to shaping the contours and dynamics of the teaching process These contextual factors may result from the institutional structures of schools and classrooms or society at large; from a teacher's psycho-emotional disposition on any given day; from the presence of a new student in the classroom; from a week-end community celebration or crisis; from just living life one day (or moment) to the next. Authentic teachers are intentional and deliberate about making their teaching behaviors to be responsive to these factors. But what exactly these factors are and how they will unfold at any particular point in time can never be predicted with certainty. Therefore, teaching must always be 'becoming,' unfinished, flexible, a work in process. Authentic teachers welcome this uncertainty and impermanence as endemic to the work they do and as stimulants for creativity, ingenuity, and the continuous refinement and revision of techniques. They engage teaching ideas and action thoroughly and imaginatively for as long as they are viable, but relinquish them willingly when they no longer serve any useful purpose, and without being disenchanted, or feeling put upon. They are motivated by the realization that diverse evolving students, settings, subjects, knowledge, and skills require multiple and continually changing teaching strategies. This is the normal thing to do, and these teachers respond to the challenges it provokes without the need to be rewarded for doing something unusual or extraordinary.

Another critical dimension of teaching authentically is caring. It involves an integration of concern, compassion, and commitment to instructional action in the service of students. This is not a passive notion or one that begins and ends in the attitudinal. A desire to do good is necessary but it is not the essence of caring. Genuine caring is action driven. It is always doing that which is for the betterment of students as learners with untapped potentiality, and as developmentally growing and socioculturally bounded human beings. This holistic nurturing requires courageous will, intellectual stamina, creative ingenuity, and persistent efforts since teachers have to always be on the alert for ways and means to better serve the students. It is complicated further, yet made even more imperative, when teachers have to cross ethnic, cultural, racial, linguistic, and social boundaries to care for students. Sometimes this means being more humane than instructionally gifted; other times caring challenges the pedagogical competence of teachers; still other examples involve relating with students on a personal level. Sometimes the issues of caring are profound, and at other times they are simple and mundane. But, they all count as part of what genuine teaching is all about, Simply put, authentically caring teachers engage continuously in intellectually rigorous and imaginative efforts to help students develop holistically and reach maximum success. They are what Judith Kleinfeld (1975) and Franita Ware (2006) call 'warm demanders' in that they have high academic achievement expectations and assist students in accomplishing them. They cultivate the social, cultural, moral, and political development of students along with the academic. They don't just mandate performance; they facilitate it.

Authentic teaching also is adventure. Adventurers prepare thoroughly for their journeys even knowing full well that they cannot ever anticipate every conceivable occurrence. They go forward with excitement and wonder that good things will happen, that obstacles will occur but will be overcome, and that success will be had. They invest mind, body, spirit, and soul in the undertaking, and pursue it aggressively, yet respectfully of all the other factors and actors involved. An adventure is never taken alone. Even when we are not conscious of companions and they are not physically embodied, they are still present symbolically. The same is true with teaching authentically. It is never done solo or in total isolation; nor do teachers ever know with absolute certainty all of the maneuvers they will engage during the process, and they cannot totally control what the other participants (students, materials, time, circumstances, etc.) will do in the dialectic interactions that constitute teaching. While the contours of teaching may be rather predictable, the actual behaviors are always 'maybes' and possibilities. They literally shift from one moment to the next. These realities do not frighten or intimidate authentic teachers. In fact, the 'partially knowns' are viewed as catalysts for creativity, innovation, and fortitude.

Accepting uncertainty as natural to teaching suggests that authentic teachers are trailblazers. They are always forging new instructional terrains. This happens on two fronts, simultaneously. One is realizing that what is successful in one time and setting probably will not be so in another. The other is going past the threshold of current capabilities in search of other possibilities for more teaching effectiveness. In the parlance of today, teaching authentically is 'going outside of the box' and 'pushing the envelope.' Individuals who do this thoughtfully and deliberately are not easily constrained, and certainly not by the prospects of being unpopular and unconventional.

Another dimension of authentic teaching similar to trailblazing is what William Pinar (1975) calls transcendence. It means striving to be better than you currently are, regardless of your level of competence. Pinar describes it as "the experience of limitless going beyond any given state or realization of being" (p. 324). Transcendence is characterized by several distinguishing dispositions and habits of behavior. Among them are hopefulness, empathy, hospitality, wonder, awe, reverence, receptivity, and helpful skepticism toward betterment as teachers and persons. These individuals exhibit an expectant openness to new and creative teaching and learning possibilities; they are eager and excited about learning, and this exuberance fuels their teaching. They question everything and cultivate a spirit of criticism, not to be negative or doubtful, but to understand more deeply and act more effectively. They have positive attitudes toward all other individuals, cultures, and social groups, are enthralled about the prospect of learning from them, and assume that all have some inherent goodness, or the potential to be so (Pinar, 1975).

Teachers engaged in transcendence do not "seek [protection] from…uncertainty, perplexity, and irremediate ignorance…try to hide behind a screen of academic presumption and professional expertise, embellished with mystifying jargon…[or] confuse the role of teacher with that of authoritative oracle" (Pinar 1975, p. 332). Instead, they share enthusiastically with students the insights and knowledge they possess, their excitement about acquiring more and novel ways for doing so, as well as encouraging students to do likewise, to be fully engaged partners in this captivating and enriching venture called learning. They approach teaching with a genuine sense of humility and insist on shifting the spotlight from themselves to the nature and effects of the teaching processes they design and facilitate. They refuse to succumb to intellectual futility and pedagogical impotence. Transcendence is not restricted to problematic individuals and events. In fact, highly competent teachers are more likely to seek transcendence than those who are having difficultly mastering their craft. Their competence allows them to approach teaching from a position of strength, confidence, and faith that good will come from their informed, caring, and trustful investments in and receptivity to transcendent possibilities, even though they do not know what the particulars of these will be in advance of their actual occurrence. Transcendently oriented teachers realize that there is no endpoint to pedagogical competence and capacity; they are continually evolving. They know that increasing one's knowledge opens up opportunities to know even more.

The same is true for pedagogical skill building. Successful teachers want to be better or at least to teach differently tomorrow than today, and they are constantly looking for ways to make this happen. This perpetual search is not prompted by any desire to be deemed exceptional or bestowed with honorific accolades, but by recognition of the fact that every teaching act is unique, and modifications (and sometimes even abandonments) have to be made for subsequent engagements. Consequently, change is an important component of and motivating force in teaching authentically. Teachers so engaged are always making choices. They know that, in the final analysis, no one else can tell them what best to do in their actual classrooms, with their particular students, on a moment-to-moment basis. The ball is in their court, and they do not shirk this responsibility or take it lightly. Yet they are not burdened down by it. Simply, it is what it is! These teachers recognize, (and accept the mandate) that they and their students are empowered (or not) by the choices and decisions they make, and that choicemaking is unavoidable. While this never-ending task is daunting for some, authentic teachers see it as ordinary and routine; nothing especially positive, negative, or unusual. They approach every choice and decision made as if it were the panacea or ultimate answer in the thoughtfulness given to it, while knowing full well that its validity is momentary; that as soon as a choice is made and its generative moment passes, another one is being formulated. This requires flexibility and openness to continually emerging possibilities.

A final point in this discussion is that authentic teachers are always personally present in their teaching. They know that who they are has a tremendous influence on determining how they teach, and they are always alert to the implications of this reality for student engagement and learning. They readily admit that their personas may sometimes be problematic for some students and facilitative for others. They don't try to remove themselves from their teaching (this is impossible anyway) but try to broaden their repertoires of personal being to generate more instructional variety and diversity. Facing ourselves in our teaching is not the easiest thing to do because we may not like what we see, and trying to change ourselves can be disconcerting. Some teachers compensate by hiding behind claims of objectivity and dispassion that their teaching has nothing to do with them as persons, that the two are totally separate enterprises. Authentic teachers know better. Because of other attributes, such as caring, self-confidence, and transcendence, they focus on knowing more about interactions between their personal being and their professional role, and heightening the complementarity between them to further enhance outcomes for students. They are not reluctant to own personal attributes that can be problematic in teaching and monitoring and modifying them to minimize their negative effects. Conversely, they use the positive parts of their person-ness as explicit resources to help them teach better, and they try to cultivate other aspects that are not yet fully developed. Thus, authentic teachers are critically conscious of themselves in their teaching, the parallel realities that exist for students. They are always seeking to understand how the insights gained from these analyses can be used to make teaching and learning more effective. For example, they want to know the effects of their own and their students' race, culture, gender, ethnicity, prior experiences, and psycho-emotional state of being at any given point in time on the dynamics of the educational process.

William Ayers (2004) made some observations that help to further clarify these dimensions of authentic teaching. He says that whatever else teachers might teach they always teach themselves because their actions symbolize their values and beliefs. Therefore, being cognizant of "oneself as the instrument of one's teaching allows for greater change and growth as well as greater intentionality in teaching choices" (p. 105). Another dimension of being personally present in one's own teaching is being a learner as well as a teacher. Authentic teachers accept the fact that they do not know all there is to be known about either their subject matter or about teaching in general, and with particular student populations. They understand that their thoughts about and plans for instruction often are not what happen in the actual performance. So they study their teaching carefully. They are not reluctant to admit, "I don't know," or that a given teaching efforts was unsuccessful, but quickly add, "I am willing to learn and try to do better." They seek effectiveness, not perfection. These commitments and actions distinguish them from other teachers who may concede that they do not know something but then proceed to try to teach without any attempt to learn, or use lack of knowledge as an excuse to do nothing.

A case in point is doing culturally responsive teaching for ethnically and racially diverse students. Many teachers claim to be willing to do this if only they knew how. But, they do not pursue the knowledge and skills needed. These are not authentic teachers. If they were, they would accept the responsibility for teaching themselves. Maxine Greene's (1984) explanation of individuals present in aesthetic encounters is a good analogy for teachers being personally present and seeking transcendence in their own teaching. She says:

> To genuinely know and experience art, we can never send someone to see it for us and come back and report. Not only are we required to be there, we are required to

be there as active and conscious beings, allowing the energies of perceiving and imagining and feeling to move out to the works at hand, to bring them into life. Yes, and we are required to be there as open and reflective consciousness, empowered to resist fixed definition, the fetish, the fraud....[S]uch works impel the awakened beholder...to break with the habitual, the customary, the merely conventional, the given. Desire is evoked by the realization of what is not yet, expressed in the yearning toward possibility. Many works of art...can never be exhausted, never finally achieved, never 'done.' There are boundaries, yes, edges, frames, but they are there to be transcended. And, to transcend, each one for himself or herself and at once along with others, is to transform the petrified world. (pp. 133–134)

When teaching acts and students are seen as 'art works,' and teachers as 'awakened art beholders' this description sounds very much like the essence of authentic teaching.

In summary, teaching authentically is intellectually, morally, and creatively demanding. But it is also exhilarating for those who have the strength, courage, conviction, commitment, and clarity it requires. It demands openness, flexibility, frequent change, and responsiveness to complex contextual factors that surround teaching. It goes far beyond mastery of subject matter content and technical pedagogical skills. It is a demeanor and a disposition, a way of being in which one is always on the alert and receptive to ideas, resources, and strategies for how to engage students in high quality, multilayered learning experiences that are intellectually stimulating, and personally inviting, validating, and renewing. This receptivity to new teaching possibilities is not limited to times when teachers are on the classroom stage or are consciously thinking about teaching. It is always present, although at times on semi- or subconscious levels. When the mind meets a promising possibility, even in circumstances that appear not to be remotely connected to teaching, it becomes fully conscious instantly, and actively processes how it might be used, where, when, and why in the next classroom opportunity. Therefore, authentic teachers are always teaching; the job is never done because it is an integral part of the person, and the person is an inseparable part of the job. The redeeming feature of this perpetual state of professional and personal becoming is that authentic teachers are as much benefactors as they are architects of their own teaching. They are constantly learning, growing, developing, imagining, creating, critiquing, experimenting, reconstructing, and enjoying themselves. In other words, they are engaged in the high quality kinds of learning expected of students. Because they have personal experience with success, they are in a much better position to provide parallel learning opportunities to their students. They teach from the perspective of "do as I do," not the more conventional one of "do as I say." What better way to model success than for teachers to be in communion and community with students throughout the entire teaching process, not just be directors of it. This connectedness with students and the continuous reconstruction of the person and the process comprise the essence of teaching authentically.

Warm regards,

References

Ayers, W. (2004). *Teaching the personal and the political: Essays on hope and justice.* New York: Teachers College Press.

Greene, M. (1984). The art of being present: Educating for aesthetic encounters. *Journal of Education, 166*(2), 123–135.

Kleinfeld, J. (1975). Effective teachers of Eskimo and Indian students. *School Review, 83*(2), 301–344.

Pinar, W. (1975). Transcendence and the curriculum. In W. Pinar (Ed.), *Curriculum theorizing: The conceptualists* (pp. 323–337). Berkeley, CA: McCutchan.

Ware, F. (2006). Warm demander pedagogy: Culturally responsive teaching that supports a culture of achievement for African American students. *Urban Education, 41*(4), 427–456.

Chapter 6

Dewey, Aristotle, and You

Barbara Morgan-Fleming

Dear Teacher,

First let me congratulate you on choosing a wonderful occupation. I use the word occupation, not because I don't view teaching as a profession, but because it is a situation in which one is fully and constantly occupied—never a dull moment. That's the good news.

It's also the bad news. Sometimes teaching can be so overwhelming that it is difficult to find the time, energy, and inclination to reflect on and learn from the situations in which you find yourself. Often in these real world crises, we might view the academic world of philosophy as Pollyanna irrelevance, important to passing a test in the academy, but irrelevant to the problems and classroom emergencies a teacher encounters in her first year. This is one situation in which the counter-intuitive is actually the case (actually not a rare event in teaching).

Although Dewey and Aristotle may use language different from what one hears in the faculty lounge, the subjects they address (e.g., What counts as knowledge? How does one decide if something is true? How does one apply moral/ethical beliefs to everyday situations?) are relevant to the decisions teachers make every day in their classrooms. It is important that these decisions be investigated, and that one's assumptions (along with the assumptions of colleagues and institutions) be vulnerable to challenge and learning. Failure to do so can lead to the cynicism that causes one to give up on one's ideals because of the difficulty of ideal enactment. It is important to remember that the classroom is filled with mortals. No one is perfect, but we can all challenge ourselves to improve and look for ways to actively enjoy the process of improvement.

I experienced this tension when I was in the dual roles of fifth-grade teacher and graduate student in a philosophy of education course. I published an article (Morgan, 1993) that offered the following conclusion:

> The tension which exists between the rigorous philosophical form of practical argument and the day-to-day practice of teaching is a useful one. The demands of teaching are complex, and teachers must be able to manage competing and at times mutually exclusive goals. That very complexity, however, can cause one to lose one's sense of meaning and reason. The use of a rigorous analytical model to reflect on teaching action then serves as a way to maintain some elevation and perspective, but no analytical framework can completely encompass the complexity of teaching performed. The ill fit between teaching practice and formal models of teaching can be mutually beneficial, pushing the teacher to make explicit certain reasoning about actions in order that such reasoning can become vulnerable to change, and challenging formal models to deal with the practice of day-to-day teaching. (p. 124)

In the following section I provide quotations from Dewey and Aristotle illustrated with examples from my teaching experience.

Dewey

In his book, *How we think: A restatement of the relation of reflective thinking to the educative process,* Dewey (1933) offers insight and suggestions for identifying and solving the practical problems that arise daily in a teacher's life. I believe his advice is still useful today, although each of you will need to process his thoughts (along with your own), and apply them to situations in your day-to-day practice.

Given a difficulty, the next step is suggestion of some way out—the formation of some tentative plan or project, the entertaining of some theory that will account for the peculiarities in question, the consideration of some solution for the problem. The data at hand cannot supply the solution; they can only suggest it. What, then, are the sources of the suggestion? Clearly, past experience and a fund of relevant knowledge at one's command. If the person has had some acquaintance with similar situations, if he has dealt with material of the same sort before, suggestions more or less apt and helpful will arise. But unless there has been some analogous experience, confusion remains mere confusion. (p. 15)

This points to the importance of three factors in teaching: experience, reflection, and conversation. You are probably realizing that teaching, in practice, is much more complex than teaching in theory. It is tempting at such times to decide that the knowledge and ideals one has brought to teaching are "ivory tower," useless in the real world. Good teachers problem solve, and invent novel ways to put their knowledge and beliefs into practice. Experience is the first step in this process. Teaching involves situated knowledge, and much of it can only be learned when one is in the role of teacher.

But experience by itself is insufficient. One must also reflect on the experience and access the views and ideas of others who are involved in similar situations. As a mentor teacher I always encouraged preservice teachers to keep a daily journal, expressing feelings, asking questions, and making tentative plans to find the answers. It is important in this process to realize that all teachers struggle and that no one is perfect. Separating ego from practice is important. Then we can focus on a failed practice without feeling the overwhelming guilt that can interfere with creative problem solving. It's important to remember that teaching is not a simple task, and it will never be perfect. It can, however, be improved every day with reflection, and that's an important goal.

It is also important to access the knowledge and experience of others in the teaching profession through multiple conversations. I urge you to form a conversational network that includes experienced teachers and other novice teachers. Much of teachers' knowledge is implicit, going straight from thought to action, so you may need to structure the conversation with questions and situations arising in your practice. It is also important to get multiple views, because there is no magic wand in teaching, and excellent teachers may approach identical situations in different ways. Include these conversations in your reflection as you blend together experience and knowledge to improve your practice on a day-to-day basis.

Dewey offers suggestions to help. He recommends that we "cultivate those attitudes that are favorable to the use of the best methods of inquiry and testing. Knowledge of the methods alone will not suffice; there must be the desire, the will, to employ them...we shall here mention the attitudes that need to be cultivated in order to secure their adoption and use" (p. 29). These ideas are presented below and illustrated with examples from my experience.

> *Open-mindedness.* This attitude may be defined as freedom from prejudice, parti-sanship and such other habits as close the mind and make it unwilling to consider new problems and entertain new ideas...It includes an active desire to listen to more sides than one; to give heed to facts from whatever source they come; to give full at-tention to alternative possibilities; to recognize the possibility of error even in the beliefs that are dearest to us. Mental sluggishness is one great factor in closing the mind to new ideas. The path of least resistance and least trouble is a mental rut al-ready made. It requires troublesome work to undertake the alteration of old beliefs. (pp. 29–30)

This is a characteristic central to long-term good teaching. Teaching is an occupation in which one has to learn to rock one's own boat. It is easy to fall into a "group think" situation, in which one only interacts with those whose beliefs and practices are similar to one's own. It's important to remember Hegel's concept of thesis/antithesis. For growth, new perspectives, and solu-tions to occur, one must seek conversations with those who see the world differently and listen to what they say.

One of the most important and least respected voices in education is that of the children being taught. I recently completed two book chapters in which I include fifth-grade students' suggestions to new teachers. When I presented the work at national conferences the response was overwhelming. Those who had spent their careers as teachers and educational researchers said the advice was the best that they had heard and that they could think of nothing to add. So make sure your conversations include a variety of per-spectives. Open your mind so that answers can come in.

> *Whole-heartedness.* When anyone is thoroughly interested in some object and cause, he throws himself into it; he does so, as we say, 'heartily', or with a whole heart. The importance of this attitude or disposition is generally recognized in practical and moral affairs. But it is equally important in intellectual development. There is no greater enemy of effective thinking than divided interest. A pupil...feels obliged to study because he has to recite, to pass an examination, to make a grade, or be-cause he wishes to please his teacher or his parents...A genuine enthusiasm is an at-

titude that operates as an intellectual force. A teacher who arouses such an enthusiasm in his pupils has done something that no amount of formalized method, no matter how correct, can accomplish. (pp. 32–33)

In this time of high-stakes testing it is important to remember that a teacher's central task is to awaken the intrinsic interests in children that will cause them to continue the study when no one makes them. My reading benchmark when I was teaching fifth grade was when a parent complained that the child had been up all night reading with a flashlight under the covers. That commitment to reading would produce more reading fluency, vocabulary, and comprehension than hundreds of worksheets, and helping a child become a lifelong reader was one of my major goals. It is important to remember that there are no multiple-choice jobs in which one sits from eight to five and bubbles. Meaningful learning helps students apply the knowledge learned in situations that have yet to be invented.

> *Responsibility.* To be intellectually responsible is to consider the consequences of a projected step; it means to be willing to adopt these consequences when they follow reasonably from a position already taken. Intellectual responsibility secures integrity; that is to say, consistency and harmony in belief. It is not uncommon to see persons continue to accept beliefs whose logical consequences they refuse to acknowledge. They profess certain beliefs but are unwilling to commit themselves to the consequences that flow from them. (p. 32)

This quotation reminds us that it is important to avoid the blame game. When a problem arises sometimes teachers blame parents, parents blame students, and students blame both. One problem with this habit (there are many) is that each puts the responsibility on someone else's shoulders, thus losing the power to improve the situation. Think instead of what the situation would be if each person listed above took one hundred percent responsibility. As a teacher it is important to focus on your practice and figure out a way to teach every kid in the room. This will require tenacity, flexibility, and commitment, and will also produce the most rewarding teaching experience— when you look into a struggling learner's face and see the light come on. It is important to remember that every child can learn, and that it is your responsibility to start the process that makes that happen.

> *Judging theirs by ourselves.* Most persons are quite unaware of the distinguishing peculiarities of their own mental habits. They take their own mental operations for

granted and unconsciously make them the standard for judging the mental processes of others. Hence there is a tendency to encourage whatever in the pupil agrees with this attitude and to neglect or fail to understand whatever is incongruous with it. (p. 60)

Avoiding this tendency makes it possible to experience one of the greatest pleasures of teaching—getting inside the mind of someone who thinks very differently than you do. I experienced this on a daily basis as a teacher. There were students who would rather go outside and run around than sit quietly indoors with a good book! I once taught a student who could look at anything and make it in origami, and who told me that the main character of Huckleberry Finn was the Mississippi. Wow! It is important to ask open-ended questions, engage in close observation of children so that you can find their strengths, and help them apply those strengths to work on things that are hard for them.

> *Undue reliance upon personal influence.* Teachers—and this holds especially of the stronger and better teachers—tend to rely upon their personal strong points to hold a child to his work, and thereby to substitute their personal influence for that of subject matter as a motive for study...an influence that renders the pupil indifferent to the value of the subject for its own sake...Satisfying the teacher instead of the problem. The operation of the teachers' own mental habit tends, unless carefully watched and guided, to make the child a student of the teacher's peculiarities rather than of the subjects that he is supposed to study. His chief concern is to accommodate himself to what the teacher expects of him, rather than to devote himself energetically to the problems of subject matter. "Is this right?" comes to mean "Will this answer or this process satisfy the teacher?"—instead of meaning "Does it satisfy the inherent conditions of the problem?" (pp. 60–61)

This quotation reminds us that it is important to make sure that each student has some reason other than "the teacher said I had to" for engaging in learning. If we want students to be life long learners, in addition to teaching them the necessary skills, we must awaken in them the curiosity, desire, and confidence that will enable them to continue the process when we're no longer around. This process might begin with accountability to the teacher, but it can't end there.

Aristotle

Aristotle is another author who had a great deal to say about teaching and learning (Thomson, 1983). Here are some of his suggestions that I believe are relevant to teaching, helping you think about your practice and develop the attitudes necessary to be a lifelong teacher and learner.

Moral virtues, like crafts, are acquired by practice and habituation.
...the virtues we do acquire by first exercising them, just as happens in the arts. Anything that we have to learn to do we learn by the actual doing of it: People become builders by building and instrumentalists by playing instruments. Similarly we become just by performing just acts, temperate by performing temperate ones, brave by performing brave ones...the causes or means that bring about any form of excellence are the same as those that destroy it....Men will become good builders as a result of building well, and bad ones as a result of building badly. Otherwise there would be no need of anyone to teach them; they would all be born either good or bad. Now this holds good also of the virtues. It is the way that we behave in our dealings with other people that makes us just or unjust, and the way that we behave in the face of danger, accustoming ourselves to be timid or confident, that makes us brave or cowardly....So it is a matter of no little importance what sort of habits we form from the earliest age—it makes a vast difference, or rather all the difference in the world. (pp. 91–92)

This reminds us of the importance of remembering why we became teachers and constantly challenging our own practices to see if they fit with our ideals. We know that students learn by doing, so we need to remember that each of us learns to be an ethical teacher by teaching ethically. Again we must keep in mind that just because we can't be perfect doesn't mean we can't be better.

In a practical science, so much depends on particular circumstances that only general rules can be given.
The agents are compelled at every step to think out for themselves what the circumstances demand, just as happens in the arts of medicine and navigation. (p. 93)

This points to the importance of constant engagement on the part of the teacher. Rules and theories can be guideposts, but not magic wands. It is true that "every child can learn," but we must remember that not every child can learn in the same way. We must constantly engage in diagnosis and problem solving. Rote learning is not helpful for our students or for ourselves.

A cardinal rule: right conduct is incompatible with excess or deficiency in feelings and actions.
We must consider this fact: that it is in the nature of moral qualities that they are destroyed by deficiencies and excess, just as we can see...in the case of health...both

eating and drinking too much or too little destroy health, whereas the right quantity produces, increases and preserves it. So it is the same with temperance, courage and the other virtues. The man who shuns and fears everything and stands up to nothing becomes a coward; the man who is afraid of nothing at all, but marches up to every danger, becomes foolhardy....Thus temperance and courage are destroyed by excess and deficiency and preserved by the mean. (p. 94)

I often tell new teachers that teaching well is like trying to keep a seesaw level—anytime you are comfortable it's time to reconsider your practice. Introspection and reflection are vital in allowing us to develop the creativity and flexibility to teach every child, engaging in the strategies and tactics necessary to make our moral commitments maintain existence in the real (complex) world.

Our virtues are exercised in the same kinds of action as gave rise to them
But besides the fact that the virtues are induced and fostered as a result, and by the agency, of the same sort of actions as cause their destruction, the activities that flow from them will also consist in the same sort of actions. This is so in all the other more observable instances, e.g., in that of (bodily) strength. This results from taking plenty of nourishment and undergoing severe training and it is the strong man that will be best able to carry out this programme. So with the virtues. (pp. 94–95)

I conclude with this quotation because it reminds us of the importance of building moral strength as well as content knowledge and pedagogical strategies. To do this one must engage in conversation, introspection, observation, and scholarship. Remember why you decided to become a teacher and use all your resources and skills to make the world of education better for yourself and for your children.

Have fun and good luck!

Barbara Morgan-Fleming

References

Dewey, J. (1933). *How we think: A restatement of the relation of reflective thinking to the educative process.* Boston: D.C. Heath and Company.

Morgan, B. A. (1993). Practical rationality: A self-investigation. *Journal of Curriculum Studies, 25*(2), 115–124.

The ethics of Aristotle: The Nicomachean ethics. Translated by Thomson, J. A. K. (1983). New York: Penguin.

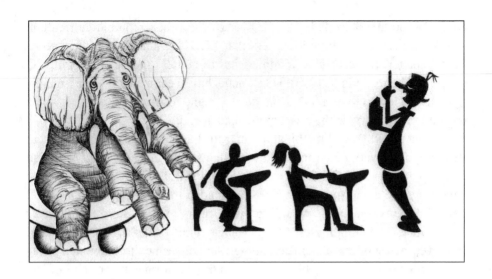

Chapter 7

An Elephant in the Classroom: LGBTQ Students and the Silent Minority

Paul Chamness Reece-Miller

Dear Fellow and Future Educators,

There is an elephant in our classrooms, and too many educators want to ignore it. In so doing, it has become a matter of life and death, so we can no longer pretend that the elephant is invisible. The elephant to which I am referring is the well-being of our lesbian, gay, bisexual, transgender and questioning (LGBTQ) students. Despite the fact that many popular television shows and movies now include LGBTQ characters, we still live by and large in a heteronormative society, where it is assumed, and even expected, that every member of society is heterosexual, and anyone who deviates from this expectation does not count or is simply ignored. This attitude is particularly noticeable in our schools, where teachers are still fired for their sexual orientation under "morals clauses" spelled out in their contracts, and where LGBTQ topics are still taboo as part of the curriculum. Even many teacher education programs exclude LGBTQ issues from their required curriculum, sending a message to future teachers that LGBTQ students and their needs do not matter. So teachers are unprepared to address the needs of LGBTQ students. The result is that LGBTQ students have become the "silent" minority who are left to live in fear and frustration and to struggle on their own as they attempt to survive the treacherous road ahead.

I want to tell you a little bit about myself. I am gay, and have known that I was gay for a very long time. I grew up in a strict, fundamentalist Christian household, where being LGBTQ is considered sinful. Growing up with these beliefs created a real struggle for me. I pretended I wasn't gay and hoped and prayed that my "gayness" would go away on its own. It didn't. So I never told anyone (including myself) that I was gay until I was in graduate school. However, many of my classmates in high school seemed to know that I was gay without my saying anything to them, and I was tormented because of it. I was called names, my locker was vandalized, I was threatened, and my clothes were stolen on many occasions in gym class. During part of my adolescence I rode a school bus, which was an even worse experience. I was constantly harassed on the bus, and often my sister came to my rescue because the bus driver was oblivious to anything going on behind the white line at the front of the bus. Because there were no teachers in my school who claimed to be supportive of LGBTQ students, and given my parents' religious views, I did not know whom I could trust. So, instead of confiding in someone, I kept these experiences and my feelings to myself. As you might imagine, I *hated* school. I did not have many friends because I was afraid of rejection. So I usually skipped lunch and hid in a cubicle in the library each day, and as soon as school was over, I went home. At one point in my adolescence, I began to feel like I could not take the ridicule anymore and wished that I would simply no longer exist. Of course, my religious beliefs forbade my even considering suicide, but I would often lie in bed at night and hope that, like Elijah, I would just vanish into thin air.

While this experience is my own personal story, many LGBTQ youth have extremely difficult experiences in school, where the classroom is not a safe, positive learning environment. In the past couple of decades, there has been some effort at addressing this problem. In 1990 Kevin Jennings founded the Gay, Lesbian, and Straight Education Network (GLSEN), whose mission is "to assure that each member of every school community is valued and respected regardless of sexual orientation or gender identity/expression"

(GLSEN, 2008, p. 1). They ensure that they carry out their mission by providing education to the community, teachers and students, as well as helping to establish Gay Straight Alliance (GSA) chapters in schools across the country. GLSEN also sponsors the National Day of Silence, and they are additionally involved in the National No Name-Calling Week in middle schools.

Despite the important work of organizations like GLSEN, research over the past couple of decades has shown that LGBTQ students, as well as those who are perceived by their peers to be LGBTQ, are still experiencing a wide array of difficulty in the classroom. In situations where youth decide to "come out" to friends and family, many studies have found that more than half of the individuals faced rejection from their friends and family, religious condemnation, and physical and/or verbal abuse (Uribe, 1994). In additional studies, many youth reported that they were uncomfortable being friends with an openly gay classmate (Lock, 2002). The discomfort of classmates, however, is unfortunately not so silent. In their nationwide, bi-annual research project, GLSEN found that a significant majority of the students in the study heard derogatory names from classmates like "faggot" or "dyke" and they also heard such expressions as "That's so gay" on a regular basis (Kosciw, Diaz, & Greytak, 2008). A myth that I have heard on numerous occasions from teachers is that things are better now in terms of the name calling. However, GLSEN's report over the past several years has shown that the word "gay" is used as much today as it was in 2001, when they launched their first study. Although there is an indication that other negative words are used with marginally less frequency now than in previous years, such words are still heard too much in the hallways and classrooms of our schools.

Perhaps more alarming for educators than name-calling is that among all sexual minority age groups, LGBTQ youth are at the greatest risk for becoming victims of violence (Lock, 2002). Kosciw, Diaz, & Greytak (2008) found that about half of the victims were physically harassed (e.g., pushed or shoved) based on either their sexual orientation or their gender expression. About one quarter of the students were physically assaulted with a weapon for the same reasons. Almost all of the students were victims of theft, vandalism, and/or vicious rumors, and about half were victims of the more contemporary form of harassment known as cyberbullying (e.g., harassment via blogs, social network sites like Myspace or Facebook, text messages and chatrooms). Similar statistics were found in a variety of studies (see Lock, 2002), many of which were reported 10 to 15 years ago; and here we are today, finding our classrooms in no better condition. In fact, based on GLSEN's 2005 report, the situation is worse now than it was even two years ago.

In fact, the situation for LGBTQ students has become quite dangerous. At times bullying and harassment has turned into murder. This sentiment is illustrated in a tragic event that took place on Valentine's Day in 2008 in Oxnard, California, when 14-year-old Brandon McInerney shot Lawrence King in the head in a classroom at their school. Lawrence was openly gay, which prompted an argument between him and Brandon the day before. While I will not pretend to know what drives a teenager to such horrific acts of violence, it is clear that homophobia played its role in the choice that Brandon made to pull the trigger, and homophobia contributes to many other acts of violence committed against LGBTQ youth across this country.

The harassment and bullying of LGBTQ students is not carried out solely by other adolescents. It is despicable and unacceptable to learn that teachers also make homophobic comments and tell homophobic jokes at school (Elze, 2003). In an interview I conducted once with a teacher I'll call Dylan, he described his high school to me, which was divided into a variety of magnet-type "small schools." One of the small schools was a performing arts school and had the reputation of being the school for all the "fags and freaks," a name used by students and teachers alike. And in one instance, Dylan overheard a colleague warn another teacher who was going to walk over to the performing arts school to be sure and "cover his butt" as he walked down their hallway. While this comment was not said in front of students, it still reveals the horrific attitude that teachers can have toward LGBTQ students.

This attitude extends beyond homophobic comments, jokes and name-calling. It is also seen in how teachers and administrators respond to the victimization of LGBTQ students. Kosciw, Diaz, & Greytak (2008) revealed that in their study less than half of the students who were victimized, bullied or harassed reported the incident to a school official or a parent, and of those who did report these incidents, half of the students reported that nothing was done or that at most the victimizer was simply told to never to do it again.

Some studies have found that only about half of the LGBTQ students, when being tormented, were able to find supportive teachers or administrators in their schools (Reis & Saewyc, 1999). Kosciw, Diaz, & Greytak (2008), however, found that eight out of ten students had found at least one teacher or administrator who was supportive. The study also revealed that the more teachers and staff are supportive of LGBTQ individuals, the greater their sense of belonging to the school community. It is, therefore, vital for teachers to make an effort to show students that they are caring and supportive, because when there is the perception that teachers and administrators do nothing in these situations, the school sends the message to LGBTQ youth that it is okay for them to be victimized or perhaps that they somehow deserve what they get. In such situations, students have nowhere to turn for support.

I have focused to this point on what takes place in the schools themselves, but trouble also exists at home, especially, but not exclusively, among families that are extremely religious (Uribe, 1994). Some research suggests that half of LGBTQ youth who come out to their parents receive a negative reaction, with about a quarter of them being completely abandoned and kicked out of the house (Ray, 2006). One such instance happened to a ten-year-old boy who hadn't come out, but whose parents only suspected that he was gay. Based solely on a suspicion, they decided that they did not even want to keep him in their home and gave him up to the state (Alexander, 2000). People came to this boy's aid, but the reality is that many LGBTQ youth have nowhere to go and end up living on the streets. But for those who are fortunate enough to at least have a home, it is important to keep in mind that they may still be struggling with their parents and other family members to get them to accept who they are. And like many other situations going on in the adolescent's life, such experiences may affect what takes place in the classroom.

As you might imagine, because LGBTQ adolescents do not often feel safe at school, coupled with the lack of support that they find at school or at home, they are at a much greater risk for academic difficulty. Kosciw, Diaz, & Greytak (2008) reported that LGBTQ students who are harassed are more likely to skip school. These same students are at a greater risk to have lower grades and choose not to pursue a post-secondary degree. LGBTQ students are also at greater risk for dropping out of school, engaging in substance abuse and other self-endangering behavior, as well as experiencing clinical depression and attempting suicide (Lock, 2002). In fact, some reports suggest that as many as one third of teen suicides may be related to struggles with sexual identity (Uribe, 1994).

I realize that I have painted a pretty grim picture of the life of an LGBTQ adolescent, but this is the stark reality for many of our students. I hope this picture has evoked in you compassion and empathy for the silent minority. Despite the negative experiences of many LGBTQ youth, some go through school very successfully. Others may experience harassment and other forms of discrimination, but because they have a strong support system, manage to handle these situations fairly well. Regardless, it is crucial that teachers and administrators be aware of LGBTQ students in their schools and that they be willing to take proactive steps to make schools safe, positive spaces for all students, regardless of their sexual orientation. This is my personal charge to you, the readers of this book.

So, with that charge, I hope that you are now asking yourself what you can do to make school a better place for LGBTQ students. A place to start is to understand a few fundamental points about what it means to be LGBTQ. Contrary to what many may think, being LGBTQ is not a phase out of which one will grow on the way to adulthood. Clinical studies suggest that the average age at which an adolescent will identify their sexual orientation is 14 years, and others report average ages even as low as 10 to 12 years (Uribe, 1994). So telling a student that he or she is just going through a phase may cause more harm than good. At the same time, one should also be careful not to force labels on students. Although many students may have a clear sense of who they are early on in their adolescence, others may take much longer to discover who they are, and labeling will only add stress to this process (Uribe, 1994). Also, labeling presents another danger, that of making such a label the single factor by which others define LGBTQ youth. They have names, likes and dislikes, hopes and fears, hobbies, unique personalities, and other defining attributes that straight people have.

Another popular misconception is that if teachers discuss homosexuality, they will in fact "make" their students homosexual. Nothing could be farther from the truth. If anything, students will benefit from honest, truthful information about sexuality, coupled with an attitude that sexual identity does not determine the value or quality of one's life (Uribe, 1994). The fear that individual teachers may have of discussing homosexuality may also be reflected in the general attitude of the school community as a whole, where the existence of LGBTQ youth is not even acknowledged. For example, a student I will call Greg revealed in a case study in which he was a participant what it was like to be invisible at his school. To him this was perhaps more significant than any negativity he experienced during his schooling. In particular, he describes how his school, in an effort to avoid facing issues of homosexuality at their prom, only allowed couple tickets to be purchased for heterosexual couples, with no provision for same-sex couples. This event was a very salient experience for Greg (Allen, 2006). Invisibility, which is common in many middle and high schools across the country, clearly sends a message to LGBTQ students that they do not matter and that they are somehow inferior to straight students.

It is clear to me that LGBTQ students need to know that they do matter and that they are an important part of our schools, but for some teachers it may be difficult to embrace this idea for a number of reasons. Teacher research has revealed that some individuals are uncomfortable and even harbor negative feelings when interacting with LGBTQ youth, and others are afraid that if they take up the "gay cause" in school, their colleagues and administrators will assume that they are also LGBTQ (Endo, Miller, & Santavicca, 2008; Sears, 1991). But the fact of the matter is that LGBTQ students are present in all of our schools no matter how invisible our society makes them. So I challenge each of you to take a step forward and refuse to allow your students to be invisible, even if this means stepping out of your comfort zone.

In addition to making LGBTQ students visible in school, I also challenge you to help put an end to the use of homophobic language in your schools. In my work with pre-service and in-service teachers, many have expressed their frustration in trying to get their students to understand why it is wrong to say "That's so gay," so I would like to share with you an approach I took to tackle this problem when I was teaching high school. But first let me preface this story by stating that I am not suggesting that anyone else use my approach. It could backfire or you could get into trouble, but it worked for me in this situation, and had an impact on the whole school, not just my own classroom. I spent several months repeatedly explaining to my students that such expressions were inappropriate, but I wasn't sure if the students truly understood what I was trying to say or if they were just avoiding the expression in my classroom because they knew I did not like it. However, there was one student, whom I will call Josh, who refused to stop using the expression. So one day I told the class that for the day they could say "that's so Josh" instead of "that's so gay." Much to my surprise, the expression went with the students to their other classes, and was used across the school for a couple of days before its novelty wore off. I had a talk with Josh along with the rest of the class and asked him how he felt, and he told us that he felt bad when people used his name like that, and he finally began to see why the expression "that's so gay" is so wrong. I was finally able to sigh with contentment that I had reached Josh, and through that example, helped others to see why such expressions are wrong. As I disclaimed before telling you this story, I do not recommend using this example in your own classrooms, but I do encourage you to be creative in establishing your own approaches to tackle this problem. While it is great to put an end to the use of expressions like "fag," "dyke," and "that's so gay," it is also important to try to help students understand why such words are harmful.

Finally, I would like to challenge you to examine closely the curriculum in your schools. The curriculum in American schools is by and large founded on heterosexism and continues to exclude LGTBQ content (Kosciw, Diaz, & Greytak, 2008; Robinson & Ferfolja, 2001). Despite the exclusive nature of the curriculum, there are many opportunities for teachers to include content that is representative of all members of society, including LGBTQ persons. I was working as a high school French teacher when it came time for my first-year students to discuss families. I made an effort to include in the content all types of families, including same-sex parents. I also included cultural elements as part of my lessons that discussed the legalization of same-sex unions, the right for same-sex couples to adopt children, and so forth. Textbooks obviously exclude this type of content, so I had to make a conscious effort to include it in my lessons. Supplementing lesson plans to make them more inclusive is a great way for teachers to address bias found in the curriculum. Of course, you may have challenges from parents or administrators, as my friend and colleague Denise did when she stepped out of the box and took a risk as part of her sociology class. Denise was teaching a unit on social stigmas and wanted to invite a speaker who was HIV positive to come and speak about what it was like living in society with this disease. She struggled to get appropriate approval, with resistance from the principal and some parents, because they were worried the speaker would focus on the fact that he was gay. But with her persuasive argument, she finally convinced the administration to allow her to invite her guest, who ultimately had a positive impact on her students' learning. One student, in fact, wrote a letter to the editor of the local newspaper to challenge the entire community's belief system. We need more teachers willing to take these kinds of risks, and make the curriculum more representative of all our students.

So I leave you with a few final thoughts. Our avoidance of the elephant in the classroom has become a matter of life and death. It is time for teachers, administrators, teacher educators, parents and all other community members to open their eyes, see the elephant, and provide the attention that all our students, even LGBTQ students, deserve. Regardless of your personal convictions or whatever else may be preventing you from acknowledging this elephant, the fact of the matter is that our youth are suffering, and some are dying. It is our ethical duty to put an end to the suffering and to provide a safe, positive learning environment for each and every student in the classroom. I like the idea of the Hippocratic Oath that doctors take as they enter their profession, and I think teachers should take a similar oath. Until that happens, I offer you one final challenge: Will you take an oath to be an advocate for the silent minority, the student that no one wants to see? I hope you will, because LGBTQ students are counting on you, and so am I.

All my best,

References

Alexander, C. J. (2000). Gay youth: More visible but fewer problems? *Journal of Gay & Lesbian Social Services, 11*(4), 113–117.

Allen, L. (2006). Trying not to think "straight": Conducting focus groups with lesbian and gay youth. *International Journal of Qualitative Studies in Education, 19*, 163–176.

Elze, D. E. (2003). Gay, lesbian, and bisexual youths' perceptions of their high school environments and comfort in school. *Children & Schools, 25*, 225–239.

Endo, H., Miller, P. C., Santavicca, N. (2008). *Surviving in the trenches: A narrative inquiry into queer teachers' experiences and identity.* (Unpublished manuscript).

GLSEN. (2005). *The 2005 national school climate survey: Executive summary of a report from the gay, lesbian, & straight education network.* Retrieved January 12, 2009, from: http://www.glsen.org/binary-data/GLSEN_ATTACHMENTS/file/582-2.pdf.

GLSEN. (2008a). *About us.* Retrieved on January 12, 2009, from http://www.glsen.org/cgi-bin/iowa/all/about/history/index.html.

Kosciw, J. G., Diaz, E. M., & Greytak, E. A. (2008). *The 2007 national school climate survey: The experiences of lesbian, gay, bisexual and transgender youth in our nation's schools.* New York: Gay, Lesbian, & Straight Education Network. Retrieved January 18, 2009, from http://www.glsen.org/binary-data/GLSEN_ATTACHMENTS/file/000/001/1290-1. pdf.

Lock, J. (2002). Violence and sexual minority youth. *Journal of School Violence, 1*(3), 77–89.

Ray, N. (2006). *Lesbian, gay, bisexual and transgender youth: An epidemic of homelessness.* Washington, DC: National Gay and Lesbian Task Force.

Reis, B., & Saewyc, E. (1999). *Eighty-three thousand youth: Selected findings from eight population-based studies as they pertain to anti-gay harassment and the safety and well being of sexual minority students.* Retrieved January 18, 2009, from http://www.safe schoolscoalition.org/83000youth.pdf.

Robinson, K. H., & Ferfolja, T. (2001). "What are we doing this for?": Dealing with lesbian and gay issues in teacher education. *British Journal of Sociology of Education, 22*(1), 121–133.

Sears, J. (1991). Educators, homosexuality, and homosexual students: Are personal feelings related to professional beliefs? *Journal of Homosexuality, 22*(3/4), 29–79.

Uribe, V. (1994). The silent minority: Rethinking our commitment to gay and lesbian youth. *Theory into Practice, 33*, 167–172.

Chapter 8

Uncovering Internalized Oppression

Angela Valenzuela

Dear Bold Teacher,

I begin by sharing a personal story that has great significance for U.S. Mexican and other children of color. Borrowing from Pizarro (2005), I suggest that teachers too rarely notice the "soul wounds" that students of color inflict upon one another. These wounds can result in internalized oppression, meaning that minority group members subscribe to the dominant group's negative stereotypes of their group (Córdova, 2005; Fanon, 1991; Memmi, 1965; Torres, 2003). Even well-meaning teachers routinely fail to help children and youth of color heal from the soul wounds that they experience at the hands of White students and adults; they often fail even to notice the ways that children and youth of color wound one another. In order to help students begin to heal from these wounds, educators need to learn from stories like this one.

I have suppressed this memory for years. I finally wrote this account on July 1, 2003, after visiting with a childhood friend, Norma, who still resides in San Angelo, Texas, my hometown. This painful memory from my seventh-grade year fills me with a deep sense of guilt and remorse, but it also reveals a larger problem of self-hatred and internalized oppression that originates within powerful societal institutions like schools, a primary site where young people internalize dominant ideologies that non-White selves are inferior (Macedo, 1994; Olson, 1998; Valenzuela, 1999).

I was in the seventh grade at Robert E. Lee Junior High School, where Mexican-origin and African American youth comprised about a third of a school population that was otherwise Anglo. I remember being small and scared. I was especially afraid of getting beaten up by a group of African American girls who would bully the smaller students for their lunch money. I recall my seventh-grade year being a continuous dodging experience and a series of narrow escapes from these threatening bullies. Consequently, I felt the need to show toughness and hang out with students who were tough. I befriended Norma, who was tougher and more physically mature than me. Whenever I was around her, I felt protected. Norma was not only attractive, but she strutted about with an attitude, wearing her stylish threads. Though from a poor family, she always dressed fashionably, primarily because she made all of her clothing herself. All of us girls admired her for her looks, and in my case, how they combined with her tough *chola* ("wannabe" gangster) demeanor.

Norma had a problem with another female student that I had trouble understanding. Although her name was Jovita, she pronounced her name "Joe-vita," an Anglicized version of her name (in Spanish, the *j* sounds like an h). Unlike Norma, myself, and the majority of Mexican-origin youth, who were Mexican American, she was an immigrant girl who spoke more Spanish than we did and wore a lot of makeup together with clothes that Norma derisively referred to as "K-Mart specials." Norma routinely ridiculed all of these things. Norma had so much power over me that I felt embarrassed and became secretive about the fact that my mother purchased my clothes from K-Mart whenever she did not make them herself. Hypocritically, I recall occasionally chiming in when Norma commented on Jovita's clothing. I drew warped, teenage pleasure in making Jovita the object of our ridicule. It seemed harmless enough in the beginning, especially since the two of us did not know her anyway.

As time wore on, Norma's antipathy toward Jovita deepened. Jovita seemed to symbolize all that Norma wanted to expunge from her own sense of self. While Mexican Americans like Norma and me also spoke Spanish at home and English at school, we distinguished ourselves as Mexican Americans from Mexican immigrants. Norma reserved her strongest West Texas twang for times when she would talk or joke about "those Mexicans from the other side" or "those Mexicans from 'ol Mexico.'" Despite our shared origins, we tended to view the less Anglicized immigrants among us as inferior distant cousins or to ignore their existence altogether. Unfortunately, I was not sophisticated enough to recognize these behaviors as manifestations of internalized oppression. I now understand that in disparaging all poor Mexican immigrants, Norma disparaged herself.

My need to be Norma's friend kept me from sharing a lot of my own Mexican-ness with her, including the fact that my mother's parents were from Mexico. I felt pressured to be Mexican American, with the emphasis on American—somehow better, superior, and "richer" than "those Mexicans" like Jovita. My relationship with Norma provided the support I needed in order to be tough. The use of profanity, especially in Spanish, became a personal strategy for securing both Norma's esteem and my survival in middle school. Thinking, acting, and feeling tough just like Norma would carry me through, I thought.

The pecking order among the Mexican girls was established in gym class. Norma would make a nasty comment at Jovita, and Jovita would snap back. They carried on this way until one day, one of them challenged the other to a fight after school. Word spread like wildfire throughout the school: Norma and Jovita were going to fight. I remember how my heart of darkness—a toxic mixture of internalized racism and teenage cruelty—desired to witness the fight. But I was unable to come up with an excuse for my mother, so she picked me up from school that day as she customarily did. I would like to think that my own sense of integrity kept me from going, but I know that had I had the opportunity, I would have gone.

The next day, the school was abuzz about the knock-down, drag-out fight that had unfolded in a secluded lot nearby. I heard from friends that the fight got really wild and crazy, with Norma giving Jovita a black eye, and how Norma peeled off Jovita's shirt and how she fought in her bra. The details of the punches, scratches, and kicking before a jeering crowd horrified me. In my adolescent mind, I agonized over the implications. What had

Jovita done to deserve this? I thought to myself. What crime was it to be Mexican and poor? Weren't we all only just a notch "above" her, if even that much? Why did Norma hate Jovita so intensely? I wish that back then I had a language for internalized oppression. I can now say with confidence that Norma's punishing of Jovita was a punishing of her own Mexican self. The hatred that many students of color today hold toward members of their own ethnic group signifies a hidden injury resulting from our country's sordid racial history. Messages about the inferiority of non-"Whites," particularly immigrants, continue to circulate openly today.

Jovita missed several days of school. Not many days remained. When she finally did return, I remember seeing her black, blue, and dark-green eye. I observed her as she walked with great poise, silently, through the crowd. She held her head up high and looked straight ahead as faces turned to catch a glimpse of the damage. Gossip and whispers filled the air as she walked through the school's main hallway, momentarily transformed into a gauntlet that perpetuated the spectacle. I remember looking at Jovita and feeling sorry for her and feeling deeply ashamed, as if I had done something wrong. I took exceptional comfort in knowing that I had not witnessed the fight, but wondered whether she knew that. I feared that the more likely case was that she saw me as a perpetrator, little different from the throng that gathered on that fateful day.

Looking back, I realize that Norma, Jovita, and all the school's Mexican Americans had to walk a tightrope of holding onto our childhood tongue and identity in a schooling context that was indifferent, even hostile, to it. Although Spanish was my first language, English assumed dominance during elementary school even as Spanish became a resource central to middle school, peer-group survival. We Mexican Americans and Mexican immigrants were subjected to English-only school policies and practices premised on cultural erasure. Texas history was particularly degrading. The way it was taught reminded us Mexicans that we were losers and that Anglos were militarily and culturally superior. Never mind that Anglos fought this war to defend their right to own slaves or that Texas Mexicans also fought and died at the Alamo.

I can now see that this experience, coupled with hearing my parents' and grandparents' stories of racism, classism, and sexism, marked a turning point in the development of my social and political consciousness. I remember vividly how I resented feeling at once vulnerable and dependent on Norma.

Thankfully, by the eighth grade, the bullies were gone and I no longer needed her for protection. While I remained friends with her, our friendship continued more on my own terms. As for Jovita, I never saw her again. Did she move to another school? Had she dropped out of school before her eighth-grade year? Did Jovita pay the price of soul wounds inflicted by internalized racism, with Norma and me as acting as its unwitting agents? Given the severe humiliation she had endured, I inferred the worst and have felt guilty about it ever since. As if in silent agreement, Norma and I never spoke of the incident again. Perhaps she, too, felt guilty.

I suppressed the whole incident from my memory. My memory resurfaced just recently upon visiting Norma, whom I had seen only twice in the last 24 years. She spoke negatively and in a scornful tone about "Mexican people" and how "they" are often not very supportive of one another. Her own self-hatred jolted me that evening, reminding me of the sentiments that fueled her animosity against Jovita. She sounded little different from bigoted Anglos who make blanket judgments about all Mexicans, constructing a dehumanizing "we/they" dichotomy that expresses their power and sense of superiority over them.

I hope that in writing this story, I can finally put this incident to rest. Experiences like Jovita's are not in vain if we as educators use these stories, first to educate ourselves about internalized racism and then to afford children of color the chance to speak and write of their own experiences of denigrating others or being denigrated as racial and ethnic minorities in a racist, sexist, and classist society.

Even educators who have not experienced internalized oppression themselves have been affected by the pejorative meanings assigned to racial and ethnic groups in the U.S. By reflecting with students on how these ideas circulate inside schools or in the media, educators can help students dissect the multiple ways that such societal institutions condition all people to hold harmful stereotypes and blanket judgments and condition many to take the oppressor role against members of their own group.

To get started, educators might discuss with students what media images of their group look like and how such images affect students' sense of themselves, as well as others. For example, they might analyze the effects that political campaigns promoting English-only policies and anti-immigrant sentiments have either on nonimmigrants' notions about immigrants or on immigrants' (or children of immigrants') thoughts and feelings about themselves (Macedo, 1994; Torres, 2003).

Educators can ask students to consider how similar dynamics of berating particular groups play out in their school. In my book, *Subtractive Schooling* (1999), I show how Mexican immigrant and Mexican American students struggle daily in schools with what to make of their "Mexican" traits in an "American" context—even in a segregated, virtually all-Mexican-origin school (Valenzuela, 1999). I show the damage done to self when a student of Mexican descent seeks in a school context to expunge those allegedly socially objectionable traits that are often associated with their *Mexicanidad* (Mexicanness). By this term, I do not suggest that a unitary "Mexican" identity does or should exist. Rather, U.S. Mexicans occupy a borderlands space characterized by constant negotiation around meanings of their hybrid and frequently conflicted identities (Anzaldúa, 1999; Anzaldúa and Moraga, 1983).

Students from all minority groups must struggle constantly with whether and how to keep or discard the group traits they see in themselves, which are so often disparaged by others that they come to disparage them themselves. My research points to schools as a key site for this struggle. Students can engage in discussions of whether and how young people are pushed to fit themselves into categories of racial difference; for example, they can consider whether in their school, as in my own junior high, youth are expected to choose between being Mexican or American in an either/or, rather than in a both/and fashion. They can discuss how it affects them personally if the cultures, languages, and histories—including women's histories—of their own groups are excluded or ignored in the curriculum. They can then start the complex process of discussing how some students, or they themselves, might come to condemn the cultural and linguistic traits that reside within their own peer networks and neighborhood community.

Long before ever setting forth to engage students compassionately in an analysis of how disparaging treatments of self can arise, educators must start becoming aware of the soul wounds inflicted by young group members on themselves. Educators' basic awareness of such dynamics promises not only to help students like Norma and Jovita but also to humanize and enrich the classroom and schooling experience for all.

Sincerely,

References

Anzaldúa, G. (1999). *Borderlands/La Frontera.* San Francisco: Aunt Lute Books.

Anzaldúa, G. & Moraga, C. (1983). *This bridge called my back: Writings by radical women of color,* 2nd edition. New York: Kitchen Table, Women of Color Press.

Córdova, T. (2005). Agency, commitment and connection: Embracing the roots of Chicano and Chicana Studies. Special Issue: Presence, Voice, and Politics in Chicana/o Studies, *International Journal of Qualitative Studies in Education 18*(2), March-April, pp. 221–233.

Fanon, F. (1965). *The wretched of the earth.* Grove Press.

Fanon, F. (1991). *Black skin, white masks.* Grove Press.

Macedo, D. 1994. *Literacies of power: What Americans are not allowed to know.* Boulder, CO: Westview Press.

Memmi, A. (1965). *The colonizer and the colonized.* Boston: Beacon Press.

Olson, L. (1998). *Made in America: Immigrant students in our public schools.* New York: New Press.

Pizarro, M. (2005). *Chicanas and Chicanos in school: Racial profiling, identity battles, and empowerment.* University of Texas Press.

Torres, E. E. (2003) *Chicana without apology: The new Chicana Cultural Studies.* NY: Routledge.

Valenzuela, A. (1999). *Subtractive Schooling: U.S- Mexican Youth and the Politics of Caring.* Albany: State University of New York Press.

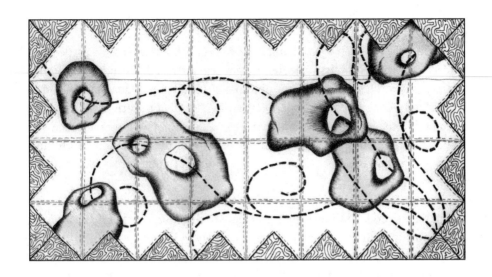

Chapter 9

The Power of Water

Mary Cain Fehr

Dear Fellow Educators,

As an agent of change, which would you rather be, metaphorically: a rock or water? In a previous job, my colleagues and I half jokingly said we would ask this question when interviewing prospective employees, since our field, instructional technology, required the ability to facilitate change. Our consensus was that water is a far more effective agent. It has the impressive ability to seep into tiny crevices and wear away resistance, subtly, gently and steadily. As a result, it can reshape rock and carve new channels for powerful forces to flow. Teaching boldly also requires the ability to facilitate change. In my teaching experiences, I have used the water approach to accomplish things that would have otherwise been met with resistance. I'd like to share two examples with you.

Sewing for Safety

In my last P–12 teaching assignment, I taught art to students in grades 3–6 whose lives were seriously affected by poverty, crime, and drugs. Taking this job was my professional choice, one that some of my acquaintances didn't understand. They expressed condolences to me, if not outright shock. True enough, it was not an easy assignment, but I quickly saw how much the students needed good teachers and the resources that the school could provide. They also needed respect, love, and teaching that considered their cultures and life situations.

One evening at home, I happened to tune into a local TV channel on which the zip codes of local sex offenders are disclosed for public awareness. After watching the criminals' information (including their specific crimes) scroll across the screen for a while, I noticed to my dismay that the majority of these individuals resided in the zip code of my school, and that most of them had committed their crimes against *children!* I wondered if our students had been given any personal safety training. My own children had, twenty years earlier, even in our suburban school district. Surely my current students had, right?

Wrong. I went to our building administrators and learned that no personal safety curriculum was in place. Our students were not learning to steer away from potentially dangerous situations, and they were not learning about community resources that help families in dangerous situations. So another teacher and I offered to take a look at some curricula to address this need and find a way to implement it. We looked online and went to the school district offices and to the regional education support center to check out their curriculum kits. We brought several to our school for teachers and administrators to consider. Only a few people took the time to preview the materials, but we made a selection nonetheless. When we made our final recommendation to the school administrators (who were replaced at midterm for unrelated reasons), we were told that we could not proceed with this plan because we teachers were not trained to handle the situations that could result from discussing such sensitive topics. I suppose they thought it would be better to allow our students to be abused or injured than to take the risk of bringing a bad situation to light or implementing a curriculum that might be controversial. That was one can of worms they were not willing to open. I suppose we were a little too direct, given the situation, the people involved, and the timing. It was perhaps the *rock* approach to facilitating change.

However, I was not willing to leave my students uneducated about ways to stay safe. So I developed a curricular unit in art that took the *water* approach. Sometimes you have to sneak things in the back door. Sometimes being subtle with a specific purpose, for the sake of your students, is teaching boldly.

I told my students that they were going to make a quilt for a special reason: We were going to donate it to the local women's shelter when it was finished. I felt it was important for my students to know that, even with as little as some of them possessed, they could still contribute something to the community. We decided that our beautiful quilt could be used by someone staying at the shelter, to provide warmth and some cheer. It just might make their day or night a little bit better. It might bring a smile to someone's face during a dark time of life.

On the first day of this project, I asked my sixth-grade students if they knew what a women's shelter was. Out of two groups of students, only one student had even the slightest idea. This confirmed my hunch that there was a need for this information. So I told them that a women's shelter is a place where women and their children could go and stay a few days, when they didn't feel safe at home for any reason. I emphasized the fact that the shelter is free and available to anyone who might feel the need to go there for protection. Although the location of the shelter is not made public for security reasons, we talked about how to telephone the shelter if there was a need. My male students wanted to know if men could go there, too, if they didn't feel safe. What an interesting question!

During the next few weeks, each student made a quilt square that featured his or her face, photographed with a digital camera and then reduced with computer software to only two tones: black and white. We printed these stylized images and then students traced them onto blocks of donated white fabric with permanent black markers. Next they created colorful geometric borders with heat transfer crayons. These self-portraits were very dramatic, and much more abstract and anonymous than the original photos. We chose black fabric for the strips between the quilt blocks and for the back of the quilt. Next, I brought my sewing machine to my art room so everyone could learn a new skill and participate in assembling the quilt. To my surprise the boys were highly interested in the sewing machine! To them it was like a car. They wanted to operate it and learn how to maintain it. I was delighted with their absence of gender bias about sewing!

One of my sixth-grade boys, Reggie (pseudonym) had been resistant in my class during the first few weeks of school. He was unmotivated and often acted out (probably my fault for not connecting with him soon enough). But when he started working on his quilt square, he became enthused and was proud of his self portrait. It was so nicely done, in fact, that I selected it for exhibition at the county fair student art show. *Reggie had turned a corner!* I went home that Friday feeling encouraged and proud of him.

On Saturday I received a phone call from a fellow teacher who told me that Reggie had been shot near the school and had died in the emergency room. I was devastated. The next week, my students used art to help process their grief by choosing to draw elaborate memorial images instead of working on our quilt. The faculty and staff took up a collection to help pay for Reggie's funeral. Even the custodian made beaded bracelets and sold them to teachers to help raise money. After the funeral, which was standing room only and heart wrenching, we had a schoolwide balloon release in memory of Reggie. Reggie's quilt square was exhibited posthumously with a memorial plaque at the art show. After the show I gave it to his mother. To this day the balloon release photo hangs in my office to remind me of Reggie and the outpouring of emotion at our school that resulted from his death. Still, the school administrators had no interest in a personal safety program.

As work on our quilt progressed, I contacted the women's shelter to tell them about our gift and to ask if a representative might come to our school so the students could formally present our quilt. They immediately agreed to send their community education specialist to our school. Exactly the person I wanted!

We continued to work on the quilt, and we made big plans for the presentation in early spring. We invited parents, school administrators, school district administrators, and the local media. I wanted my students to know that they had done something important! We arranged to have punch, cookies, and a presentation/celebration in the school's library.

Five weeks after Reggie's death we were stunned by another loss. This time it was a multiple loss. Three of our students, twin brothers and their sister, and their mother were beaten to death in the middle of the night in their home. Just imagine the anguish that struck our hearts and our school community.

I asked myself over and over, "If they suspected impending danger, could they have been saved by going to the women's shelter?" The culmination of our project seemed too late for them. One of the deceased children, a third grader, had drawn the cutest picture of himself for me a few weeks before this horrifying event. The crayon figure had a speech bubble coming from his mouth, proclaiming, "I'm happy!" Around its neck was a gold necklace. The necklace is enlarged in an inset box in the lower right corner of the page—a pretty sophisticated visual idea for a third grader, I thought! When DeShawn (pseudonym) first brought his drawing to me, the enlarged necklace incorporated the word "pimp." I quietly said to him that maybe this was not an appropriate word to write on schoolwork, so he went back to his table, changed the necklace to say, "I love you," and then presented the drawing to me as a gift. That drawing also hangs in my office now, and it always will.

Time passed. Wounds began to heal, and we finished our quilt. It was so visually striking that other teachers stopped by the art room to preview it and compliment my young artists. Finally, the time came to present it to the women's shelter. I made final arrangements with the shelter's education specialist. We sent formal invitations to parents, building administrators, teachers, central administrators, and the local media. My students decided who among them would hold the corners of the quilt to display it during the presentation, who would read the presentation script, and who would assist in other ways.

On the big day, we filed into the library and took our places. A few parents assembled, as did a few central administrators, and several of our building administrators. Teachers who had conference periods at that time also attended. My students sat politely, eyeing the punch and cookies. The shelter representative arrived, and we began our ceremony. After the presentation, she talked with my sixth graders about the purpose of the women's shelter and about how to detect warning signs and avoid potentially violent situations. She explained that physical abuse usually begins as verbal abuse. She explained that it can begin at very early stages in teenage relationships and adult relationships. Then she passed out brochures that described a "Dating Bill of Rights." She explained that each person in a dating situation has the right to help decide what happens, or does *not* happen, on a date; that a person does not have to engage in risky or dangerous behavior simply because another person pressures her or him to do so. It was an enlightening presentation and a timely one, since my socially advanced students were rapidly developing an interest in romantic relationships. The representative also described what the shelter has to offer and answered many questions from students, including the one about men coming to the shelter for protection. Her answer was affirmative. It was a healthy educational experience that upset no one. While I am not sure that anything has changed in the school district where I taught, it should be noted that in 2007, a Texas law was passed requiring school districts to help protect students from emotional or physical abuse by their girlfriends and boyfriends. After two of its teenage students were murdered by their significant others, Austin Independent School District now teaches students about "safe and respectful relationships," starting in elementary school (Austin American Statesman, 2008). It's not too early.

A newspaper reporter attended our presentation, took notes, interviewed several students, made photos, and produced a full page color spread in the newspaper a week or so later. My students felt like superstars! I privately celebrated the fact that they were now informed on at least one personal safety topic and the administrators never blinked. We had their full support from the beginning because the lesson was couched in a harmless service project. In fact, they were proud of the whole event and posted a laminated copy of the newspaper article outside the front office. The *water* approach had succeeded. It was slow, gentle, and innocuous, but it carved a mighty channel.

Using Fiction to Avoid Friction

After teaching at the school described above, I began my second year as a doctoral student and became a full-time instructor in a college of education where I am now an assistant professor. I knew that I wanted to be a teacher educator, so it was a perfect opportunity to immerse myself in these intertwined endeavors. My recent challenges in public school teaching caused me to wonder how prepared our brand new graduates were to teach diverse students. Even with a decade of teaching experience at five dissimilar schools, I had felt unprepared for *this* job during my first few weeks as the art teacher. There had obviously been a gap in my own teacher preparation related to meeting the needs of students whose lives were so different from my own. I struggled and searched for strategies to teach more effectively. I wondered, "If *I* felt unprepared, as a veteran teacher, how could brand *new* teachers possibly survive unless they were specifically prepared to teach diverse students in ways that are responsive to their life situations and unique needs?" In my quest for strategies, I discovered one called *culturally responsive teaching* (Gay, 2000) or *culturally relevant teaching* (Ladson-Billings, 2001) that appeared to promise solutions. It seemed to fit my situation and answer my questions better than any other approach had. It made *sense*! I read everything I could find on this topic, began a collection of books and articles, and realized that this interest was steering my graduate studies in a specific direction. I was on a mission.

During my last year as a doctoral student, I taught a Capstone course, a weekly seminar course taken by student teachers. I had taught this course many times during the previous few years, and it was always the same. The curriculum had been established by someone who preceded me, and it had been continued, unaltered, by many instructors for many years. It was a good curriculum except for one thing: It did nothing to prepare preservice teachers for the realities of today's diverse classrooms. After surveying my students, I found that they knew virtually nothing about culturally responsive teaching. Many of them had never heard of it and could not define it. So I set my sights on making this topic part of *my* Capstone course. It was my last chance to inform this group of young women who were about to embark on their teaching careers. Rather than *rock*-ing the boat for everyone by making a big issue of this, I quietly went about weaving this information into my course, like water trickling through a pebbly stream, exploring possible routes and adapting as conditions changed. Eventually the water from such streams makes its way to the mouth of the river and into the ocean.

Knowing how busy student teachers are, and knowing that they would not have time to read another textbook for the Capstone course, I decided to write a story about a fictional first-year teacher who has a very challenging teaching assignment: *Christie's Journey: Becoming a Culturally Responsive Teacher*. Christie (named for the typical White, female, middle-class, monolingual student in our teacher education program and many others like it), is unprepared for this task and is having a rough time as the story opens. In fact, she is clueless and feels like a failure within the first few weeks of school. The story follows Christie through her first year of teaching as she is mentored by her colleagues about culturally responsive teaching. Each chapter addresses an important topic in culturally responsive teaching in a sequence that mirrors the likely sequence of concerns of a first-year teacher. Chapter one addresses culturally responsive classroom management. Subsequent chapters address caring and high expectations; communication; culture and the community; culturally responsive pedagogy; and culturally responsive curricula. Although culturally responsive teaching includes many additional important topics, this selection was appropriate to the time frame I was working with and the readiness levels of my students.

Each week, my students read one chapter from the story. Each chapter is prefaced with guiding questions and followed with reflective questions to which they responded via e-mail messages to me. The reading load was light and enjoyable because humor is sprinkled throughout the story, and as my students said, "Christie is a *case!*" She's dedicated, good hearted, and well intended, but she is also *very* fallible. This fallibility provided a safe space for my students to reflect on their own gaps in understanding, their biases and mistakes, and to "discuss" them in the reflective responses. Each of my students went on a vicarious journey with Christie and identified with her along the way. In many of their reflections, they said that they recalled events from the story while handling situations in their own student teaching classrooms. They thought about how Christie had handled similar situations and what her mentors had instructed her to do.

Without feeling like they were doing extra work, my students were learning about a very crucial teaching strategy, one that will serve them well in the future (and may already be doing so). I call it edutainment. They concurred that it was like watching a TV show, a 'dramedy' (drama/comedy). One student said that she had printed out the entire story from the Web site where I had posted it and had packed it up with all her lesson plans and books, to use it as a reference in her classroom-to-be. Many stated that the story had given them new ways to interpret classroom situations and to respond to their students' individual needs in culturally responsive ways. When I surveyed my students again at the end of the semester, they demonstrated a much improved understanding of culturally responsive teaching.

I suppose I could have suggested to the powers-that-be that we rewrite the curriculum for the Capstone course and mandate that we implement it in all sections. But that's the *rock* approach, and it probably would not have been approved. It would have mandated an unwelcome change. Instead, my water approach succeeded once again, and news of *Christie's Journey* has begun to seep into the crevices. Other professors have expressed an interest in it. My current students are reading it, laughing and learning. In fact, they are performing it as a reader's theatre in class. I'm still on my mission! Someday I hope every student who graduates from our teacher education program understands the value and the strategies of culturally responsive teaching. May this gentle little trickle of change eventually make its way to the sea of teacher education. If you don't know about this way of teaching, I *urge* you to begin your own journey toward becoming a culturally responsive teacher! It will change your life and the lives of your students.

Best wishes,

Mary Cainfehr

References

Gay, G. (2000). *Culturally responsive teaching: Theory, research, & practice.* New York: Teachers College.

Ladson-Billings, G. (2001). *Crossing over to Canaan: The journey of new teachers in diverse classrooms.* San Francisco: Jossey-Bass.

State steps up efforts to stop dating abuse. (2008, September 19). *Austin American Statesman,* p. A1.

Chapter 10

Aesthetics of Confrontation:
From the Streets to the Classroom

Sheng Kuan Chung

Dear Teachers,

Not long ago a fellow teacher in a scholarly forum questioned my pedagogy, which centered on controversial social issues. She pointed out the unease caused by bringing unpleasant subjects into the art classroom, which she believes should be a joyful learning haven for children to create aesthetically pleasing objects. I was not surprised by her query. I pondered the same question years ago.

The fascination of American public schooling with student testing and the preoccupation of art teachers with formalist pedagogy have marginalized art education as a non-essential school discipline. Particularly, the failure of art teachers to reconceptualize art education for meaningful practice reminds me of an age-old Zen tale of a master teaching his student:

Toyo, a 12-year-old, was one of Mokurai's most advanced students. One evening, he went to meet with his master Mokurai....The master said: "Toyo, show me the sound of two hands clapping." Toyo clapped his hands. "Good," said the master. "Now show me the sound of one hand clapping." Toyo was silent. Finally, he bowed and left to consider his problem. The next night he returned and struck the gong with one palm. "That is not right," said the master. The next night Toyo returned, and...for ten nights, Toyo tried new sounds. At last, he stopped coming to the master....(Peter Pauper Press, 1959, p. 25)

This ancient anecdote illuminates how we respond to the outside world in ways to which we are accustomed. Toyo thus could not realize that one hand clapping is a sound without sound. His initial solutions to the problem are not surprising given that we use the cognitive tools we have accumulated to solve problems. Because living is about learning to use tools, adapting to the environment, and assuming particular ways of being, disapproval can easily surface when we encounter a foreign situation such as an unfamiliar way of teaching art.

A major problem in education is the disconnection between classroom instruction and the contemporary world. Some scholars argue that teachers teach as they were taught when they were young. Although education majors often are taught new content and pedagogy in their teacher preparation programs, their childhood learning experience does seem to impact their classroom behavior, perhaps subconsciously. Additionally, changing that classroom behavior can be as difficult as changing one's identity. All of us who teach can benefit from examining how much of our teaching is driven by taken-for-granted educational notions, to what degree this limits what our students learn, and whether we have become so comfortable with it that we do not see the need to change it.

In response to my fellow teacher's question, I will use street art by the British artist Banksy to illustrate my point that it is virtually impossible to understand real-world art without considering controversial social issues. Specifically, I will discuss a Banksy stencil painting and the issue of homosexuality that it raises. Finally I will share some of my students' (mostly preservice art teachers) personal and professional views about homosexuality as triggered by Banksy's work. I will conclude by encouraging you to engage your students with issues-based art, thereby helping them to develop critical consciousness, aesthetic sensitivity, and a sense of social responsibility for the collective social well-being.

Banksy's art can be found in urban city streets; it is categorized as street art. Street art embodies the desire of human beings to mark traces of their existence. It is generally regarded as a post graffiti movement (MacNaughton, 2006). In contrast to government-commissioned public art, street art is illicit, subversive, and antisystem in nature. Ironically, the institutionalized art world has begun to embrace street art, exhibiting and auctioning pieces by street artists who are notoriously anti-artworld. Street art encompasses a wide array of media and techniques such as traditional spray-painted tags, stickers, stencils, posters, photocopies, murals, paper cutouts, mosaics, street installations, performances, and video projections displayed in urban streets. What motivates individuals to render art in the street varies from self-expression and reclaiming street rights to illuminating social issues and empowering the disenfranchised. Street artists emphasize what their art does and not what it is; in other words, they focus on the process of public interaction, intervention, and discourse. Imagine a creative arena with no regard to standards, censorship, or established traditions. Unlike art sanctioned by the institutionalized art world, street art reflects the unedited world in which we live. As street-art author Matthew Lunn observes, "[Street art] has a rawness you don't get through other forms of media. It is the voice of the world around us" (Lunn, 2006, p. 4).

Street artists like Banksy prefer urban sites as their artistic platforms, and most integrate their pieces into urban sites that maximize their subversive messages. Street art is often replaced by other street art or dismantled by city officials; it is ephemeral. Indeed, the inspiration for street art is its ability to prompt public discourse. For street artists, the public's interactions with their work often outweigh concerns of ownership or the legal risks involved in its production. Many street artists, including Banksy, use pseudonyms to avoid legal prosecution for vandalism.

Although Banksy (his real name is either Robert Banks or Robin Banks) is a household name in London, is internationally known, has traveled across the globe to create site-specific pieces, has exhibited in major museums and galleries, and has auctioned his art at Sotheby's, his identity remains mysterious. He refuses to be interviewed or show his face publicly. Banksy's stencil art is highly popular at auction houses, selling for up to half a million dollars per work; however, he rarely offers his art for sale.

Using postmodern methods of subversion, cultural jamming, and guerrilla communication,[1] his art, like other street art, raises provocative questions about current wars, poverty, gentrification, capitalism, imperialism, and corporate globalization.

Banksy's pieces challenge the power of the corporate-dominated media to serve the interests of the powerful few who control what we know, how we see the world, and our public spaces. They remind us that public space is becoming less a free space that serves the common good, and more a profit-driven arena for the private sector. To stimulate discourse about public space and challenge the London city council on graffiti issues, Banksy once posted "This wall is a designated graffiti area" signs on several London street walls as if they were official public notices issued by the city. Days later, these walls were covered with graffiti. Banksy maintains, "The people who run our cities don't understand graffiti because they think nothing has the right to exist unless it makes a profit" (Banksy, 2006, p. 2). In response to graffiti vandalism, Banksy argues,

> The people who truly deface our neighborhoods are the companies that scrawl giant slogans across buildings and buses trying to make us feel inadequate unless we buy their stuff. They expect to be able to shout their message in your face from every available surface but you're never allowed to answer back. Well, they started the fight and the wall is the weapon of choice to hit them back. (Banksy, 2006, p. 2)

Banksy disguises himself while working on his projects. Like other street artists, Banksy does not sign or title his work because its purposes are to challenge public perceptions and stimulate discourse. Because his work is antiestablishment, it delivers thought-provoking messages to the viewer. Banksy travels across the globe to promote alternative political conversations on topics such as AIDS, zoo practices, art institutions, and the Israeli West Bank security wall. He does this by creating site-specific art, often in combination with stenciling techniques, using methods by which the art becomes inherently part of the street. His work speaks directly to the masses by being humorous and visually stimulating, yet thought provoking. His stencil art provides a voice for those living in urban environments and those marginalized by the art establishment. Banksy's work leads viewers to consider what is art and what is vandalism.

Interestingly, despite being regarded as graffiti vandalism and therefore illicit, the city of London allows some of Banksy's art to remain in place, due in part to public support and in part to the powerful constructive messages it delivers.

In a university art methods class, I showed several examples of Banksy's art to my students (mostly preservice art teachers) and instructed them to focus on one particular stencil image (Figure 1). This life-sized stencil piece portrays two London policemen in uniform passionately kissing each other on the street.[2] This provocative image can be seen in several London city locations and compels passers-by to consider their conceptions of homosexuality and masculinity. In this way Banksy's work restores the function of public art to force viewers to examine

Figure 1. Adapted from photo by Richard Holt; used with permission.

their surroundings. The image of kissing policemen is so thought provoking that analyzing it formally seems silly without exploring the issues it raises. While showing this piece, I asked my class of twenty-five to write down anonymously their reactions to it, what they think of homosexuality and whether they would address this issue in the art classroom. Afterwards, I facilitated a class discussion about the concept of heteronormality.

Overwhelmingly, my students responded to the first question positively. For example, one stated, "I have more gay friends than straight friends. It's a social prejudice that disgusts me." Another elaborated,

> I have no problem working with gay people and feel that I have no reason to judge how another person lives their life. There are bad relationships among all groups. I would rather one of my students grow up in a happy home with two fathers than in an unhappy home with a mother and father. My gay friends have always been just as loving and caring as my heterosexual friends.

Another echoed the same position: "People are predispositioned and...no one should judge another human being—regardless of their own personal beliefs or religion. I think they should be allowed to marry, share benefits, and adopt children." It was encouraging that most of my students have a strong stance on equality rights and social justice. However, a couple of them approached this question differently, maintaining respectively that "Satan has free reign in our world [and has thus] influenced the concept of homosexuality," and "It is a choice that people make. It is not a gene, nor a permanent disposition, but a personality choice that is made according to the influences."

Education is critical to understanding differences among people, regardless of what makes them different. Ironically, ours is an advanced, democratic society in which most parents do not discuss homosexuality with their children. Nor would they allow teachers to do so. Few of my students mentioned the importance of teaching children about this issue, but one wrote this:

> It is sad that homosexuals have to hide their feelings. I think it's sad when they are told they can't raise children. I think gay issues should be talked about in schools so people will be educated and not make decisions based on ignorant nonsense.

Another revealed, "I was very fortunate to have parents that taught me from an early age that homosexuality is okay. My favorite teacher was gay and it didn't make a bit of difference to me."

We perhaps can anticipate a new generation of teachers who, like most of my students, will support equal rights and social justice for all. However, as far as teaching gay issues is concerned, my students' overwhelmingly positive feedback does not translate well into what they would actually implement in the classroom. As two of them stated, "I probably would not teach gay issues because I don't want to cause trouble in a district that might be more conservative," and "I would probably focus on acceptance of differences and different types of families." Another echoed, "I would take a more general approach and discuss stereotyping or discrimination as a broad issue, but not specifically focusing on homosexuality." One summarized, "I would teach gay issues in the context of social tolerance—not just about gay issues but all issues leading to stereotypical biased opinions." Most said they would not specifically teach about homosexuality or designate a learning unit on gay issues; rather they would focus on diversity and difference and teach about stereotyping, acceptance, respect, and tolerance, or talk about it if they "see disturbance in the class concerning gay students." In addition to regular class discussion, this type of anonymous reflection allows me to learn more about my students' views on homosexuality and further identify the challenges surrounding this issue.

To facilitate a class dialogue about gay issues, or specifically the concept of heteronormality, Banksy's kissing policemen can easily ignite a political discussion. Example questions for class dialogue might include:

- What do you think about this picture?
- Are policemen authoritarian figures in our society?
- Would you still see policemen as authoritarian figures if you saw them act like this on the street?
- Are there other implicit messages in this picture?
- Is it more socially acceptable if one of the police officers is a woman, and if so, how?
- What do you know about gay people?
- How does American society discriminate against gay people?
- What can we do to make America a truly equal society?

Another approach is to introduce the concept of heteronormality. In other words, students need to understand that heterosexuals, as the dominant group in society, hold the political power to legitimize their own educational agendas. The dominant group defines and polices norms such as sexual relationships, marriage, family structure, and parenthood from its heterocentric cosmology. Heterocentric gender roles have permeated mainstream ideology, which controls almost every aspect of social practice and portrays gay people as deviant; this in turn has a detrimental effect on gay youth as they struggle to understand themselves and become constructive members of society. In America, heterosexuals are free to show their affection in public, while public displays of affection are considered a social taboo for homosexuals. Banksy's kissing policemen is antiheteronormality. In American schools, it is not uncommon to see school children use homophobic language to humiliate peers or deliberately make malicious jokes. Students uninformed about homosexuality are likely to have prejudiced attitudes and behave offensively toward gay people. The lack of discussion about gay issues in schools has imposed homophobia on children. Owing to ignorance and intolerance, discrimination based on sexual orientation is legal in several U.S. states.

Nothing is more culturally relevant than confronting students with issues that impact their everyday existence by teaching art found in their own neighborhood. Urban youth look to the streets for authenticity and inspiration. Because street art is a vernacular art form circulated in young people's everyday visual culture, it can serve as a powerful source of images for involving students in political discourse about contemporary life and art. As Banksy once visualized,

Imagine a city where graffiti wasn't illegal, a city where everybody could draw wherever they liked. Where every street was swashed with a million colours and little phrases. Where standing at a bus stop was never boring. A city that felt like a living breathing thing which belonged to everybody, not just the estate agents and barons of big business. (Banksy, 2002)

I believe that many of you, like Banksy, constantly imagine new possibilities for changing the lives of your students. We can cultivate in school children an aesthetic sensitivity and a critical mindset by engaging them in analyzing, interpreting, evaluating, and producing art within the context of social and political struggle. We can teach school children skills and techniques to make art for aesthetic enjoyment while at the same time engaging them in critical thought to enhance democratic participation and cultural emancipation. We can bridge the gap between classroom art instruction and contemporary art practice if we are open to inspiration from contemporary art that tackles unjust social conditions. To answer my fellow teacher's question about my emphasis on socially responsive art pedagogy, I cannot imagine how students would understand the art of our time without framing it within the context of sociopolitical struggle. We as art teachers can inspire and empower school children to transform their world if we are willing to challenge them to critically explore their everyday aesthetic sites/sights, negotiate dominant values and ideologies, and construct alternative artistic expressions that advocate social justice and equal rights for all. We can certainly be seen as key players in the public school arena if we are willing to tackle important social issues in our own classrooms.

With my best wishes,

Shng Chng

Notes

1. Guerrilla communication is both a communication method and a political intervention through street performance/events or public engagements designed to disrupt or change the public's perceptions. For a definition of subvertizing and cultural jamming, visit http://en.wikipedia.org.

2. This piece is stenciled on the street wall, making it appear as if the policemen were doing so on the corner of the street.

References

Banksy, R. (2006). *Banksy.* London: Random House.

Banksy, R. (2002). *Existencilism.* England: Weapons of Mass Distraction.

Lunn, M. (2006). *Street art uncut.* Australia: Craftsman House.

MacNaughton, A. (2006). *London street art.* London: Prestel.

Zen Buddhism: An Introduction to Zen with stories, parables and Koan riddles told by the Zen Master. Mt. Vernon, NY: Peter Pauper Press, 1959.

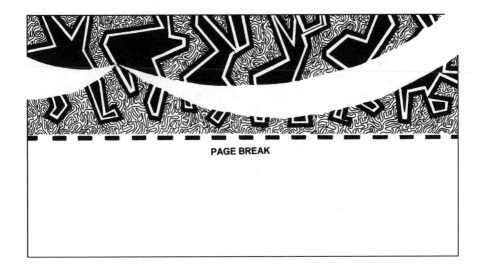

Chapter 11

The Limits of Schooling

George Wood

Dear Teacher or Future Teacher,

While I was in the airport waiting for a flight to Omaha to write about assessment in Nebraska, my wife reached me with news every educator hates to hear: 'Tina' (not her real name), a 1998 graduate of my high school, had been killed, falling from a fourth-story window. Foul play was suspected.

One of the strengths of a small school is that you come to know your students well—perhaps too well. Tina had been a success story following a rocky start. She came to us from a neighboring school when she was in ninth grade. Dad had been murdered years before. The family was fleeing overdue rent and disciplinary action against a sibling who had thrown a desk at the principal. Mom wasn't sure we could help the sibling, but she had hopes for Tina.

Tina's sibling never did graduate, but Tina found a home at our school. She played softball and loved school; actually, she loved *learning* and told me that every chance she had. She graduated on time and left us in the spring of 1998, headed for community college.

Things happened after she left: An abusive boyfriend. A baby. No more money for gas to get to college. Dropping out. Brushes with the law that landed the boyfriend in prison and cost Tina custody of her child.

In the summer of 2006 I ran into her. She was near the bottom—overwhelmed by legal troubles, broke, without a car or even a drivers license, and unable to see her boy.

We talked about what had transpired in the eight years since she had left school, and just as we did then, we made a plan. For sixteen months the plan worked: She paid her fines, performed community service, regained her license, got a job, bought a car, received permission to visit her son, set a court date to restore custody, and re-enrolled in community college.

But then something, one thing, went terribly wrong. And now she is gone.

There is a larger story here, and that is that schooling has its limits. Tina was a school success. She did well while she was there. After she left us, however, she had only a dysfunctional family to turn to. The community college did not provide the level of support that our public schools can (including transportation to and from school), and our legal system provides inadequate counsel to the poor. Tina's chances of success plummeted.

For all of their limits, U.S. public schools are places that still try to serve each student, to catch every child left behind. Unlike any other American institution, we take in all comers regardless of income, background, or ability to succeed. Sometimes, when faced with odds that we simply cannot overcome, we are blamed for 'failing' our children.

Let's be frank. Our schools have not failed us. In fact, my organization, the Forum for Democracy in Education, found in a study on traditional schools versus private schools,[1] that students attending traditional public high schools are as likely to perform as well academically, go to college, be satisfied in their jobs, and be engaged in civic life as are students who attend private schools.

No, public schools are not failing America; America is failing its public schools, and consequently, its children. We live in a nation where parents have to turn to the courts for adequate school funding while cities build lavish sports arenas, and states give tax breaks to multinational corporations; where teachers struggle to get by on pay that qualifies their children for free school lunches while steroid-assisted sports stars and inebriated celebrities make millions; where our government can spend between $7 and $10 billion *a month* on a war but cannot find $7 billion *a year* to pay for the S-CHIP program that provides health care for our children.

Meanwhile the national debate over education is focused on the No Child Left Behind Act, a reauthorization of the Elementary and Secondary Education Act first passed in 1965 as *one part*, and the smallest part at that, of Lyndon Johnson's War on Poverty. This act, intended to provide housing and food to improve the lives of our poorest children, has become one of the few things we do. And rather than help these children by providing the resources and support schools need, NCLB is all about test scores, sanctions, and taking money away from schools to pay for private tutoring companies, scripted reading programs, and test preparation booklets.

The distance from the death of Tina to national policy seems wide only if one thinks the schools alone are the answer to the challenges our children face. For Tina and so many other young people, school is part of the answer—but only part. Until America realizes this, our schools will continue to struggle heroically to make differences in the lives of all the children who walk through our doors, knowing that these children have no guarantee of help after they walk out.

In the meantime, in every city, town, and neighborhood in the U.S., teachers will continue to teach our children with the hours they are given. They will do this for each child knowing that their efforts will be lost on some for one painful reason or another, because they know that by teaching boldly, their successes will be measured one child and one life at a time—no matter how short that life may be.

Sincerely,

Notes

1. For more information on this study, see http://www.forumforeducation.org/node/97.

Chapter 12

Nonviolence: A Philosophy and Method for Teaching Boldly

Carolyn Erler and Susan L. Allen

Dear Fellow Teachers,

In this chapter I do something that in other circumstances might seem foolish. I share with you a painful episode in my teaching career that at the time felt very much like a failure. All of us go through this, especially when we're thrown into new situations. Rather than try to forget what happened, however, I sought the help and advice of another teacher whose work I greatly admire. This teacher is Susan L. Allen, media anthropologist and tireless advocate for violence awareness and nonviolence education on the campus of Kansas State University in Manhattan, where she has been developing nonviolence-related programs for nearly 30 years. Last November, I contacted Susan out of the blue. To my surprise, she was open to talking with me. When I invited her to a dialogue about her path-breaking work in education and community organizing, her response was immediate and affirmative.

What she didn't know at the time—perhaps what I didn't even know—was that I was seeking answers to some of the most troubling questions facing teachers today. I now share this dialogue with you, in the hope that you will learn, as I did, from this amazing and masterful educator.

Nonviolence: A Philosophy and Method for Teaching Boldly

The position I filled during my first year as a public school teacher had been created after the start of the school year to comply with the state's class-size amendment. Despite the title of critical thinking teacher, my actual role was to fill in the gaps and overflows created by the school's high enrollment.

Teaching without a classroom was not easy, but then most teachers start out that way, or so I was told. I had a harder time accepting that the school principal was an officer in the army. He was new to the school, and had made many changes since his arrival: a compulsory moment of silence for our fallen soldiers after the Pledge of Allegiance; a "Wall of Heroes" in the cafeteria; American flags in every classroom and hall; and the visible presence of young members of the Junior Reserve Officer Training Corps. I began to dread all these things—most of all, Richard Wagner's "Ride of the Valkyries" blasting through the loudspeakers before school, after school, and between every class while school was in session. There was simply no way to escape Adolf Hitler's favorite composer.

To explain my feelings, I must relate a little of my own past. I was a public middle school student during the last years of the Vietnam War. There was a clear understanding on the part of my elders that the war was a drastic strategic mistake and waste of human life. During Watergate my older brother, who was of draft age, rejoiced at the downfall of the gloomy president and his corrupt, despicable regime. One of my clearest memories from middle school was of my eighth-grade history teacher, a lanky old socialist named Mr. Worstel, forcing us to watch the Watergate hearings. I remember him saying that our country had almost fallen into the hands of fascists. Even though I did not understand what this meant, the words stuck.

What a difference a draft makes. Wars of choice fought by volunteer soldiers and mercenaries require heavy psychological conditioning of the young and impressionable. I came to see my job as that of a state functionary, pressed into service for a mass psychological operation. The fact that I had such a view of my work rendered my teaching of critical thinking problematic, to say the least.

I dealt with my discomfort by trying to teach nonviolence. Drawing from my background in art education, I chose to approach the subject of nonviolence through visual media. The work of anime masters Isao Takahata and Hayao Miyazaki offered fertile ground for such an exploration. Feature-length films such as Takahata's *Grave of the Fireflies* (1988) and *Nausciaä of the Valley of the Wind* (1984) by Miyazaki are distinguished by themes such as humanity's relationship to nature and technology, and the difficulty of maintaining a pacifist ethic (McCarthy, 1999).

One scene in *Nausciaä of the Valley of the Wind* (1984) shows the main character befriending a wild cat. At first the cat bites her and Nausciaä gasps. But Nausciaä does not react violently. The cat soon relaxes and begins to lick Nausciaä's wound. "There," she says to the cat, "you were just frightened." Thereafter, the two are good friends.

After watching this scene, I asked my students to imagine the outcome if Nausciaä had reacted violently. We listed behaviors that the character chose and those she did not choose, and discussed the consequences attached to each choice. Perhaps not surprisingly given their age, some students complained that lack of violence was "boring." Other students said that it was easier to practice nonviolence with animals than with humans. As one boy expressed it, nonviolence in a violent world would only get you killed. Of course, they all understood and respected Dr. Martin Luther King, Jr., but King, they said, "was different." When I tried to press them on *how* or *why* King was different, no one answered.

It took me a year to get "Ride of the Valkyries" out of my head. Now in a university academic setting, I help art education majors learn from their student teaching placements in local schools. Some wonder if they can "teach boldly" within the constraints of the public school system. I tell them they can, and this is how: Teach nonviolence.

I direct them to the writings of Susan L. Allen, who has devised teaching methods for children and adults that include memory aids, analogies, stories, equations, and drawings. A dedicated practitioner and inspiring author, she is currently finishing a book about what she calls *"Every Day Nonviolence,"* and a children's book showing that "Nonviolence is not passive but something one can DO." Allen and I recently had a chance to get together to discuss her teaching methods. Our dialogue follows.

The Dialogue

S.A.: When I read your intro I realized "teach boldly" must mean something like, "teaching as a subversive activity," which was one of my inspirations. I still use that phrase occasionally because working to change the status quo is what I do, and of course nonviolence (NV) is subversive in that it WILL change the status quo if accomplished.

C.E.: You just started a new semester in which you will be teaching Intro to Nonviolence to a new group of students. In "Organic Balance" (Allen, 2003), you mention that most young people you work with "do not think about the role they play with respect to balance within the whole system," which is not surprising. Now, like me, you are teaching young adults of college age. I'm curious about how many of your Intro students, on average, come to you with some prior knowledge of NV as a practical philosophy and methodology.

S.A.: Our students think of nonviolence as something huge: peace and justice, Gandhi and King—something, they aren't sure what, that is accomplished by famous people in drastic, global circumstances...nothing real people could do; certainly not themselves. Yet, they are drawn to enroll because something strikes them as hopeful. Most of them have experienced imbalances in the world, such as injustice, oppression, or exploitation, in their own relationships and homes, and they watch the news and know we need to do something to correct it.

What I try to do is go underneath specific circumstances to show that all relationships are systems; that systems are holistic not dualistic; and that injustice or unfairness reveals imbalance in a system. Basically, because systems are abstract and nonthreatening, I can show that a bully is a bully whether we're talking about a dictator or an abusive husband or humans polluting the earth. The global NV axiom, "if you want peace, work for justice" translates locally to, "if we want safe homes or safe dates or safe communities, we need to work for fair relationships." It actually is an equation: Want healthy, sustainable systems? Work for balance.

In *The Uses of Enchantment* (Bettelheim, 1977), we are reminded that a child's mind contains "a rapidly expanding collection of often ill-assorted and only partially integrated impressions" and that "fantasy fill the huge gaps in a child's understanding" (p. 61)....If we exchange the word *child* for *peo-*

ple and remember that we all continue to mature throughout life, this insight becomes a psychological rationale for the use of anthropologically oriented information, or nonviolence information, as a basis for a holistic perspective....Due to a lack of information, we have gaps in our own understanding that are filled with fantasies about ourselves and our world...often in the form of prejudice and fear.

I argue that information and insights from anthropology could be catalytic to...affective development...in the same way Bettelheim (1977) argues that fairy tales can affect development of the mind. According to Bettelheim, fairy tales are nonthreatening because they are removed from "ordinary reality" (61). As such, a tale can affect development through the subconscious....Anthropology can share insights in the same way by removing us from the immediate and the emotional. I think the information and insights of nonviolence works similarly. It feels nonthreatening...but in fact 'subversively' helps important ideas seep in, uncoerced.

Today I suggest that nonviolence teachings function in the same way fairy tales and anthropological perspectives do: to cultivate a more flexible spirit that is better able to adapt to change and more willing to accept differences and ambiguities, thus encouraging us to act to preempt many of the causes of violence. Then...I try to be very practical and work on direct experience projects.

C.E.: I want to talk about your direct experience projects in a moment. But first—of the students who already have some experience/knowledge of NV, do you know if they learned this at home, at school, or in a religious context?

S.A.: Some of our students have traveled and come upon perspectives beyond their "given" cultural frame of reference. But the major source is religion. We can talk about religion some time. In our day-and-age establishment religion has been the only source for human beings who sense they have a relationship with the universe and want to investigate it. This is another value of nonviolence language. EDNV or Every Day Nonviolence language gives us a nonmoralistic, impersonal and, perhaps most importantly, logical way to talk about that relationship that, again, goes underneath the status quo cultural stories and allows us to see them in an inclusive context.

I might add, happily, that students on this campus and in the community often have heard of the Campaign for Nonviolence (CNV) through various events because this is our eighth year. That basic *awareness* of nonviolence is prerequisite to changing expectations—and, in my opinion, changing *expectations* is the second key step in changing from a community that expects violence and organizes around it and to a community that expects nonviolent interactions and will step up to make that happen.

The third step is *skills building* and for that we plan activities that help build skills around levels or concentric circles of relationships. These include our inner life, our interpersonal relationships, the community, the globe, and beyond, to the environment and universe, which in fact completes the circle back to our inner life.

We have an outdoor social justice film series; we offer free yoga and meditation; we have a 500+ member SafeZone (SZ) program, and lots of other projects people have heard about and/or participated in. SafeZone is the quintessential local nonviolence movement, by the way. Average students, faculty, and staff have volunteered to be trained as visible allies for fellow citizens who are troubled or who are in trouble.

We also teach academic Nonviolence Studies courses and hold nonviolent communication trainings. The CNV even adopted a highway this year to illustrate that taking care of the environment is yet another way to bring healthy balance to a human relationship system.

C.E.: Your years of organizing around nonviolence issues have obviously dramatically increased the level of violence awareness on the KSU campus. Can you estimate about how many students, faculty, and staff participate in large events such as the Campaign for Nonviolence?

S.A.: I appreciate that you think we are making a dent in the enormous challenge of changing from a violent to a nonviolent culture. The reality is that creating lasting social change moves slowly, especially for those of us who think it is so important.

I have a current list of 170 people who attend yoga fairly regularly. Others wander in and out, of course. Meditation is still growing, but we have six or eight to a dozen most Mondays. SZ is big…and I think the reason it is so popular is because it gives people a real job that they can feel. It is so rare in our money-oriented world to sense your positive power—and do it for free! We've trained over 500 K-State students/faculty/staff; we helped the local high school start its own SZ. Even the district superintendent took training, and we've trained some local Job Corps staff and teachers from other towns so they can start a SafeZone. People who have participated in some kind of event number in the thousands—we usually have 200 or more at Movies on the Grass, the social justice film series; lots of people stop to get info or watch the international news TV at our SZ/WC/CNV kiosk in the student union. We produced a "win-win" public service announcement, read strategically by our popular football coach...that was aired on several TV stations around the state a couple of years ago; and we had 64 community members read one of the 64 "ways" to practice nonviolence on the radio one year. Lots of people wear CNV "peace + 63 other ways to practice nonviolence" t-shirts. We've sent dozens of those t-shirts to groups and individuals—a couple of local businesses wear them on Wednesdays during the season; a peace group in Dallas found us on the Internet and bought some; a school in Honolulu wanted posters. We send posters out to anyone who asks. This year we made a Spanish-language 64 Ways poster that has been popular. This year for the first time state extension offices in our 105 counties will have our posters available. We don't do direct political action in the name of the CNV because it cuts off listening by those primed to disagree—so the Spanish-language poster is a subtle way of encouraging a more inclusive definition of "All the people" in our democracy. The truth is everything we do has political intent but don't tell anyone.

C.E.: Just so our readers know, the 64 days between the assassination anniversaries of Mahatma Gandhi on January 30 and Dr. Martin Luther King, Jr. on April 4 were designated as the Season for Nonviolence in Los Angeles in 1998. Each of the 64 days was linked to a "way" to practice active nonviolence. Since then, the Season for Nonviolence has grown into an international grassroots campaign dedicated to demonstrating that nonviolence is a powerful way to heal, transform, and empower our lives and our communities (SNV-LA, 2008).

S.A.: Yes. And to do this we rely on volunteers. Not only are institutions tied to "fighting violence with violence," funding agencies have been locked into grants to 'clean up the mess' after violence, and we, or I, have just not been good at getting money....They want to know how many acts of violence occurred before the CNV and after the CNV. We don't know! Reporting is problematic, for one thing. For another, the movement is toward culture change and that's hard to count. Surely these participation numbers are getting high enough that KSU can get some grant money one of these years. I think we're ready to walk through that door. Maybe even find some understanding donors.

C.E.: This gets me so riled up. Have you seen the 2005 film by Eugene Jarecki, "Why We Fight"? It shows how the defense industry, what Eisenhower called "the military-industrial complex," dictates U.S. foreign policy and practically runs the global economy. So of course there's no money for nonviolence education. As you said in "Activist Anthropology in a Women's Center" (Allen, 2001), we spend so much time and effort 'mopping up the blood' that we never get to address the causes of violence against women, for example. When I think about it, I get very angry.

S.A.: I'm not sure why many bright women do not acknowledge, or perhaps perceive, the problems most women face. I used to think Phyllis Schlafly and her ilk were motivated by simple 'survival-of-the-fittest' fear. They saw as clearly as feminists do that women live their lives in institutionalized economic and physical jeopardy; but instead of reacting with anger they react like threatened mother lions and fight to maintain the status quo because they've been taught our present system assures that they have one man and perhaps his brothers to protect them.

The reality that one in every two or three women experiences violence herself leads me to believe the real reasons are more complicated and include privilege, socialized self-blame and a kind of willed naiveté that looks a lot like denial. In addition, many women do not want to "make matters worse" by complaining or calling attention to themselves, and the myths go on.

On a university campus, as in the world at large, change doesn't come because it is the "right thing." In a society that continues to benefit financially from discrimination against women, privilege for men, institutional financial and political inequities, abuse of power and even the use of violence to solve its problems, we who are assigned the tasks associated with stopping violence are rarely in positions with enough power to change anything. Certainly we cannot do so in traditional ways. Change means sharing power, and that is just too threatening to those for whom the status quo works just fine.

C.E.: I want to get back to concrete teaching methods—drawings, metaphors, analogies, equations—that can be used with kids. And can you tell us why early childhood nonviolence education is so important?

S.A.: Yes, strange as it may sound, I believe humans can consciously choose to evolve; we can look rationally at our predicament and decide to change our individual and collective mind about how we resolve conflict.
Coleman McCarthy uses this quote in his book, *I'd Rather Teach Peace*:

> Q: Why are we violent but not illiterate?
> A: Because we are taught to read.

Exactly. We need the notes for music, the alphabet to read. When we focus on the "ABCs of nonviolence," we'll see their value and adopt them....I think sensing the need to correct the course of imbalanced relationships for our own well-being must be a "fail safe" mechanism built into human beings—like pulling yourself back from a fall just before completely losing your balance on the mountain side or falling off a bike. Maybe we humans can change our minds before we all end up with the polar bears.

Even though technology now makes it possible for us to recognize we live in a "global village" and also allows us to communicate among all its inhabitants for the first time in history, human beings and human cultures have not absorbed the fact that we live in an interdependent whole system of relationships. Lessons necessary for recognizing whole systems include learning the difference between stasis and balance; recognizing healthy equilibrium as functioning more holistically like a gyroscope or a mobile rather than dualistically like a teeter-totter; recognizing relationships, large and small, as interconnected, interdependent systems that are analogous to the human body; and realizing that what individuals do, consciously or not, is "passed forward." We can see the interconnected nature of systems for the first time in human history, now, from photos of the earth from space, from the unending spiral of the DNA double helix, from an MRI that shows *your* brain mirroring *my* heart beat when we touch.

My favorite analogy for talking about nonviolence is the human body. To address "dis-ease" in relationship systems with the holistic practices of nonviolence is parallel to applying a wellness or public health model to treatment of disease in the body. It is using holistic, preventative measures rather than waiting for the system to begin to fail before we act.

I do believe that if people see that relationship systems function similarly to the human body, then nonviolent methods that help us keep relationships on course, instead of waiting for the crisis, will be adopted just as good nutrition practices are being adopted. It makes sense. It is about survival not sentiment. I think it can happen like the changes in behavior, concerning potato preparation, that happened with the monkeys on that infamous Japanese Island (Watson, 1979). When 'enough' healthy well-balanced people recognize the power of nonviolence within their own life, we'll become the "100th monkey." We will become the critical mass that can turn human beings into nonviolent problem solvers.

C.E.: How do you make your ideas visual, or visible, for your students?

S.A.: Lots of ways. I draw swirls to illustrate an invisible force like the wind as a watermark on the "64 Ways to Practice Nonviolence" (SNV-LA, 2008) poster. I try to show the "force" in things like patterns: the migration of birds, the development of a baby, the color wheel, the path of a spotlight; I especially like black birds in their fall swirls and schools of fish. The formulation of thoughts inside a brain illustrates the entropy and redundancy of life. I think those patterns and other kinds of patterns in poetry and math illustrate a force more powerful that people can begin to see themselves being a part of, and tap into without the need for creationism.

C.E.: Yes, patterns. Patterns are the very structure of the universe at the micro- macrolevels. By tapping positive, life-sustaining patterns and concretizing them into practices, some of which have strong mnemonic effects, you have, as I see it, designed a toolkit for learning sustainability. Conscious, self-reflexive learning is the process through which humans evolve, and this involves choice. So the lessons of sustainability and NV must be chosen for the reason that nothing else makes sense. NV must become the new common sense.

S.A.: Exactly. I think of my anthropological take on nonviolence as an "ecology of relationships."

C.E.: What advice do you have for teachers who are struggling to implement nonviolence education in authoritarian institutional settings such as the middle school where I taught?

S.A.: I've come to think that our only shot at breaking into this entrenched and increasingly out-of-balance organizational structure requires a mix of 'civil disobedience,' taking advantage of help from a growing number of female and male sympathizers who care about justice in the administrative hierarchy, and teaching as a 'subversive activity.' Maybe there are many ways this can be accomplished, but I'm particularly excited about teaching nonviolence.

Until we can teach and practice nonviolence in the 'real' world, beginning in kindergarten or before then, what better place than at our schools to try an approach that, among other things, has the potential to get ahead of some of the violence and is so positively framed that it can suit even the public relations office? In my opinion, our great challenge is to make nonviolence "cool" as it competes for attention beside the daily drama of violence. For example, maybe we can find ways to frame nonviolence as "green" relationships. I should say that even some of my best friends have doubts about trying to practice nonviolence on a campus. "It's too 60s;" it "Sounds like Gandhi and King;" and "Are we going to the president's house in a VW microbus and have sit-ins?" are some of the comments I have received.

C.E.: It reminds me of my middle school students, who seemed to be saying that MLK was made somehow less relevant by 9/11.

S.A.: In my opinion, the one critical point these people are missing is that Gandhi and King were right in the 1930s and 1960s, and they are right today. The power and the potential of nonviolence are real, which is why it has not been embraced by the establishment, and those who are serious about ending violence shouldn't be embarrassed to give it a try. The world has yet to make a sincere attempt to contest violence with nonviolence as a pragmatic set of tactics and tools as well as a philosophy that is far different from our naïve view of it as pacifism or "passive-ism."

We have to remember we are creating our futures as we speak. We can't go back and undo past imbalances that have led to violence, such as injustice and misuse of power, but we can examine current problems within the context of whole systems, identify connections, discern precursors, and work to preempt a future crisis. The positive action we take to correct the imbalances is my definition of "every day" nonviolence.

Nobody said it would be easy. My conviction though—one that I learned from the holistic perspective of anthropology—is that if we can nudge the perspectives of a critical mass of citizens to a high-enough hill, changes in behavior may follow like the flow of a river. (End of dialogue)

Carolyn Erler: Conclusions

The most painful part of my job at the middle school was that I wanted to teach nonviolence, but I didn't know how. The fact that I was an experienced educator who had always done well in the classroom added to my frustration. The lingering pain of defeat was what pushed me to seek out nonviolence educators such as Susan Allen. I wanted to know what I had overlooked so that I could change.

What I didn't take into account was the transformative nature of learning. Susan did not tell me how to fix my mistakes; she gave me a new paradigm, a higher ground from which to think about, practice, and teach nonviolence. From this new place, I saw my "failure" as a teacher as a symptom of a narrowly focused, politicized notion of nonviolence. I had cut the meaning of nonviolence for my students to the size of my own thinking; or, as Susan put it, I had not gone "underneath specific circumstances," which can be threatening, to lay the conceptual groundwork.

During the Vietnam War, peace was a moral stance, a movement and critique of power, just as today activists challenge the war in Iraq on grounds of nonviolence. We are familiar with peace as a form of antiestablishment discourse. But how many of us equate peace and nonviolence with healthy functioning ecosystems, the basis for life on earth? How many of us view nonviolence as the essence of sustainable relationships and the backbone of social justice? When we open ourselves to the wholeness of systems and recognize our crucial presence and role within them, we appreciate that nonviolence is another word for and a way to achieve balance.

For teachers, the elegance of Susan's broadminded conceptualization of nonviolence is its relevance to math, science, social studies, language arts, music, art, and physical education in equal measure. If as teachers we can prepare our students in multiple ways and on multiple fronts to act on the global imperative of nonviolence, I believe that we will have taught well—and boldly.

Thank you for letting me tell my story. I hope that in some small way, I have encouraged you to share your stories—even stories of perceived failure—with other practicing teachers. This is how we "do" solidarity as people committed not only to educating children, but also educating parents, administrators, and communities about the issues that trouble—and inspire—us the most. If you "pass forward" one idea from this dialogue with Susan, let it be this: Teachers are the leading edge of human evolution.

Peace,

To continue learning about the Nonviolence Education Program at Kansas State University, and to read articles by Susan L. Allen, visit http://www.k-state.edu/womenscenter/NonviolenceWorks.htm

References

Allen, S.R. (2003). Organic balance as a conceptual framework for social change movements. In T.D. Dickinson (Ed.), *Community and the world: Participating in social change* (pp. 261–280). Hauppauge, NY: Nova.

Allen, S.R. (2001). Activist anthropology in a women's center. *Voices: A Publication of the Association for Feminist Anthropology, 5*(1), 11–16.

Allen, S.R. (Ed.). (1994). *Media anthropology: Informing global citizens.* Westport, CT: Bergin & Garvey.

Bettelheim, B. (1976). *The uses of enchantment: The meaning and importance of fairy tales.* New York: Knopf.

Jarecki, E. (2005). *Why we fight* [Motion picture]. U.S.A.: Sony.

L.A. Season for Nonviolence. (2008). Nonviolence Works. Retrieved September 12, 2008, from www.nonviolenceworks.com/snv/.

McCarthy, H. (1999), *Hayao Miyazaki: Master of Japanese animation: Films, themes, artistry.* Berkeley, CA: Stone Bridge.

Miyazaki, H. (Writer/Director), & Takahata, M. (Producer), (1984). *Nausicaä of the valley of the wind* [Motion picture]. Japan: Topcraft.

Sharp, G. (1973). The methods of nonviolent action. *Peace Magazine* [Archive]. Retrieved
    Februrary 1, 2008, from http://peacemagazine.org/198.htm.
Takahata, M. (Writer/Director), & Nosaka, A. (Writer). (1988). *Grave of the fireflies* [Motion
    picture]. Japan: Studio Ghibli.
Watson, L. (1979). *Lifetide: The biology of the unconscious.* New York: Simon & Schuster.

Chapter 13

A Marshall Plan for Teaching:
What It Will Really Take to Leave No Child Behind

Linda Darling-Hammond

Dear Present and Future Teachers,

I want to share a word with you about a law that will color your professional life even after it is gone—the No Child Left Behind Act. Views on it are currently as divided as Berlin before the wall came down. Whatever one thinks about the Act, it's clear that developing more skillful teaching is a sine qua non for attaining more equitable achievement for students in the United States. If we do not have sophisticated skills for teaching challenging content to diverse learners, there is no way that children from all racial/ethnic, language, and socioeconomic backgrounds will reach the academic standards envisioned by the law. For this reason, one of the most important aspects of NCLB is its demand for a "highly qualified" teacher for every child.

Research indicates that expert teachers are the most important—and the most inequitably distributed—school resource. In the U.S., however, schools serving more than one million of our highest-need students are staffed by a parade of underprepared and inexperienced teachers who know little about effective instruction, and even less about teaching English-language learners and students with disabilities. Many of these teachers enter with little training and leave soon after, leaving instability in their wake. Meanwhile, affluent students receive teachers who are typically better prepared than their predecessors, further widening the achievement gap.

Some argue that this longstanding condition is not really a problem—that the revolving door of unprepared entrants is plenty good enough for the students in poor schools. This argument was made again recently by the Hoover Institution, which published an article by researchers Kane, Rockoff, and Staiger looking at teachers' pathways into the New York City public schools. The study found that, while uncertified and alternatively certified teachers initially did less well in producing student achievement than certified teachers, especially in reading, most of the differences disappeared by the third year of teaching. Therefore, the article concluded, we need not worry about teacher training and certification for the teachers of disadvantaged students.

This argument is not supported by the study's own data. In fact, most of those who survived through year three had, by then, completed training and achieved certification. Many did not last that long. About three-fourths of the Teach for America recruits and half of the other uncertified teachers had already left. This constant attrition of underprepared teachers creates a harmful cycle in which students in poor schools are constantly learning from inexperienced and less-effective teachers. With estimates of the costs of beginning teacher attrition averaging about $15,000 per candidate, those who left also cost the city millions of dollars in wasted resources. With the same policies, an ongoing stream of new recruits will undereducate thousands more students stuck in schools that routinely hire these kinds of teachers.

The study also dropped from its analysis classrooms serving large numbers of special education and limited-English-proficient students, those who most need teachers with greater levels of skill. In a study that colleagues and I conducted, we found that uncertified recruits did particularly poorly with limited-English-proficient students.

This is not smart policy. The notion that we can remain a world-class economy while undereducating large portions of our population—in particular students of color and new immigrants who are fast becoming a majority in our public schools—is untenable. Mostly because of these under-investments, the U.S. continues to rank far behind other industrialized nations in educational achievement: 28 out of 40 nations in mathematics in 2003, for example, right behind Latvia. Meanwhile, leaders of countries like Finland that experienced a meteoric rise to the top of the international rankings have attributed their success to their massive investments in teacher education.

Most of the higher-achieving countries we consider peers or competitors now provide high-quality graduate-level teacher education designed to ensure that teachers can effectively educate all of their students. Preparation is usually fully subsidized for all entrants and includes a year of practice teaching in a clinical school connected to the university. Schools receive funding to provide coaching, seminars, classroom visits, and joint planning time for beginners as well as veterans. Salaries are competitive with other professions, offering additional stipends for hard-to-staff locations.

If we are serious about leaving no child behind, we need to go beyond mandates to ensure that *all* students have well-qualified teachers. Effective action can be modeled after practices in medicine. Since 1944, the federal government has subsidized medical training to fill shortages and build teaching hospitals and training programs in high-need areas—a commitment that has contributed significantly to America's world-renowned system of medical training and care.

Intelligent, targeted incentives can ensure that all students have access to teachers who are indeed highly qualified. An aggressive national teacher quality and supply policy, on the order of the post-World War II Marshall Plan, could be accomplished for less than 1 percent of the more than $300 billion spent thus far in Iraq; in a matter of only a few years, it would establish a world-class teaching force in all communities.

First, the federal government should establish *service scholarships* to cover training costs in high-quality programs at the undergraduate and graduate level for young and midcareer recruits who will teach in a high-need field or location for at least four years. (After three years, teachers are more likely to remain in the profession and make a difference for student achievement.) Because fully prepared novices are twice as likely to stay in teaching as those who lack training, shortages could be reduced rapidly if districts could hire better prepared teachers. Virtually all of the vacancies currently filled with emergency teachers could be filled with well-prepared teachers if 40,000 service scholarships of up to $25,000 each were offered annually. (Price tag: $1 billion per year.)

Second, *recruitment incentives* are needed to attract and retain expert, experienced teachers in high-need schools. Federal matching grants can leverage additional compensation for teachers with expertise and/or additional responsibilities, such as mentoring and coaching. If matched by state or local contributions, stipends of $10,000 for 50,000 teachers annually—based on systems that recognize teacher expertise, such as National Board Certification, standards-based evaluations, and carefully assembled evidence of contributions to student learning—could attract 100,000 accomplished teachers to high-poverty schools to serve as mentors and master teachers. An additional $300 million in matching grants would improve teaching conditions in these schools, including smaller pupil loads, adequate materials, and time for teacher planning and professional development—all of which keep teachers in schools. (Price tag: $800 million a year.)

Third, as in medicine, the Marshall Plan should support *improved preparation*. Incentive grants ($300 million) should upgrade all teachers' preparation for teaching literacy skills as well as standards-based content, and for teaching special education students and English-language learners. An additional $200 million should expand state-of-the-art teacher education programs in high-need communities that partner "teaching schools" with universities. As in teaching hospitals, candidates study teaching and learning while gaining hands-on experience in state-of-the-art classrooms. Effective models have already been created by universities sponsoring professional development schools and by school districts offering urban teacher residencies that place candidates with expert teachers while they complete their coursework. These programs create a pipeline of teachers prepared to engage in best practice, while establishing demonstration sites for urban teaching. Funding for 200 programs serving an average of 150 candidates each at $1,000,000 per year per program would supply 30,000 exceptionally well-prepared recruits to high-need communities each year. (Price tag: $500 million.)

Fourth, providing *mentoring for all beginning teachers* would reduce attrition and increase competence. With one-third of new teachers leaving within five years, and higher rates for those who are underprepared, recruitment efforts are like pouring water into a leaky bucket. By investing in state and district induction programs, we could ensure mentoring support for every new teacher in the nation. Based on the funding model used in California's successful Beginning Teacher Support and Assessment (BTSA) Program, a federal allocation of $4,000 for each of 125,000 beginning teachers, matched by states or local districts, could ensure that each novice is coached by a trained mentor. (Price tag: $500 million.)

Finally, preparation and mentoring can be strengthened if they are guided by a high-quality *teacher performance assessment* that measures actual teaching skill. Current tests used for licensing and federal accountability are typically paper-and-pencil measures of basic skills and subject matter knowledge that demonstrate little about teachers' abilities to practice effectively. Performance assessments for new teachers in states like Connecticut and California have been strong levers for improving preparation and mentoring and for determining teachers' competence. Federal support to develop a nationally available performance assessment for licensing would not only provide a useful tool for accountability and improvement, but would also help teachers move more easily from states with surpluses to those with shortages. (Price tag: $100 million.)

In the long run, these proposals would save far more than they would cost. The savings would include the more than $2 billion now wasted annually because of high teacher turnover, plus the even higher costs of grade retention, summer school, remedial programs, lost wages and prison sentences for dropouts (another $50 billion, increasingly tied to illiteracy and school failure). A Marshall Plan for Teaching could help ensure within only a few years that the U.S. can place well-qualified teachers in the schools that most need them and give all students a genuine opportunity to learn.

Best,

Linda Darling-Hammond

Chapter 14

Teaching Boldly in Timid Schools: Reflecting on Knowledge Access and Knowledge Control

Linda McSpadden McNeil

"Teaching is awesome! Our job is to make something awesome happen for that child every day! If you're not prepared to work hard to make sure something awesome happens for that child every day, then maybe teaching is not for you."
-Connie Floyd, a teacher

"What piece of the universe will your students touch today?"
-Dr. Bruce Alberts, editor of Science magazine

Dear Caring Teacher,

When I was hired to teach sophomore and junior English at Hillsboro High School in Nashville, Tennessee, I thought they hoped I would become the kind of teacher who had inspired me to teach: strong, intellectually alive, infinitely curious, passionate about literature, and more confident in us— their students—than anyone would have thought reasonable. These teachers believed that their classrooms could be places where ideas could thrive, and that our lives—and theirs—would be richer for it. I would soon learn that what they really wanted was someone to "cover" three sections of sophomore English and two of American literature. But by the time I figured that out, I had already found kindred spirits among the faculty who, like me, carried high aspirations for ourselves and for our students. As we made common cause, shared ideas (and three-prong adapter plugs!) and got involved in the school, I'm afraid we came to be viewed more as troublemakers than as bold teachers.

I entered teaching with another preconception. As a White teacher assigned to a White high school in a biracial, very segregated southern city, I was aware of stepping into a highly discriminatory, unequal system. Never having lived in the South, I nonetheless knew that my generation of teachers carried the obligation to chip away at the discrimination that we had inherited. I had few illusions that my generation could eliminate all inequalities, but our charge to try was at the heart of what it meant to be a teacher in the late 1960s and early 1970s. Teaching boldly in that day was to challenge the status quo, raise questions with our students, make changes in the curriculum, and ally with those outside of schools who were working to change the discriminatory conditions of children and their families. Tiny but tangible steps toward greater equality, taking place in parallel with major civil rights legislation, made me believe that by the time my own children were growing up, the world would be a fairer place. It never occurred to me that during my lifetime, the policies governing our schools would be creating —even mandating— new forms of inequality. But that is getting ahead of the story.

For thirty years, I have studied and written about two oppositional forces in our schools: the goals of knowledge access and the mechanisms of knowledge control. By knowledge access I mean that great purpose behind our teaching: to open the world of human knowledge to our students and to foster in them many ways of knowing. In the words of Dr. Bruce Alberts, of the National Academy of Sciences and, currently, *Science* magazine, we teach so that today our students can touch another piece of the universe. The possibilities for what we teach are limitless. Never in human history have the grown-ups had so much to teach the children, not limited by geography, by language, or by one's own education. The whole world—all of accumulated human activity—is literally accessible to us and available for us to share with the children. And if we do bring them into this exciting world of learning, they can grow and develop in ways we have yet to imagine. An awesome responsibility, indeed.

Knowledge control is more subtle. It encompasses those things that put barriers between what we hope to teach and the children's learning. The lock the textbook industry has had on course content, the reluctance to teach anything controversial, the America-centric nationalism so pervasive in our historical narratives, the exclusion of the voices of people of color have created barriers that have sometimes been very explicit and formalized and at other times been so taken for granted that we do not notice them. Sometimes we become aware of these barriers, of these controls, often at times of great upheaval or social change.

It is true that my doctoral studies in critical theory with Michael Apple, and studies in the history of schools and school knowledge with Herbert Kliebard and John Palmer, at the University of Wisconsin-Madison helped give a vocabulary to my curiosity about the factors shaping school knowledge. And all my work since then has been aimed at analyzing the factors shaping, or inhibiting, what is taught in schools, and to whom. But my firsthand acquaintance with the tension between knowledge access and knowledge control came before—from being an idealistic young teacher in a southern high school. In many ways, the working conditions for teachers were quite different from what you face today. "Accountability" was heard in reference to settling up the paperback book orders at the end of the semester. Assessing student learning, like creating the curriculum, was the work of teachers, not bureaucrats and certainly not testing companies. Teachers were viewed as the subject-matter experts, choosing the novels in English classes, the themes to emphasize in history courses, the experiments for science labs.

And we taught accordingly. Our group of new young English teachers immediately connected, in part out of desperation for ideas. We soon found support from several remarkable experienced teachers who were all too happy to open their files full of teaching ideas. We knew we had no idea what we were doing, but that didn't stop us from getting together after school, over the summer, and always on snow days to create new materials for our students, to seek out novels the sophomore boys would like, to figure out ways to make sure our students (all 165 per teacher) wrote every single week.

We innovated. Because most of the teachers loved teaching upper-level courses, the sophomores had received little attention. We created a sopho-more language arts lab, full of wonderful paperbacks and reading corners and small group centers. We petitioned to team teach, horrifying parents who were sure this new venture would bring down SAT scores (it did not) and irritating a principal who would have to make the necessary room changes. American literature was teamed with American history; Patsy Sloan, the his-tory teacher in the team, brought Joe McCarthy memorably to life (I still re-call her description of his uncouth behavior on the Senate floor), assuring that in our English classes *The Crucible* would have its power as social commentary as well as drama.

Our search for great things for our kids to read was immensely enriched by the bookstore across the street from the high school, owned by the father of one of our students. On a number of occasions two of us would legiti-mately play hooky from school, telling the school secretary we needed to check to see if the paperbacks for our classes had come in. (I'm very grate-ful, looking back, that we could not check by e-mail; we needed those out-ings to hear Mr. Zibart tell us what we absolutely had to read next. Playing hooky occasionally is essential to teaching boldly!)

We also knew what we didn't know. It became immediately apparent that the American literature anthologies were completely inadequate. They contained no Black poets or other Black writers. They did include the Van-derbilt poets, Robert Penn Warren and Allen Tate and their colleagues. But there was no mention of African American literature, even though up to that time, almost every major African American writer had been a student, a pro-fessor, or a writer in residence at Fisk University, just across town. A Fisk professor had anthologized African American poetry; his volume became our source as we White teachers delved into this rich literature and made copy after copy for our students. (I am embarrassed to report that we were too shy or too uninformed to call this professor and invite him to our classes.)

It may have been these explorations into Black literature, a literature so notably missing from the "Southern Literature" sections of the official an-thologies, that most visibly brought us up against barriers to our goals of opening up new knowledge to our students. We had purchased several titles personally, including the Black poetry anthology. I had also come across a wonderful recording of Langston Hughes' dramatic monologues read by Ruby Dee and Ossie Davis. It was stirring in its own right and perfect for pairing with the dramatic monologues of Robert Browning, a mainstay in the textbook.

But to build a really good set of novels, short-story collections, biographies, and poetry by Black writers was beyond our personal budgets. We began requisitioning purchases for the school library from this burgeoning list of newly published and classic works in Black literature. Week after week I'd send a student to see if these books were in. Our lesson plans had been built around the choices students would make among these new titles. Week after week the reply was "they haven't come in yet."

They had not come in yet because they had not been ordered. Instead, the librarian had replaced each of our requests with an order for a recording of a Shakespeare play. To this day, I think I am responsible for the largest collection of Shakespeare play recordings in any public high school in America. (And yes, we did end up purchasing many of the requested titles out of our own pockets.)

More experienced teachers, upon hearing about the unordered books, kindly pointed out our naïveté. The library was for the librarian, not for the students and definitely not for new teachers. It was well known that she hated to have the books checked out; it disturbed the order of the shelves. She did not trust students or new teachers with any of the audio-visual equipment, so the message always came back "not available" though there were perfectly good projectors and overheads sitting in the library storage room.

The storage room also held "banned" books. I smile to this day to recall that the librarian put the book *Blood Brother*, on the back shelf. This middle-school level novel is about an American Indian boy and a White boy who prick their fingers to mingle their blood as a seal of friendship. The librarian (who apparently had never opened the book) thought it meant "soul brother" and thus banned it from circulation as potentially radical. She did not want to order books published later than the end of World War II lest they be too controversial or "inappropriate." This time frame belied the fact that the school itself was built in the 1960s.

It was easy at first to see these barriers to our teaching as personal, not so much personal against us, but as the actions of individuals. We of course attributed the refusal to order Black literature or to shelve *Blood Brother* in the stacks to the librarian's age, to the Old South mentality that she and the teacher closest to her shared from having grown up in the White culture of this region. That teacher, an English teacher, taught her students that Jesus spoke King James English; she truly believed it because the words of Jesus were printed in red in her King James version of the Bible. We imagined that change might come generationally, accelerating only after this older generation retired. Then we met the biology teacher, younger than we were, who had never heard of evolution, and the even younger business teacher who, though the school was to be integrated the following year, bought a Confederate flag the width of a city street for the band to march behind and didn't understand why anyone would object.

I learned of the flag when Patsy Sloan, a history teacher who later became mayor of a city in Kentucky, sent a student runner to my classroom with an urgent message that I come to her classroom to look out the window. We proceeded to the principal's office to explain "this isn't how we do." By then I was beginning to have a better understanding of the structures of schooling that lie behind the personal interactions. This was not just a matter of a young, clueless drill team sponsor unaware that the racial divisions in the city and the pending school desegregation made her purchase not only inappropriate but harmful. The library purchases, the Confederate flag, the attention to dress code but not the quality of math instruction, were organizational issues. The principal deferred to the librarian because, as he admitted, he was intimidated by her and it was "her library." He refused to discipline a boy who was absolutely out of control, disrupting every class, because "why, I know his daddy—I know his granddaddy," de facto evidence that he was not a problem.

The school system was not hierarchical by today's standards. In their classrooms, teachers were the curriculum developers, the designers of assessments, the subject-matter experts. But the organizational structure exemplified in the principal's decisions was one of timidity. The principal's main rationale for decisions were "keeping things running smoothly" and keeping the Fathers' Club, made up of civic and corporate leaders, happy.

The timidity extended to keeping the school running smoothly even if it meant ignoring serious problems. The drama teacher was brilliant and well-loved, especially admired for her courage as the wife of a soldier on active duty in Vietnam. She was one of the first African American teachers hired in the year prior to integration of the students. Staying late for drama practice, this teacher made an appointment to get her hair done at the salon in the up-scale department store across from the school. When she arrived, she was at first told she didn't have an appointment, then grudgingly whisked into a back room, out of sight of other customers. We activist young teachers couldn't threaten to withhold our business because none of us could afford to shop at that store. The principal refused to take any action because he (and I'm sure he intended no pun) "didn't want to make waves." A few of the mothers of our students took up the cause and made the store change its racially restrictive policies. But to the administration, "school was school," and what happened in the shopping center was not "school," thus needed no action even though the teacher was "on this side of town" because of her willingness to stay after hours for our students. (That this amazing teacher and a Black literature teacher educated in England known for her brilliance were reassigned to White schools, while some of our weaker teachers would the next year be sent to historically Black schools, was not lost on our students.)

Our group of eager young White teachers felt the administrative timidity when a letter we sent to the school board was published in the city's conservative afternoon newspaper (the same paper that had run a banner headline, "It's Time to Use the Nukes" in Vietnam). Our letter had recommended that the attendance zone of a new junior high be drawn such that the school would be naturally integrated, an important precursor to the pending desegregation of all the city's schools. A Black reporter, having no school news that day, had found the letter in the school board in-box and upon seeing it was written by teachers at the White high school found it noteworthy enough to publish. Fathers began calling the school when the paper hit the newsstands; we signers all received ominous notes to report to an emergency meeting at the last bell. The principal was visibly shaken and angry. He could not sanction us for writing our opinion. But the fact that we identified ourselves as teachers at the high school that would one day receive that junior high's students crossed a line. Everything at Hillsboro High was supposed to stay "in the family." The message was clear: the few but influential parents who had called to complain wanted us fired or transferred to a Black high school. That those schools had no openings, and that we would need a long learning curve to be good teachers for their students, was moot. Our letter had caused a disruption—the disruption and public embarrassment, not the issue of race and equality, or of teacher's voice, were the "problem."

Our students were not so timid as their fathers or our principal. They were for the most part wonderfully curious. Many felt a real pressure to learn. The world was changing dramatically, and they were struggling to figure out their place in it. The Vietnam War had not yet ended; the boys in our classes faced the draft right after high school if they did not do well enough to get into college. Even if headed for college, they struggled with the ethics of war. Studying Gandhi, Martin Luther King, Jr., and Thoreau was not a mere academic exercise; they wanted to know when civil disobedience was appropriate—and when it was imperative.

They were passionate about Earth Day and the environment. They struggled with the dilemma of wanting to picket a local paper company, a known polluter, though the company paid the best wages in the area to African Americans. On more than one occasion, if the principal passed my classroom and heard these discussions, he would remind me that I was supposed to be "teaching English." I learned two things from such encounters: the best teaching is often what takes place in asides and tangential discussions, and "smooth running" doesn't necessarily mean educational.

Two contrasting teaching moments embody the tension between knowledge access and knowledge control that I experienced but did not yet have a name for. Both involve student voice.

Students who had loved the discussions and varied readings in our team-taught classes became concerned after they got to senior English and found themselves spending six weeks on an expurgated version of Chaucer. They were applying to good colleges and were afraid that if admitted, they would not have read as extensively as their peers from private academies or East Coast public schools. They proposed a book group to meet after hours to read and discuss more contemporary authors and international literature. When they found they were spending more time preparing for these voluntary seminars, they petitioned the school board for academic credit. It was the first student-initiated, student-designed course to be awarded credit by the Nashville schools; two of us taught it, guided it, without additional pay and it continued for several years after we left the school.

By contrast, a turn at judging submissions to an essay contest introduced me to content-free teaching, an oxymoronic preview of things to come in education policy. I was to screen student essays for a contest being held by a local college. It was interesting to read papers from other teachers' students until I got to the last pile. Paper after paper was very strange. They had no misspellings, no comma faults, no sentence fragments. They also had nothing to say. My colleague Claire Stockard, with whom I team-taught sophomore honors, couldn't keep from laughing. "Oh, you got to Mrs. L.'s students. Of course they don't say anything. She teaches the five-paragraph essay." Claire explained that each essay was to have five paragraphs of five sentences each. There was no requirement that the paper have anything to say; the point was to be able to write error-free prose in this artificial framework. Reading the papers was frankly creepy—so much nice round handwriting, so many well-placed adjectives, but no ideas. The teaching of writing had long since moved to writing for meaning, writing to develop a writer's voice. This formulaic exercise was a waste of students' time, the appearance of learning without the substance.

I hadn't thought about the five-paragraph essay in years. My research followed the questions I encountered at that school: What are the factors shaping what is taught in schools, and to whom? Who decides what knowledge is of most worth and what gets left out? What ways of organizing schools give teachers support for insightful and imaginative teaching, and give students opportunities for powerful learning? What forms of schooling, policies, or social conditions inhibit our most knowledgeable teachers, limiting children's access to knowledge?

I began this letter to you by saying that we, the grownups, have never had more to teach the children. And never before has so much been understood about how children learn. This should be the most amazing moment in all of human history to be a teacher. And it should be a magical moment to be a child in school.

We must ask, then, why have we—as a nation—chosen this moment of greatest possibility to limit what we teach to what can be measured on a computer-scored test made by a corporation far from our students and their families? Why have we minimized the potential of this moment by having children, as a requirement of law, write in the form of an easily scored five-paragraph essay? Why have we adopted a management system that works, that is, produces positive indicators, only by dumbing down the curriculum to fit bubble-in answers and by triaging out of our schools those students whose scores may bring down the school ratings? Why did we take this moment of greatest student diversity to legislate an education system that in many cases creates, rather than reduces, inequalities?

The current system of educational accountability is based on the same kinds of fears that made my old principal let the librarian keep kids from checking out books. There is the fear that if we get serious about equity, we will have to first make the inequities public and have very public discussions about how to address them. Better to test all the children the same and create the appearance of equity. We can't trust principals to make teachers work hard unless we pay the principals a bonus if their school scores go up. And as you are very aware, there is talk in Washington, and maybe in your state, of tying teachers' pay to their students' test scores, as though teachers can't be trusted to teach unless we have a way to measure what they do, even if everyone knows that the children's test scores are a poor proxy for teachers' work.

The barriers to knowledge access my colleagues and I encountered were grounded in fears that old ways were passing, that long-stalled racial integration would destabilize the familiar, and that keeping youth from studying social issues would somehow postpone social change. The barriers your generation of teachers faces are even more formidable because they carry the force of law. It is harder to teach boldly if the principal walks the halls (as some have been known to do) to see if all teachers are on the same page or are using test-prep drills as their curriculum. It is harder to teach boldly if the principal spends scarce school dollars on practice tests, comparing at regular intervals which teachers' students are likely to assure the principal a cash bonus, or put his or her job in jeopardy. And now, under No Child Left Behind (and likely, its successor), teachers know that if their children don't score well on the state tests, their school can be closed or even turned over to a for-profit company to run.

How shall we teach boldly under such a controlling system? The very acts that seem bold today were once just called good teaching. When I asked a prekindergarten teacher what it would mean for her to teach boldly, her reply was immediate: "recess!" What does it mean that in many school districts today, letting children go out to play is a bold act, an act of resistance?

To be a teacher is to be that knowledgeable, caring adult who represents the entire community to the children. It is to be that person who knows not only how children learn, but how these children, here in this classroom, think and puzzle and question and amaze. It is to be the person who knows the children's families and works every day to learn more about their cultures, about what they and their families value. It is to be so excited about learning that you can't keep from sharing new ideas with the kids. It is to be that person who says, about that Confederate flag, or five-paragraph essay, or culturally empty textbook, or stack of test prep booklets, "This isn't how we do."

To be a bold teacher is to ask, "Wait a minute? Is this good for the kids?" If we do this today, will we be releasing their imaginations? Will we be expanding their universe? In the words of Maxine Greene, will we be helping them become more morally wide awake?

And to be a bold teacher is to have someone standing with you when you ask these questions. In writing these reflections on my teaching, I remember and I write as one of a group, a group of us the principal sighed to see coming into his office, a group of us who learned to laugh at the absurdities and cry out of sight of our students and librarian. Standardization, by design, silences the teacher's voice, renders the child a number without cultural identity or personality or stage of development or thoughts. Standardization shifts decisionmaking far from those who know the children. To teach boldly under such a system is to make common cause with those at your school and across your community who understand that teaching is helping children touch the universe. It's about helping them find and write their own stories. It's about connecting your story and your voice to theirs. It may not be possible to make something awesome happen every day for every child. But when it happens, it will be because a teacher did something bold.

My best to you in your work on behalf of the children,

Chapter 15

Dare to Be Positive!

Donalyn Heise

Dear Teachers,

I want to commend you for choosing this important profession! You are about to embark on one of the most rewarding and essential professions: educating future generations. Although you will have challenges, you have everything you need to be an effective, efficient educator. You are competent in content and pedagogy and will soon be confident as an emerging teacher. The first few years may be difficult, and at times may be stressful. Just as you may feel anxiety as an emerging teacher, your students may also feel anxiety and the uncertainty related to the turmoil they may be experiencing in their lives. With societal issues, threats of violence, economic challenges, and peer pressure, students need you more than ever to stay positive about their growth and learning, and to help them feel a sense of purpose as contributing members of society. They need you to care enough to listen and hear them, to stay the course, to be responsive, and devote energy and insight toward their educations. I urge you be positive, to transform the teaching environment, foster positive relationships, and create authentic learning that links school to life. I hope the insights and suggestions presented here will help you stay positive, enthusiastic, and realistic, while creating a nurturing learning environment that is meaningful for all students.

Transform the Learning Environment

As teachers, we have the ability to transform the learning environment through courageous acts of teaching. We can transform the classroom into a place that challenges students to care about their educations and put forth their best efforts. We can transform school to be a welcoming place that fosters life-long learning. Courageous teaching means being willing to take risks as a teacher and mentor. It means being brave in curricular and instructional strategies.

Use positive emotions to transform the learning environment and enhance student motivation. Long- and short-term memory is connected with the experience of the learner. Students remember longer if you make content exciting, fun, happy, nurturing, silly, or perhaps even a bit startling. Emotions can be created by classroom attitudes, innovative instructional strategies, and praise. Be bold. Try doing something unexpected or outrageous.

Education renewal cannot exist if schools are unwelcoming, boring places where kids do not want to be. So think creatively to transform learning. Consider instructional play as a framework for transforming the learning environment. Instructional play is an enjoyable activity or game that results in learning. It can involve independent or collaborative activities, with or without manipulatives. Try incorporating play into every lesson. Envision a school where all students are *required* to play. Children have an innate desire to learn, to solve problems, to become independent. Re-instill that passion. Witness their request to learn the skills and information necessary for meeting challenges of play. Play can involve all the senses and address the cognitive, behavioral, and affective domains. Play can incorporate problem solving, real-life learning, and attention to the challenges of the game. It just may create a generation of people capable of adapting to a rapidly evolving world.

Teach Students to Care about Themselves and Others

The classroom teacher is in the most influential position to get our young people to care about themselves and others. We can create new ways of reaching students by developing innovative, authentic curricula that address academic standards while motivating students to care about their own educations. Forget about helping struggling students by focusing on their self-esteem. Self-esteem is a feeling and feelings come and go. Help them develop self-respect; it is built on actions. Help students develop pride in themselves through successful actions. What can you do on a daily basis to empower students to value effort and actions?

I once heard a student say, "Its hard to care, when you don't." Students won't put forth effort if they don't care. As teachers, we can challenge students to think critically, and we can create experiences that encourage empathy. We can create opportunities for all students' voices to be heard. One way to do this is to challenge their presuppositions. Create an intriguing discussion prompt and ask students to respond to it and defend their response. For instance, if teaching an interdisciplinary lesson centered on the theme of commemorating important events or people in our lives, you may display the following statement: "War memorials should be created by war veterans." Ask students to think, and then discuss their reactions to this statement. Do they agree or disagree, and why or why not? Then show them images of Maya Lin's Vietnam Memorial and share the controversy surrounding her design for this public art. Allow all students to voice multiple viewpoints, and then ask, "Who decides?"

During these dialogues, you can remain value neutral. Your opinion on a controversial topic is not important; rather it is important that students practice discussing, hearing, and accepting varying views and learning how to live in a democracy. It can help students understand the important balance of individual and collective identities.

This example links learning to real life. Not only can it increase student engagement, but it can give all students opportunities to have a voice in the community conversation, to participate in civil dialogue, to ask tough questions, to hear different perspectives. It helps promote skills, habits and dispositions necessary for living in a democracy. It can teach them about consensus or how to agree to disagree. Avoiding controversial issues in the classroom means that students may grow to adulthood having never practiced civil dialogue and may be incapable of tolerating diversity of ideas and issues. Therefore, create a nurturing learning environment that fosters empathy and understanding by linking learning to real life issues. These opportunities are treasured platforms that you have to pursue with great sense of purpose.

Create Authentic Learning

Teach students to care about learning by linking the learning to their own lives and adapting your teaching methods to be more responsive to them. One of the most effective teachers I know is a small, soft-spoken middle school teacher who facilitates authentic learning in a nurturing environment. In this low-income school where students enter boisterously from loud hallways, shouting at one another and exhibiting disrespect for others, students walk through her classroom door and immediately demonstrate an attitude shift. They enter and follow the classroom routine, behaving responsibly. They seem not to operate or behave out of fear, but rather out of a sense of belonging. They seem sincerely happy to be there. They respect the teacher and other students, and seem engaged in learning. How did she create this atmosphere of caring, kindness, and desire to learn? This teacher cared enough about her students (our students) to give them boundaries while providing positive feedback. But she also maintained high expectations and a curriculum that linked lessons to real life situations. She dared to address societal issues while teaching interdisciplinary units that met the academic standards. When we link learning to real life, we help students learn about themselves and their place in the world. Authentic learning helps instill lifelong learning and a sense of purpose.

Another authentic way to educate for life and make learning more memorable is to make learning enjoyable. Think of something you learned outside of formal education. Where did you learn it? Who taught you and how? Chances are you enjoyed learning because you were an interested, engaged, active learner. The best lessons are those that are so enjoyable that the students forget that they are learning something.

Avoid Negative Attitudes in Media and in Others

It is difficult to stay positive about the teaching profession when we are surrounded by negativity. With current challenges to the education system, teachers and administrators may face pressures from declining budgets, high-stakes testing, decreased parental support and an increase in school violence. These pressures can create frustration, and frustrated teachers often make a habit of sharing negative comments about the profession. Some environments are toxic and should be avoided. Steer clear of negative conversations and create a habit of focusing on the positive.

Dare to be positive by focusing on the potential for effective teaching and learning. Keep a positive attitude by being selective. Be careful of what you listen to and what you say. Decide where you will spend your time, thoughts and energy. We are all interconnected, so pursue educating with a sense of purpose, realizing that, collectively, little things matter. Small changes can make great contributions, so dare to remain positive despite negative conversations you might encounter.

In addition to the negative comments of colleagues, the media may also remind us of the ills of education: school violence, bullying, gang activity, absenteeism, high drop-out rates, and lack of student motivation. Rarely do we hear the many successes of education in the media, the teacher who mentors and inspires students to reach their potential, or the school that supports authentic learning. Our perceptions can become our reality. So, avoid negative attitudes of others and surround yourself with other optimistic, enthusiastic educators who are committed to making a difference in young people. Counteract negativity by informing the media of the powerful learning taking place in your classroom. Notify them of student success.

Avoid Labeling Kids as BAD

Many education graduates hope that they will be offered a good job in "a good school." There is no such thing as a bad school. There are, however, schools with great potential and students longing for quality education. And quality education comes from great teachers like you. There is also no such thing as a bad kid. There are, however, students who exhibit anger, rudeness, defiance, or other inappropriate behavior. These kids are testing us to see if we are worthy of their trust. They are desperately seeking mentors who won't give up on them. They require patience, fortitude and sustained efforts. There are no quick fixes to these problems. Educating is a process that takes time. Understand and learn ways to respond to the challenging behavior of troubled youth. Separate the behavior from the child. Remember that misbehavior is often a cry for help, or a mask for the fear and uncertainty they feel inside.

Whether you find yourself in an urban classroom, teaching in a rural area, or private school, you may encounter students representing a variety of needs, interests, and abilities. Students who learn differently are often labeled. Consider it a privilege and an honor to be able to work with these diverse populations. You may teach some students who struggle academically or exhibit inappropriate behaviors. Do not label these kids as "bad." You may also have some students who sit quietly in class. All have the potential to fall through the cracks of our current education system. Even the students who sit quietly, follow the rules, and complete their work can be at-risk. Students who make superior grades and rarely disrupt can have needs and abilities that are not addressed. Some are not reaching their potential. While we spend time with struggling students, these high-ability students are often given busy work or asked to teach others. While peer tutoring is an excellent instructional strategy, it can be overused. All students deserve the opportunity to advance academically and emotionally from where they are to where they can progress. I encourage you to set up a video camera on a tripod in your classroom and periodically record your teaching. (Check school district policies about photographing students first.) Then critically reflect on your teaching practice. Do you give all students attention, or do you tend to spend your time and energy on a selected few? Do you inadvertently label students? You may gain valuable insights from critically reflecting on your teaching.

Schools, courts and the mental health profession are often preoccupied with negative, deviant behavior of youth and their deficits, instead of focusing on their strength and resilience. Some youth are labeled delinquent, disordered, dysfunctional, disturbed, or deprived. Some adults consider youth at-risk, damaged goods, punks or psychopaths. Yet troubled children and youth are often clever and resourceful. Some are resilient, capable of surviving trauma, rejection and uncertainty. These are skills that can be useful and beneficial for society. Our challenge is to channel students' energy and creativity and help them develop a sense of purpose. All children have some positive characteristics such as autonomy, self-determination, persistence, creativity, cleverness, resourcefulness, or energy. Focus on these positive traits, and articulate these qualities as positive in your communication with students, parents, and administrators.

Employ an asset model instead of focusing on students' deficits. Focusing on assets empowers individuals to realize their strengths and abilities and celebrate the things we can control in our life. Quality education has the power to transform the lives of individuals and communities. Through innovative teaching, we can help release human potential, build empathy and foster resilience. We can facilitate learning about the meaning of life, the human spirit, and our relationship to our world.

Don't let the reputation of the school or the student population be your excuse for ineffective teaching. You have the power to transform the culture of your classroom and the culture of the school. Change is a sustained effort that takes time. If you want something badly enough, you can find a way to make it happen.

Foster Positive Relationships

Cultivate constructive relationships with other teachers, staff, and administrators in your school. Learn the culture of your school and how to communicate and work with others. Explore ways to collaborate with other teachers and support student achievement. Establish ongoing communication with administrators before there are any incidents that require student intervention. Investigate collaborations with others that result in attaining mutual goals. Contact your assigned mentor or supervisor when you feel overwhelmed, or have questions or concerns. Your professional organization can provide a network for brainstorming solutions. Its members are there to help you.

Foster positive relationships in your classroom as well. Use effective classroom management strategies to promote a culture of respect among your students. Teach students to respect materials, space, and others. Does your classroom reflect your positive attitude toward teaching, attitudes toward your students and positive expectations for learning? Is it visually stimulating? Are principles of respect encouraged? Focus on the intended outcome that you wish to achieve and make sure that your actions are helping you move toward that goal.

Speak the Actions You Want to See

We often hear that we should keep student expectations high, but how do we accomplish that in the classroom? I think if we assume students are capable of extraordinary achievement, they may exhibit those behaviors. But simply believing won't make it happen. We have to do something. The threat of low grades may not motivate all students to achieve. Some students are not motivated by grades. Many will work harder for our approval than for high grades or the threat of punishment. But we have to clearly communicate academic and behavioral expectations by articulating them regularly, not in a threatening tone, but through positive reinforcement. We have to help them understand the importance of school. We have to guide them to see learning and its connections to real life issues. Praise them for their efforts and attitudes.

In addition to academic behaviors, you need to articulate the behaviors expected for a respectful classroom environment. Speak with your actions and words. Exhibit and articulate the virtues you want to cultivate in your students: kindness, understanding, decency, humor, persistence, and vision. Let your students see you being proactive, promoting justice, and advocating for quality and excellence. Model life-long learning. Be bold; be courageous in content and processes of quality education. Let them see you take risks. Even if that risk results in failure, students will have an opportunity to see you learn and grow. Challenge yourself and challenge your students. Understand your students and learn with them.

Promote Your Program and Your Students' Work

Be proactive and disseminate all the good things you and your students accomplish. Don't wait for someone else to promote your success. Exhibit student work at the school board office, legislators' offices, local libraries, galleries, coffee shops, and community businesses. Send press releases to the media to cover your school successes. Send newsletters to parents, and make phone calls to parents to inform them of the positive things their child has accomplished. The time you spend calling parents to share the positive will pay off tenfold in the long run!

Finally, **be positive** and don't accept defeat as inevitable. Seek positive qualities in your students and acknowledge their sustained effort and positive attitude. You are an asset to your students, the community, and the profession. I am honored to be a part of your professional development journey and proud to have you as a colleague in the education profession. Becoming an effective teacher is a process that takes time. Give yourself that time.

Remember, all schools have challenges. All schools have students who need a great teacher, one who is optimistic about every student's potential and brave enough to teach courageously. All students deserve the best, and that is you! May you always remain enthusiastic and energetic as you transform challenges into opportunities. Dare to be positive!

My best,

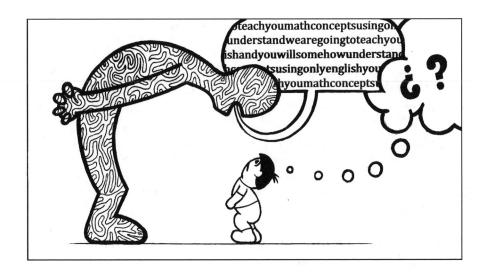

Chapter 16

Teach Outside the Classroom

Kara Mitchell

Dear Teachers,

Linda Darling-Hammond (1997) wrote, "I have always felt that the most exciting thing any person could do is to learn and the most challenging and satisfying thing anyone could do is to teach....Learning, I have always felt, is as essential as breathing" (p. xi). Learning, as essential as it is, is not confined to classroom and school walls. And teaching, as challenging and satisfying as it is, shouldn't be confined within classroom and school walls either. Teachers need to be our society's educators and for this to happen, teachers must teach both inside and outside their classroom and school walls. To explore this idea of teaching outside the classroom, I will discuss an investigation of why teaching outside the classroom is so important and of tools to start doing it.

Why Teach Outside the Classroom?

The current political and societal context is leaving teachers behind. For instance, when No Child Left Behind (NCLB), the current version of the federal Elementary and Secondary Education Act, was created, educators and educational researchers were widely excluded (DeBray, 2005). Additionally:

> Many political and educational leaders are attempting to shut down public education and teacher education. They do not believe that teachers are capable professionals, and they are generally not interested in working with teachers to learn that standardized, high-stakes tests may not be the best way to assess *literacy* instruction and achievement. (Burns, 2007, p. 57)

In this climate where teacher knowledge is overlooked and blatantly ignored, teachers need to work to help community members, politicians, and business leaders understand the depth, expanse, and utility of teacher knowledge. Learning and teaching are intricate endeavors and teacher knowledge is essential in making decisions that effect classroom practice. If teachers act as educators for our whole society, the professional knowledge of teaching can affect public opinion and help our communities understand the complexities of the issues we face inside classrooms.

Many facets of education are complex and difficult for those outside of teaching to truly understand. These misunderstood intricacies can lead to ineffective policies that both tie teachers' hands and disregard the experience and expertise of teachers. One clear example of this is found in looking at the issues, policies, and practices surrounding the teaching of bilingual learners, often referred to as English Language Learners (ELLs).

As most educators can attest, first- and second-generation immigrants comprise the fastest growing segment of the current student population (Suárez-Orozco & Suárez-Orozco, 2001). These students are often discussed and identified in terms of their ability to navigate school in English. However, as Garcia (2008) and Brisk (2006) point out, by discussing these students only in terms of their English-speaking level, integral parts of these students' linguistic skills, cultural identity and background knowledge are overlooked: their bilingual, sometimes even multilingual, abilities, and development. These students have been referred to in the past as Limited English Proficient (LEP), English Language Learners (ELLs), and English Learners (ELs). However, to support the bilingual identities, opportunities, and development of this growing student population, I will refer to them as bilingual learners.

The methods of instruction used to work with bilingual learners in U.S. schools are highly politicized and often misunderstood. As teachers know, based on prominent sociocultural theories of learning, students learn best when new knowledge is built on what pupils already know and can do (Oakes & Lipton, 1999). Most students, including those who are not yet proficient in English, come to classrooms with extensive background knowledge and language skills. Unfortunately, there is sometimes a mismatch between the linguistic, cultural, and academic knowledge students bring to the classroom and the types of knowledge they are expected to engage with and master in the school setting (Heath, 1983). This mismatch may at times even impede the accessibility of the curriculum for bilingual learners and students from nondominant language backgrounds (Schleppegrell, 2004). For this reason, bilingual education, an instructional method utilizing various amounts of students' home languages for the purpose of advancing English proficiencies and grade-level content knowledge (Brisk, 2006), is considered by experts and language-teaching specialists to be the most effective means of providing quality educational opportunities to bilingual learners (Crawford & Krashen, 2007; Rolstad et al., 2005; Slavin & Cheung, 2005).

Though extensive research as well as teacher experience and expertise point to the value of utilizing home languages in instructional contexts for bilingual learners, bilingual education has been outlawed in California, Arizona, and Massachusetts through voter referenda. Common contemporary American thought positions English as an inherently superior language, bilingualism as a deficit, and quick immersion into English-only classrooms as the cheapest and most efficient method to solve the "problem" of heritage languages (Brisk, 2006; Meskill, 2005). These pervading myths coupled with widespread anti-immigrant sentiment (Suárez-Orozco & Suárez-Orozco, 2001) make bilingual education a highly political issue that a majority of voters in the cases of California, Arizona, and Massachusetts voted against.

In addition to ending bilingual education, these voter referenda call for only one year of sheltered immersion English for bilingual learners. To the general public, one year of specialized English instruction appears to be enough time for bilingual learners to learn English. However, teacher knowledge and expertise prove otherwise. In fact, educational research has shown that bilingual learners may need between two and four years to speak conversational English at the same level as their native-English-speaking peers. Yet the more complex form of English used in classrooms, generally referred to as academic English, may take between five and eight years to master at native-speaking levels (Crawford & Krashen, 2007).

Teachers and educational researchers working with bilingual learners can quickly attest to the difficulties these students often encounter in reading and writing academic English, even when they are incredibly proficient in social and conversational English (Scarcella, 2003). Experts in language acquisition have shown how bilingual learners are really doing "double the work" (Short & Fitzsimmons, 2007) of their native-speaking peers by learning both grade-level content and a complex language and therefore need more time to develop academic English proficiencies. Teacher experience also shows how students held to high expectations, offered quality educational opportunities, and given explicit academic language instruction can excel and master difficult content (Zwiers, 2008). These things that are so obvious to educators and researchers working in classrooms with bilingual learners are not obvious to those outside the classroom who often think English can quickly be mastered. In order to combat such prevailing myths, especially when they can lead to policies that limit instructional options for teachers and learners, teachers must share their knowledge and teach outside the classroom.

Though not all attempts to teach outside the classroom, especially with regard to fighting those who oppose bilingual education efforts, result in desired outcomes, teachers and other bilingual learner advocates in Colorado illustrate the importance of teaching outside the classroom. Escamilla et al. (2003) analyzed the events and campaign surrounding the 2002 defeat of the anti-bilingual education initiative in Colorado and found ten lessons for advocates of bilingual education to consider. All ten of these lessons are useful, but the first two lessons clearly demonstrate the value in sharing teacher knowledge outside of classroom walls. They also expose the value of teaching outside the classroom for any issue and any purpose, not just to improve the opportunities of bilingual learners in schools.

The first lesson Escamilla et al. (2003) found was that "all politics are local." In Colorado's efforts to defeat the opposition to the bilingual education initiative, "it was necessary to create a message that would appeal to all Colorado voters, to devise a strategy to get the message out across the state, and to conduct a well-organized grassroots campaign" (p. 365). Organizations like "English Plus" and "Colorado's Common Sense" were created and worked to put this plan of action into place. Teachers and education leaders played crucial roles in these organizations, in creating the message and getting it out across the state. In fact the authors note, "Making the situation local necessitated the involvement of local school districts" (p. 366). Teachers working locally to share their knowledge and expertise outside of the classroom were pivotal to the success of this campaign.

The second lesson Escamilla et al. (2003) discuss is "the importance of long-term, multifaceted strategies" (p. 367). The various strategies used in Colorado to defeat the referendum that opposed bilingual education included legal, political, and educational approaches. All of the strategies used in the campaign were important for the ultimate success of defeating the English-only initiative, but the educational strategies were an incredibly important part of that work. "The educational component included strategies and specific initiatives to educate the state legislature, the general public, the media, the voters, and educators in all fields" (p. 367). This is a specific example of teachers taking their knowledge and sharing it outside of the classroom in order to support best practices in teaching and learning inside the classroom. Though the work of teachers teaching outside the classroom cannot alone account for the success of the campaign, imagine the difficulty in fighting a voter referendum without this kind of work. Teacher knowledge and expertise shared outside of the classroom is essential in such cases.

Not all teachers live in states facing such referenda, nor do all teachers have expertise in working with bilingual learners. However, all teachers have knowledge and expertise about what is happening in their classrooms and schools and can share that knowledge in their local communities to promote both quality working conditions for teachers and educational opportunities for students. At a time when teachers are paid less than their college educated counterparts in other professions (Taylor, 2008), experiencing serious retention problems (Yost, 2006), and struggling to provide quality educational opportunities to students from low-income and linguistically and racially diverse backgrounds (Berliner, 2006), the complexities and depth of teacher knowledge on all aspects of the broad range of educational issues facing our country need to be shared.

Additionally, educational change experts have long shown that school reform efforts rarely succeed when not utilizing teacher knowledge and expertise. "Much more could be done if researchers, policymakers and administrators worked *with* teachers rather than *on* them" (Bailey, 2000, p.

113). By teaching outside the classroom, teachers proactively engage in conversations, campaigns, programs and policies that can positively affect the work they do inside the classroom. Teaching outside the classroom is a way to change the tide of unworkable and harmful school reform efforts being thrust at teachers. By freely offering teacher knowledge and expertise to create workable policies and plans, teaching outside the classroom will improve teaching and learning for both teachers and learners in our schools.

How Can One Teach Outside the Classroom?

First, start with the very literal act of teaching outside of your classroom. Who can you talk to about the difficult realities and challenges of your work? Who will listen? Who will join your efforts to improve these conditions and issues? An obvious place to start is with your friends, family, neighbors, colleagues, and community, but you can expand to the level of school board members, district officials, legislators, business leaders, and newspaper editorial staff. What coalitions can you form with community members in other professions? How can you collaborate across the local community? Informing your community about the realities of teaching can help to provide the public with insights that aren't often shared or understood. The more you share of your expertise and knowledge about what happens inside the classroom, the more you can do to help improve your own working conditions and the experiences of your students.

Second, when you teach outside of your classroom, share your experience as a teacher by focusing on reasonable solutions to the various issues you face. Sharing solutions rather than complaints is an effective way to build coalitions and find local support. Additionally, teachers are often painted as whiners, which can negate effective efforts for teachers to be society's educators. Teaching outside the classroom should be a solution-focused exercise.

Third, to teach outside the classroom, recognize that you are the solution. Whatever educational issue you would like to focus your energy on, the solution to that issue is within your grasp. Your expertise, experiences teaching, and knowledge about teaching and learning are where solutions to educational issues should be found. By finding solutions for the educational issues you care about in the contexts you know best—your own classroom, grade, department, school, and district—you can use your experience and expertise to truly improve the world of teachers and students as well. But your work doesn't have to stop at the local level. You can also work to find solutions for state and national issues.

Fourth, in efforts to teach outside the classroom, look for opportunities to learn. Teaching outside the classroom can be a two-way endeavor and information exchange of your expertise and teaching knowledge and the expertise of those with whom you meet. As teachers well know, teaching and learning are intricately connected and by working to share information about the realities of classrooms and schools, teachers may also need to learn about the realities of policy creation, legislative imperatives and fiscal restraints. Though teachers have limited time, spending an hour with education specialists working on state and federal legislation can provide a two-way opportunity for teaching and learning. Teachers don't need to be policy experts to contact policy makers. Meetings with school board members, district leaders, and legislative offices do not have to be preceded with extensive investigations into policy matters. These meetings can be an opportunity for you to share your knowledge of teaching and learning and the issues you face in your work. It is an opportunity for those outside of teaching to share their work in creating the policies that affect your classroom. Additionally by approaching meetings with those outside of teaching with humility and willingness to learn, broader and more comprehensive solutions to educational issues can be formed.

Fifth, in teaching outside of the classroom, represent your expansive knowledge and expertise with confidence. Though teachers often receive messages of inferiority from the world around us, teacher knowledge matters and must be shared. Teaching is exceptionally important work and many teachers are working hard to do it very well. Represent your profession with confidence and poise. Confident messages are more powerful than those delivered with insecurity. Regardless of all the things you don't know, you have the pivotal expertise of a teacher and that needs to be shared with gusto.

Sixth, planning is essential for successfully teaching outside the classroom. There are few things more precious to a teacher than time. And teachers truly never have enough of it. Teachers have so many demands placed on their time that they must become experts in priority setting and time management. This same realm of expertise needs to be tapped in order to teach outside the classroom. By setting aside one hour a week to teach outside the classroom, teachers can positively influence the world we live in and the policies that affect teaching practices. In order to create that one hour of time each week to spend teaching outside your classroom, consider altering your grading system, doing more collaborative planning, or getting student volunteers to help you with tasks you can delegate.

By teaching outside your classroom, you can be in a position to create positive change and promote valuable policies to aid you in your work inside the classroom. The world doesn't change overnight, but it does change. It wasn't that long ago when women, 71% of the current teaching profession in the U.S. (U.S. Census Bureau, 2004), couldn't even vote. Change is possible, but it won't happen without challenging the status quo. Freire (2005) discussed this, saying:

> 'What can I do? Whether they call me *teacher* or coddling mother, I am still underpaid, disregarded, and uncared for. Well, so be it.' In reality, this is the most convenient position, but it is also the position of someone who quits the struggle, who quits history. It is the position of those who renounce conflict, the lack of which undermines the dignity of life. There may not be life or human existence without struggle and conflict. Conflict shares in our conscience. Denying conflict, we ignore even the most mundane aspects of our vital and social experience. Trying to escape conflict, we preserve the status quo. (p. 83)

It is time to fight the status quo. And it's easier to do than you may think.

My own experience teaching outside the classroom began in the spring of 2007 with a deep concern that NCLB would quickly be reauthorized with minimal changes. This concern led me to contact my U.S. senators and representative's local offices. It was surprisingly easy to set up appointments with the office staffers who worked on education and was even easier to find other concerned educators to accompany me on these visits. Each meeting was unique and varied in length and specific topic of discussion, but each interaction helped me gain confidence and feel that I actually had a voice.

I'm not a policy expert, but I know what it is like to watch bilingual learners struggle with a standardized test they have no chance of passing or even understanding and be defeated by the experience. If I didn't tell my representatives about those experiences, who would? My local visits prepared me to join a lobbying effort by the National Education Taskforce and the Institute for Language and Educational Policy in Washington, D.C. I was amazed at how incredibly easy it was to set up appointments with education staffers in the offices of representatives and senators from my state as well as with members of the House and Senate Education Committees. These meetings were truly two-way exchanges during which I was able to learn about the legislative process, the compromises necessary to satisfy the demands of so many different constituencies, and the efforts underway to improve NCLB. I was able to teach about my experiences researching and working with bilingual learners under the constraints of NCLB. Lobbying in D.C. and at the state level shouldn't be left to large corporations, organizations, or politically powerful unions. We can each lobby individually for what we feel is important in education. And imagine how strong the voice of teachers in policy and program creation could be if all teachers made an effort to share their knowledge beyond the classroom walls.

By teaching outside the classroom, teachers can use their expertise to enter the contemporary discourse and fight for more professionalism, recognition, better teaching conditions, and higher quality educational experiences for students. Teaching outside the classroom is something teachers both can and must do.

Will you please join me in fighting the status quo by teaching outside your classroom?

Affectionately,

Kara Mitchell

References

Bailey, B. (2000). The impact of mandated change of teachers. In N. Bascia, & A. Hargreaves (Eds.), *The sharp edge of educational change* (pp. 112–128). New York: Routledge/Flamer.

Berliner, D. C. (2006). Our impoverished view of educational reform. *Teachers College Record, 108*(6), 949–995.

Brisk, M. E. (2006). *Bilingual education: From compensatory to quality schooling* (2nd ed.). Mahwah, NJ: Lawrence Erlbaum Associates.

Burns, L. D. (2007). A practical guide to political action: Grassroots and English teaching. *English Journal, 96*(4), 56–61.

Crawford, J., & Krashen, S. (2007). *English learners in American classrooms: 101 questions, 101 answers*. New York: Scholastic.

Darling-Hammond, L. (1997). *The right to learn: A blueprint for creating schools that work.* San Francisco: Jossey-Bass.

DeBray, E. H. (2005). Chapter 2: Partisanship and ideology in the ESEA reauthorization in the 106th and 107th congresses: Foundations for the new political landscape of federal education policy. *Review of Research in Education, 29,* 29–50.

Escamilla, K., Shannon, S., Carlos, S., & Garcia, J. (2003). Breaking the code: Colorado's defeat of the anti-bilingual education initiative (amendment 31). *Bilingual Research Journal, 27*(3), 357–382.

Freire, P. (2005). *Teachers as cultural workers: Letters to those who dare teach.* Boulder, CO: Westview Press.

Garcia, O., Kleifgen, J. A., & Flachi, L. (2008). *From English language learners to emergent bilinguals.* Teachers College, Columbia University.

Heath, S. B. (1983). *Ways with words: Languages, life and work in communities and classrooms.* New York: Cambridge University Press.

Meskill, C. (2005). Infusing English language learner issues throughout professional educator curricula: The training all teachers project. *Teachers College Record, 107*(4), 739–756.

Oakes, J., & Lipton, M. (1999). Contemporary theories of learning: Problem solving and understanding. *Teaching to change the world* (1st ed., pp. 66–94). Boston: McGraw-Hill College.

Rolstad, K., Mahoney, K., & Glass, G. (2005). The big picture: A meta-analysis of program effectiveness research on English language learners. *Educational Policy, 19*(4), 572–594.

Scarcella, R. C. (2003). *Academic English: A conceptual framework* (Technical Report No. 2003–1) University of California Linguistic Minority Research Institute.

Schleppegrell, M. J. (2004). *The language of school: A functional linguistics perspective.* Mahwah, NJ: Lawrence Erlbaum Associates.

Short, D., & Fitzsimmons, S. (2007). *Double the work: Challenges and solutions to acquiring language and academic literacy for adolescent English language learners - A report to Carnegie corporation of New York.* Washington, DC: Alliance for Excellent Education.

Slavin, R., & Cheung, A. (2005). A synthesis of research of reading instruction for English language learners. *Review of Educational Research, 75*(2), 247–284.

Suarez-Orozco, C., & Suarez-Orozco, M. M. (2001). *Children of immigration.* Cambridge, MA: Harvard University Press.

Taylor, L. L. (2008). Comparing teacher salaries: Insights from the U.S. census. *Economics of Education Review, 27,* 48–57.

U.S. Census Bureau (2004). *Facts for features: Special edition.* Retrieved July 5, 2008, from http://www.census.gov/Press–Release/www/releases/archives/facts_for_features_special _editions/001737.html.

Yost, D. S. (2006). Reflection and self-efficacy: Enhancing the retention of qualified teachers from a teacher education perspective. *Teacher Education Quarterly, 33*(4), 59–76.

Zwiers, J. (2008). *Building academic language: Essential practices for content classrooms.* San Francisco: Jossey-Bass.

Chapter 17

Recognizing Diversity in Asian Students

Hidehiro Endo

Dear Teachers and Future Teachers,

I am writing this letter to expand your thinking about Asian students in the U.S. educational environment. East Asian students (such as Chinese, Japanese, Korean, and Taiwanese) and Southeast Asians (such as Cambodian, Hmong, Indonesian, Laotian, Malaysian, Myanmarese, Filipino, Singaporean, Thai, and Vietnamese) are often seen as "model minorities." Even though you may have not heard the term model minority, you can probably think of racial stereotypes, particularly positive ones, about Asians such as being hard workers and math geniuses. This model minority image of the Asian population is attributed to their economic and academic achievement shown in statistical data. Although the term "model minority" appears to be a flattering racial remark, the model minority image, in reality, shadows the reality of who Asians really are (Lee, 1996). This image constructs a myth that tells us that the majority of Asian students are smart, quiet, nerdy, and studious. The model minority image also perpetuates an erroneous idea that Asians are homogeneous in nature. Consequently, this positive image hinders people from becoming aware of Asian students' *real* educational experiences and educational needs and most importantly who they are. In truth, many Asian students struggle with the model minority image, and their voices are often overlooked in U.S. education. Of course, model minority stereotypes are not the only issues of which you need to become aware in order to understand Asian students' educational needs. Some other impediments involving social, cultural, racial, historical, and political issues have an impact on Asian students' educational experiences.

In order to help you become an informed educator, I would like to introduce to you some of the history of Asian immigration in the U.S. and discuss the nature of positive racial stereotypes of Asians in this country. I will also share with you some of my personal experiences as I discuss the heterogeneity in Asian people. As a person of Japanese descent, I hope this letter helps to enrich your understanding of the Asian students you are currently serving or whom you will be serving in your culturally diverse classroom.

The term Asian is often used to identify a person from East Asian, Southeast Asian and South Asian countries or a person whose family originally came from these countries. According to the 2007 American Community Survey, approximately 13.2 million Asian people are currently living in the U.S. and about 4.4 % of the total U.S. population is Asian (U.S. Census Bureau, 2008). The Asian population in this country has been gradually increasing over the last several decades.

I would like to briefly introduce the history of Asian immigration in the U.S. so you can better understand how the model minority myth, the positive racial stereotype of Asians, has come about in the U.S. In the mid-18th century the first large influx of Asian immigrants, the Chinese, began landing in the U.S. The Japanese also started to migrate in 1868 (Morimoto, 1997). The majority of the early Asian immigrants went into the railroad business, farming, coal mining, fishery, and lumber work as labor contractors (Ichioka, 1990). As the number of Chinese and Japanese immigrants grew, they were seen as a peril that endangered the power of White Americans (Bhattacharyya, 2001). In fact, Asians were depicted as the "yellow peril" for a long time. The notion of the yellow peril was constructed with the purpose of oppressing Asians (Bhattacharyya, 2001; Jones, 1955; Suzuki, 1977). Unlike immigrants of European descent, Asian immigrants are not racially assimilable into White America. Additionally, the rise of Asian immigrants in the late 19th century was viewed as a cultural, political, and economic threat by White supremacists (Kawai, 2005). Consequently, two of the historically crucial exclusion acts against Asians, the Chinese Exclusion Act in 1892 and the 1924 Immigration Act, which prohibited Japanese people from immigrating to the U.S., were enacted (Kitano & Daniels, 1995; Morimoto, 1997). These acts represent the anti-Asian sentiments in the U.S. at that time.

Following the end of World War II, immigration from Asian countries resumed, although the number was limited. In 1952, the McCarran-Walter Act, the first immigration act that abolished racial restrictions subsequent to World War II, was enacted. Furthermore, as a result of the promulgation of the 1965 Immigration Act, the number of Chinese and Koreans as well as Southeast Asians such as Filipinos, Vietnamese, etc. grew significantly (Kitano & Daniels, 1995).

Along with the increase of Asian immigrants in the U.S., a positive image of Asian Americans began to appear in the 1960s, inaugurating the term, "model minority." The positive representation of Asian Americans was attributed to the popular press that paid attention to the success stories of Asian Americans in a variety of contexts (Wong & Halgin, 2006). By focusing on the positive picture of Asian Americans, model minority stereotypes such as *Asians work hard in order to succeed in American society in the face of adversity* were constructed.

However, it is too optimistic to believe that the model minority image was an improvement to the yellow peril image, which had been implanted in White American society for a little more than 100 years. As Suzuki (1977) stated, Asian Americans were initially content with the positive image that implied they were finally accepted in White American society; however, after a while, they came to realize that this positive image would not raise their actual social, political, and economic status. The success stories of Asian Americans were disguised by the idea that regardless of one's racial background and socioeconomic status, everyone has equal opportunities to succeed in the U.S.... the "American dream." This concept denotes that one's academic and economic success is fundamentally attributed to one's work ethic. However, it absolutely rejects other significant factors that impinge on one's academic and economic accomplishment in U.S. society, such as one's social class, gender, race/ethnicity and educational attainment. Moreover, the model minority stereotype transformed into a social burden not only for

Asians, but also for other minority groups. Some scholars claim that the model minority stereotypes were constructed to send a political message to the social justice movement, saying that Asian Americans climbed up the social mobility ladder without governmental support. This movement culminated in the Civil Rights Act of 1964 (Ng et al., 2007; Osajima, 2000; Suzuki, 1977). What is more, the model minority image was exploited to label other minority groups as failures (Takaki, 1993). This image began to oppress other racial minorities by suggesting that they were to blame for not being able to obtain better economic mobility.

Importantly, this positive racial image disregards the fact that Asians are not homogeneous. Of course, the lack of knowledge regarding the differences among Asians is not solely attributable to the spread of the positive racial image of Asians. In general, the presence of Asian people in U.S. media is very limited. Additionally, the portrayal of Asians in U.S. media is often a debatable representation that exaggerates the stereotypical image of Asians such as martial arts specialists, culturally insensitive businessmen, or nerdy students who love playing video games, to name a few. The limited media image prohibits people from developing an awareness of the diversity that exists among Asians. The unawareness of who Asians are and their heterogeneity can be a hazardous impediment for many Asians of school age, because the manipulated representation hinders teachers from becoming aware of who their Asian students really are.

Let me talk about the heterogeneity of Asians in the U.S. for a moment. At the beginning of this letter, I briefly mentioned the regional classification of the Asian nations. Although Asians share some physical traits and cultural characteristics, Asians are ethnically different. In the U.S., East Asian groups such as the Chinese, Koreans, and Japanese are more visible those of Southeast or South Asia. Even East Asians have significant cultural differences such as languages as well as social, economic, political, and historical differences among the ethnic groups. Similar differences exist among Southeast and South Asians. For many Asians, especially the first generation to live in the U.S. and the foreign-born population, their ethnic identity is more meaningful than their racial or pan-ethnic identity. However, in U.S. schools, where little attention is paid to Asian students' diverse heritage customs and languages, the maintenance of their ethnic identity is often disregarded. One of my Japanese friends who married an American man shared with me a story regarding their son's schooling experience. Given that he is a multiracial U.S. citizen, his experience of becoming conscious of his racial/ethnic identity differs from those of foreign-born Asians. This story may seem to digress from the discussion of the heterogeneous nature of Asians, but I think it demonstrates how hard it is for racial/ethnic minorities to sustain their heritage cultures in U.S. schools. Moreover, since the number of interracial couples is increasing in U.S. society, the experiences of their multiracial children also need to be discussed in terms of educational equity.

My friend's son was a second grader when the incident occurred at his elementary school. One weekend, his mom made *Onigiri*, Japanese rice balls, a popular Japanese traditional rice dish that is enjoyed as a takeout lunch by many Japanese people. She wanted her son to become familiar with Japanese customs even though he had grown up in the U.S. He greatly enjoyed eating the rice dish. Since he liked *Onigiri*, she decided to make more for his school lunch the following Monday. On that Monday evening, she opened his lunch box and found that the *Onigiri* was still in the box. She asked her son why he did not finish eating his lunch. He told her that at the school cafeteria, as he started eating his rice balls, some of his peers began to make fun of his *Onigiri*. Following the onset of the mockery, he stopped eating the Japanese traditional dish and put it back in his lunch box. He told his mother, "I don't want *Onigiri*. I want a peanut butter and jelly sandwich for my lunch."

There are several ways to analyze this incident. Some may think that his peers' reactions to the *Onigiri* are normal and teaching about Japanese food is not a teacher's responsibility. But as a result of the incident, my friend's son learned that eating the traditional Japanese rice dish is not an acceptable cultural practice at his school. This bitter cultural lesson taught him that he needs to bring a "standard" school lunch as his peers do, in order to fit in. I believe that the majority of racial/ethnic minorities regularly experience such hidden cultural lessons in schools. One of my biggest concerns regarding the incident is that there appears to be no curriculum to help children understand racial/ethnic and cultural diversity in U.S. society. It is important to re-examine the current school curriculum and incorporate to help students become accepting of social identities different from their own, such as race/ethnicity, gender, class, religion, and sexual orientation. Moreover, teachers should be role models for students. You, as a teacher, are a very influential figure for students, and what you say, think, and believe can have an impact on how your students see diversity in our society. It is very important that you become aware of diversity in U.S. society and that you understand and are tolerant of our diverse social identities. Your understanding can guide racial/ethnic minorities such as Asian students to build their self-esteem and to be proud of their heritage.

There is significant diversity among Asian students other than their countries of origin, including age at the time of arrival in the U.S., generation, purpose of coming to the U.S. (voluntary or involuntary), parents' educational attainment prior to their arrival, and parents' socioeconomic status. The 2007 American Community Survey shows that out of approximately 13.2 million Asian people, 8.9 million are foreign born (U.S. Census Bureau, 2008). Given that the Asian population increased following the 1965 immigration act, it is not surprising that many Asians are foreign born. However, in addition to 4.3 million U.S.-born Asians, about 5 million people out of the entire foreign-born Asian population hold U.S. citizenship (U.S. Census Bureau, 2008). That is to say, about two-thirds of the total Asian populace in the U.S. holds U.S. citizenship, whether by birth or by naturalization.

The relationship between U.S. citizenship and Asians brings to my mind the conversations I had with one of my Southeast Asian students to whom I taught the Japanese language at a university in the U.S. One day, after class, she asked me what I study. I told her that I am doing research on Asian immigrant youths' educational experiences since their voices are often overlooked in U.S. society. She seemed to find my research very interesting and started sharing with me the struggles she went through as an Asian student in her high school. I asked her if she was an immigrant. She said "No." Then, I asked her if she was born in the U.S. She said, "Yes, I was born in the U.S., but I am not an American. I am an Asian who happens to have U.S. citizenship. That's how I see myself." I was well aware of the "perpetual foreigner" status of Asians in the U.S. In U.S. society, in spite of the growth of the Asian population, "Asianness" is still strongly associated with "foreignness" due to the small population, physical traits, cultural differences, geographical remoteness, political and historical background, and English-speaking status, among other things (Harvard Law Review Association, 1993; Jo, 2004; Ng et al., 2007). Thus, a question like, "where are you from?" is frequently asked of Asian individuals, often just because they look "different." Even though I know many Asians struggle with discovering who they are due to the perpetual foreigner image entrenched in U.S. society, the impact of directly hearing my student's perceptions regarding her national identity was profound.

Experiences such as this measure the present U.S. educational system's White, ethnocentric curriculum. The result is an image of national identity that is strongly tied to White ethnocentrism embedded in U.S. society. For culturally marginalized but racially inassimilable Asian Americans, constructing and maintaining national identity and becoming an "American" are complicated practices. In order for you, a teacher, to help Asians construct, through their school experiences, identities of which they can be proud, it is important that you become aware of the diversity among Asians and understand the struggles they face as a group of culturally marginalized people. You must challenge the ethnocentrism existing in U.S. schools.

I would now like to talk to you about the diversity of Asians in the U.S. in terms of why they immigrated and their socioeconomic status. Many Southeast Asians immigrated to the U.S. as war refugees or for political asylum after 1975, at the end of the Vietnam War. The circumstances of those who migrated as war refugees or those seeking political asylum (involuntary immigrants), and Asian immigrants who voluntarily come to the U.S. as professionals, differ in many respects. Involuntary immigrants, as well as their children, are usually not prepared to begin new lives in the U.S., and they often carry very heavy social and cultural burdens such as language barriers. What is more, involuntary Asian immigrants generally bear a serious socioeconomic burden, unlike those who already have jobs and a place to start their new lives prior to their arrival. Involuntary immigrants usually start new lives with no money, no home, very limited (if any) English language ability, and/or job skills. Lower socioeconomic status (Anyon, 1981) as well as limited social, cultural, political and linguistic knowledge (Cummins, 2001) impinge on the academic achievement of immigrants' children. The 2007 American Community Survey indicates that approximately 27% of the Vietnamese, 34 % of the Laotian, 38% of the Cambodian, and 39% of the Hmong people who are 25 years and older in the U.S. do not hold a high school diploma, compared to 15.8 % for the total U.S. population (U.S. Census Bureau, 2008). The average percentage of the three East Asian groups, Chinese, Korean, and Japanese, who hold high school diplomas is 11.2% (U.S. Census Bureau, 2008). The academic struggles that many Southeast Asians face are often overlooked due to the positive racial stereotypes of Asians. Furthermore, they have a hard time articulating their academic and psychological problems because of the stereotype of Asian students as smart and self-determining. Teachers must understand this and take on the responsibility of determining the needs of each of their students, including their Asian students.

I thank you for taking time to read this letter. I hope it has helped you to understand the presence of diversity in all Asian peoples in the U.S. and the damaging nature of the current positive racial stereotypes of Asians. I hope it helps you to polish your multicultural lenses to enable you to see the differences among Asian students more clearly than before. You probably are a caring, responsible, talented, and well-motivated individual; otherwise you wouldn't have chosen teaching as a career. Please keep extending your knowledge regarding who Asian students are and the educational issues they face so you can listen to the silenced voices of Asian students. Please keep developing your awareness of the diversity in your classroom and become accepting of these differences by examining the ethnocentrism entrenched in U.S. classrooms. Your awareness and tolerance of this diversity is a key to helping Asian students have better school experiences. Again, thank you and have a wonderful, never-ending journey to becoming a better teacher.

Best wishes,

References

Anyon, J. (1981). Social class and school knowledge. *Curriculum Inquiry, 11*, 3–41.

Bhatacharyya, S. (2001) From 'yellow peril' to 'model minority': The transition of Asian Americans. Paper presented at the Annual Meeting of the Mid-South Educational Research Association. (ERIC Document Reproduction Services No. ED 462462).

Cummins, J. (2001). Empowering minority students: A framework for instruction. *Harvard Educational Review, 71*(4), 649–655.

Harvard Law Review Association (1993). Racial violence against Asian Americans. *Harvard Law Review, 106*(8), 1926–1943.

Ichioka, Y. (1990). *The Issei: The world of the first generation Japanese immigrants, 1885–1924.* New York: First Free Press.

Jo, J-Y. O. (2004). Neglected voices in the multicultural America: Asian American racial politics and its implication for multicultural education. *Multicultural Perspectives, 6*(1), 19–25.

Jones, D. (1955). *The portrayal of China and India on the American screen, 1896–1955.* Cambridge, MA: Center for International Studies, MIT.

Kawai, Y. (2005). Stereotyping Asian Americans: The dialectic of the model minority and the yellow peril. *The Howard Journal of Communications, 16,* 109–130.

Kitano, H. H. & Daniels, R. (1995). *Asian Americans: Emerging minorities.* Englewood Cliffs, NJ: Prentice Hall.

Lee, S. J. (1996). *Unraveling the "model minority" stereotype: Listening to Asian American youth.* New York: Teachers College Press.

Morimoto, T. (1997). *Japanese Americans and cultural continuity: Maintaining language and heritage.* New York: Garland Publishing.

Ng, J. C., Lee, S. S., & Pak, Y. K. (2007). Contesting the model minority and perpetual foreigner stereotypes: A critical review of literature on Asian Americans in education. *Review of Research in Education, 31,* 95–130.

Osajima, K. (2000). Asian American as the model minority. In M. Zhou & J. V. Gatewood (Eds.), *Contemporary Asian America: A multidisciplinary reader* (pp. 449–458). New York: New York University Press.

Suzuki, B. H. (1977). Education and the socialization of Asian Americans: A revisionist analysis of the "model minority" thesis. *Amerasia Journal, 4*(2), 23–51.

Takaki, R. (1993). *A different mirror: A history of multicultural America.* Boston: Little Brown.

U.S. Census Bureau (2008). 2007 American community survey 1-year estimate. Retrieved December 31, 2008, from http://factfinder.census.gov/servlet/IPCharIterationServlet?_ts=248875086430.

Wong, F. & Halgin, R. (2006). The "model minority": Bane or blessing for Asian Americans? *Journal of Multicultural Counseling and Development, 34,* 38–49.

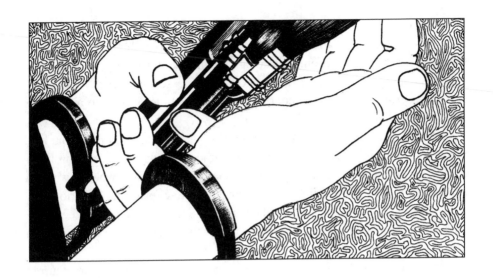

Chapter 18

Loving the Thugs

Dennis Earl Fehr

Dear Fellow Educators,

I would like to share with you a couple of stories from my life that have shaped the unusual way that I prepare people to teach.

As an able-bodied, straight, White male in the U.S., I learned early the commerce of oppression in two ways, both of which seemed within the natural order of things (Fehr, 1993). In the first way, that of the isolated, patriarchal, religious community of my childhood (our neighbors called us "Mechanized Amish" because we used cars and tractors rather than horses), I was born to advantage, such as it was. I did, however, spend my childhood feeling that I was looking at the wide, wicked—and therefore attractive—world through a knothole in religion's fence. At one time the sect's children were made to drop out of school under conditions suggestive of an automobile warranty—on their sixteenth birthdays or when they gave their lives to Christ, whichever came first.

In mainstream culture I observed the advantages that resulted from my maleness, straightness, and Whiteness. My association with a 'weird cult', on the other hand, was a profound disadvantage in that, during my public school years, it taught me the taste of mockery. This lesson, however, would become one of my life's most important—I draw its bitter taste into my mouth when I write, speak, and teach.

The stress of this environment, combined with a dysfunctional home life, manifested itself in school. By seventh grade I had become a 'problem child,' spending much time in detention hall—on the days when I went to school at all. My earliest linguistic contribution to Western civilization was to name my gang of detention hall misfits "The Zoo." By spring the name had made its way into the teacher's lounge, where my teachers teased each other about having Zoo Duty.

In eighth grade I was expelled from school due to an event that occurred in science class. That day, as circumstances would have it, I happened to be holding a loaded squirt gun under my desk, which was pushed against the front wall, separated from the class. This location assured me the attention of my classmates, and I wished to reward them. Each time our teacher shuffled past my seat, I jetted a stream of water at his fly. His baggy pants made him oblivious to the expanding blotch, so I tallied several handsome shots before he noticed.

I might have been suspended rather than expelled had I not earlier that day thought it was a good idea to toss a lit firecracker in the boy's locker room at a classmate's bare feet with the command, "Dance, Tom!" Some days are just better than others. Tom danced splendidly, and I was expelled.

The point of this frank account of my wayward youth is to illustrate that I do not belong to the demographic that typically enters the teaching profession: The well behaved and academically successful. I was a thug. This has enabled me to form a view of teacher preparation that differs from the norm. I should add that my mother (who rarely angers but when she does is a force of nature) "requested" that the principal readmit me, and as my sixteenth birthday approached I decided to finish high school.

In twelfth grade I took my first art class, which confirmed an ability I had suspected was inside me. I decided to go to college. The elder of the congregation had said nothing when I decided to finish high school, but at this point he admonished me about the dangers of being educated. I ignored him and applied to the University of Illinois (I was sequestered enough to know of only two universities in Illinois). I majored in accounting for two…well, minutes, and then transferred to art.

My brief but terrifying brush with accounting resulted from widespread disagreement within the church about my decision to become an artist. I would be looking at naked women in life drawing class (a prospect that this 17-year-old freshman did not find troublesome). Furthermore, my maternal grandparents' attitude toward art was clear: art objects were graven images, idolatrous and vain. This extended to family photographs. My parents did, however, display some art. In fact, my parents are self-taught artists. My father's magical transformations of blank paper into likenesses of Beetle Bailey and Dagwood formed my introduction to drawing. My mother's crocheted clothes hangers, potholders, and Christmas ornaments taught me of our human need to make the world more beautiful.

At the university I became a member of that minority in the U.S. who grasp the power of imagery. I didn't know it then, but my career path was set. Meanwhile I experimented in ways that, again, separated me from the teacher demographic. I became a biker and a percussionist for local bands, enthusiastically embracing the party lifestyle. I lived in a house trailer with my motorcycles parked out front. But art had become my guiding star, and it led me to what I do today: Prepare people to teach art.

To this day most of our teachers regardless of discipline are White, middle- or working-class females. Most had successful academic and behavioral experiences school. Few hung out with the thugs. I remember the crowd in my high school who would have been likely to become teachers; they disliked, looked down on, and even feared us. It's no wonder that students such as I frustrated teachers then and frustrate them now.

Why do our teacher education programs fail to prepare our teachers for these students? Why are so many of our diversity courses so inadequate? Because university education faculty often come from the same demographic pool as our teachers: well-behaved, middle-class, White people.

So what can we do about this? One successful strategy I devised is to create semester-long field experiences for my advanced undergraduates at our county's juvenile justice center, where incarcerated youth are taught, and at Project Intercept, the alternative school for youth who have been removed from their schools for disciplinary reasons.

These two sites are invisible to the community. Both facilities are in remote parts of the county, which is symbolically fitting, because the children inside them are beyond the purview not only of the education field, but of nearly every sector of society except the police. Even their families are often "out of sight."

Educators resist becoming involved with incarcerated populations. "Why," many teachers and teacher educators ask, "should we expose ourselves to thugs? They're where they are because they're dangerous lawbreakers!"

Here is why: That attitude is an example of how a stereotype can 1) hinder a teacher's professional development, 2) inhibit the noble goal of educating of all of our children, and 3) increase prejudice against a group that is already viewed with disfavor (see McDonald, 2005, for a description of the need to integrate social justice into teacher education programs).

I remember the conversation on day one of the first semester I offered this course. It went something like this, as described in an earlier article I wrote on this subject (Fehr, 2006).

Conversation One

"Hello, everyone, and welcome to ART 4362. Let's start with a question that's none of anyone's business: How many of you have served time for breaking the law? Raise your hands. Listen to that laughter. No hands. Okay, then raise your hand if you ever were expelled from school. No hands. How about suspended for a couple days? No hands. This is getting so boring. Ever get a detention? Three hands out of 15. Anybody ever been inside a jail? Even if just to visit? No one.

"What if I told you that in this course you are going to develop social theory-based art curricula for middle- and high-school students who are incarcerated? And that you will divide into pairs and go out to the County Juvenile Justice Center each Monday to teach actual inmates who are locked up for everything from marijuana possession to armed robbery?"

Uncomfortable silence. Then, "I would not like that at all."

"Why?"

"Because obviously those kids are dangerous."

"Are they different from the kids you would teach in an ordinary middle or high school?"

"Some public school kids are as dangerous but some are not. In the Justice Center they all are."

"Let me write that on the board. 'All the kids in the JJC are dangerous.'

A few days ago I met with the director. He told me that most of his inmates are in there for drug possession. You don't have to answer this out loud, but have you ever been in a situation where you could have been busted for pot? I suspect that some of you have. Maybe last weekend. Are you dangerous?"

"I see your point, but what about the ones who are in for armed robbery?"

"Good question. If you end up teaching middle or high school, is it possible that you will teach some students who have committed armed robbery?"

"Possibly."

"But there would be two differences: One, you wouldn't know they did it. Two, you would be the only adult in the classroom. At the JJC you will be with your teaching partner and the classroom teacher, and several trustees will be walking the halls."

"*Will* be? This is a done deal? We have no voice in this?"

"Excellent point. No, you don't, and I'll tell you why. If I offered this as a choice, let's say with the alternative of teaching in an ordinary high school, raise your hand if you would pick the JJC. See, one out of 15. So 14 would not have this experience. Yet, as you pointed out, you might end up in public schools teaching kids like these who just didn't get caught. Have you ever felt nervous about managing a classroom by yourself? I'm pretty sure that no course you ever take will give you more confidence than this one. So I, with my years of experience, am imposing this challenge on you. I predict that you will look back with gratitude on your time spent at the JJC."

"You're right about one thing. Some of us don't believe you."

With that auspicious start, we were off. After each teaching session to "JJ" or "PI" we meet to reflect on how things went. Many conversations stay in my mind. Two of them went something like this:

Conversation Two

"Okay, your first teaching experience is over. How did it go for you? Who will start?"

"I will. I did a drawing lesson. It was better than I thought it would be."

"You had a room full of boys." (The sexes are segregated at both facilities.)

"Right. The first request was a Harley-Davidson eagle. As you might have noticed from how I dress when I'm not at the JJC, my husband and I are bikers. Teaching him the eagle was a piece of cake. I had to do it one line at a time but it wasn't a problem because all of them gathered in a circle and watched the whole thing. That kid will love me forever. The next one wanted to know how to draw a champagne glass with bubbles coming out, so we did that. By then they were grabbing paper and pencils and following along on their own. Next I got asked how to make curling ribbons. So we made swooping horizontal *S*-lines with short verticals on the outside ends of the curves and then parallel *S*-lines underneath, you know how that goes. Some-one else—this 11-year-old who's in because he stuck up the ice cream man with a loaded pistol—wanted the Superman symbol. Then it was cartoon characters. One of them wanted to draw hearts in the margins of his letters to his girlfriend, but he could never get the second half of the heart to match the first half. So I taught him how to make the two sides match. They loved that. They're all going to write letters covered with hearts to their girlfriends. En-velope and all. We never ran out of ideas and the 90 minutes flew by. I can't wait to go back."

The class bursts into applause.

Conversation Three

"How did your lesson on families go?"

"Not so well. I did my lesson specifically on rethinking the ideal family. A lot of these girls don't have their biological mom and dad and 2.4 siblings waiting for them at home—not that we necessarily do either, but anyway, my goal was for them to realize that an ideal family is one that is very loving regardless of its make-up. So I started by asking them what makes an ideal family. They basically gave me the Mom/Dad/Sissy/Bubba/Fido/picket-fence model. Not a word about love being part of the ideal family. And I'll bet that some of these young women are mothers who miss their babies. So we talked about how giving and receiving love whenever we can is the important thing, not technical family-member titles. I thought the discussion was going well the whole time. Next we looked at art that combines realism and abstrac-tion—specifically Jaune Quick-to-see Smith, Larry Rivers, and Australian Aboriginals—to provide avenues for both the skilled and the unskilled draw-ers, and then proceeded to make multimedia images of our versions of the ideal family. I was hoping for interesting blends of realism and abstraction that reflected their home situations, but I didn't get them. First, they were so timid that they avoided abstraction altogether (one said the abstract art we looked at was ugly). But when they tried for realism, their rendering skills were so weak that the parts they intended to be realistic were abstract in an unintentionally cubistic way. I thought those drawings were interesting, but they happened by accident. Some teacher I felt like. But the worst part was that none drew her actual family. They reverted right back to the picket-fence model. I was disappointed. In fact I literally have lost sleep over it."

"Hm. I'm not sure it was such a bad lesson. How many minutes did you teach?"

"The full 90 we were scheduled for."

"How old were they, on average?"

"I'd say 14, 15."

"So they had 15 years to learn the picket-fence stereotype. It sounds like you did a superb job, but one brilliant 90-minute lesson is not likely to dislodge an idea with roots 15-years deep. That raises an important point: We need to repeat and repeat the same themes, each time in a way that keeps students' attention, in order to dislodge unhelpful attitudes. I'm pleased with the job you did—you taught a lesson built on great social theory, and it involved important discussion, well-chosen art viewing, and an appropriate studio project. You embodied my approach to art ed."

Additional Successes

My talented students have produced other great lessons. One had her group of girls transform a standard bicycle into a customized low-rider bike. They had to choose as a group how to customize it and learn how to order the parts online. They saw that this primarily Hispanic art form deserves study in a school art class, and they learned that girls can use tools.

One student had her students put on blindfolds and sculpt clay animals using only touch. They experienced an hour of visual impairment, and they also learned that art is accessible to the blind.

My students have taught boys to knit, quilt, and make rugs. After the predictable resistance to these challenges to their rigid gender definitions, all three processes become popular. On another occasion, following a lesson on money management, the students made wallets from brightly colored duct tape. Many lessons involve mixed media to illustrate that different kinds of materials, like different kinds of people, can combine to yield superior results.

Over the course of the semester, my students learn to differentiate between *misbehavior* and *unfamiliar cultural norms*. One day at Project Intercept, which permits students to leave at the end of the school day, a student fell asleep at his desk. During our reflection time my student mentioned that she felt disrespected. I pointed out that some of these young people do not always know where they will be spending the night.

At other times my students have pointed out how frequently the young people's art contains tributes to friends and family members who are in prison or have been killed. Such awarenesses shock my students.

They also learn about art as well as teach it. They might teach linear perspective drawing and in turn be taught by the inmates how to write their names in graffiti styles.

At the end of each semester my ART 4362 students speak glowingly about their Project Intercept experiences. The following comments, transcribed from five years of anonymous course evaluations, are representative:

- "This course was particularly helpful in teaching us how to blend art with a social issue. Teaching at the JJC was an experience I will never forget!"
- "My teaching at the JJC was the best experience I've had at Tech."
- "Teaching at the JJC was my favorite experience so far. I hope there's an opening when I graduate."
- "The class is very beneficial to our major. It gave us the opportunity to teach students otherwise forgotten by the school system. It helped us grow as future educators and role models."
- "I loved the JJC. Great class! It helped my understanding of social theory enormously. We learned a new way of teaching art in public schools. Lots of enthusiasm in the class."
- "Project Intercept was awesome. Thanx!"
- "This course was extremely important. I loved teaching at Project Intercept. I think it was the most useful experience of all our courses. I learned so much more from the students than I taught them."

Negative comments have been few, and they tend to address my lack of organization (a problem that will never be fixed). In fact, the experience itself has yet to receive a negative comment. (Fehr, 2006, pp. 258–281)

Observations

I too have learned important things from this course: (1) my students' confidence as classroom managers skyrockets; (2) the Otherness with which they regarded incarcerated people disappears; (3) they become skilled at blending social theory with art; (4) their students are impressed by the fact that someone cares enough about them to teach them interesting things; and (5) on a practical note, telling prospective employers about this experience has brought some of my students immediate job offers. This last point illustrates the need in our profession for such expertise.

The world is hungry for peace. Audiences around the world have asked me to show them how to embrace our invisible students. If you already are a practicing teacher, may this letter motivate you to review your attitude toward your 'problem' students. If you are university education faculty—of any school discipline—may it inspire ideas for developing or modifying courses. And finally, if you are an education major, may you rethink your preconceptions. Teach boldly. Such shifts of vision can help us understand a group that misbehaves in part because it is out of sight.

Warm regards,

References

Eisner, E. (1981). On the differences between scientific and artistic approaches to qualitative research. Educational Researcher, *10*(4), 9.

Fehr, D. E. (2006). How to draw a heart: Teaching art to incarcerated youth. *The Journal of Social theory in Art Education, 26,* 258–281.

Fehr, D. E. (1993). *Dogs playing cards: Powerbrokers of prejudice in education, art and culture.* New York: Peter Lang.

Glesne, C. (1999). *Becoming qualitative researchers* (2nd Ed.) New York: Longman.

McDonald, M. (2005). The integration of social justice in teacher education: Dimensions of prospective teachers' opportunities to learn. *Journal of Teacher Education, 56*(5), 418–435.

Chapter 19

Contextualizing Teaching and Learning

Etta R. Hollins

Dear Teacher,

I am writing this letter to you because you have chosen the most important and influential career in our society. Teachers influence the future of our nation and the quality of life of every citizen. This is true because teachers enable individuals to think critically, develop problem solving skills, develop creativity, care about and respect themselves and others, be active and contributing members of our society, and value democracy, freedom, and social justice for all members of our society. The young people you teach will find their place in occupations and professions that serve the society; they will construct new knowledge that will solve social and political problems in the future; and they will provide for the needs of their own families. In order to do your best as a teacher you must strive to think deeply and to learn all you can about your subject matter, pedagogy, and about the students you will teach each year of your career.

I would like to share things that I have learned over the course of a very long career as a teacher and teacher educator that might be helpful to you on your journey. What I have learned that informs my teaching comes from many sources including my students, dialogue with colleagues, my own preparation as a teacher, reflecting on my own classroom practice, from scholarly literature, and from my own research and scholarship. Each of these sources has deepened knowledge of myself, my students, and my practice as a teacher.

Perhaps, among the most important things I have learned in my career is how to learn from and about my students—how to learn what they know and how they know it, what they value and why, what interests and what concerns them, what they find easy and what is difficult and why, what they share among friends that makes their relationships last, and what makes them comfortable and uncomfortable. This is a process that begins when I meet a student, continues until the student moves on to whatever comes next in his or her educational journey, and begins anew with each new student or new group of students. This ongoing learning from and about my students has enabled me to continuously improve my practice through seeing common themes and patterns in my students' learning, social relationships, values, and perceptions. This knowledge has been helpful to me in providing meaningful learning experiences for my students and creating a supportive social context for learning.

Another important thing I learned as a teacher is how to learn with my students—how to be an active participant in the learning process while teaching. Whether I am teaching new subject matter for the first time or have taught the content multiple times, my students bring new experiences and new perspectives that help to deepen my understanding of the subject matter as we examine ideas together. This is true regardless of the level of complexity of the subject matter or skill or the age or educational level of my students. One very good example comes to mind. Once when I was teaching a junior high school history course there was a student who sat in the back of the room reading a romance novel. Rather than scolding her for not attending to the topic under discussion, I decided to have the librarian locate historically based romance novels for this student to read. The student was excited about this opportunity to participate in the class discussions without giving up her favorite leisure time activity. In discussions with this student I acquired a deeper understanding of the powerful influence of romance and other social relationships on the course of history. I learned a great deal about the convergence and divergence of fact and fiction in this literary genre. This student learned a great deal about historical inquiry as she used different texts to differentiate fact from fiction. It was this process of learning with my students that has deepened my understanding of the meaning of the social dimension of learning and of knowledge as distributed across members of a group. In many ways this student knew and was learning much about history that other members of the class could benefit from knowing— she brought to our discussions a new and interesting perspective on how to make sense of the past.

There are things that we know intuitively about teaching and things we learn from a variety of sources; however, the way we make sense of and apply what we know in a coherent way is framed by theory and ideology. In the process of learning about, from, and with my students I came to better understand the meaning and value of learning theory. Observing the patterns in my students' approaches to problem solving, social interaction, ways of making sense of subject matter, and ways of acquiring skills led me to draw conclusions about teaching and learning, to question the conclusions I had drawn, and to explore the scholarly literature on various learning theories— to go beyond the survey course from my teacher preparation program and to dig deep into these theories. In this process I came to understand that learning theory is a powerful guide for planning instruction and interpreting students' responses. It provided a way of going deep into my own teaching practice to develop the coherence, continuity, and consistency that fueled my continuous development as a teacher and that enable me to better facilitate learning for my students.

Over time, I have become increasingly aware of the need for a deep understanding of what it means to *construct and reconstruct knowledge in practice*. This means that initial plans for teaching in a new context are always tentative. New knowledge about the learners and the context will fuel *reconstructing knowledge in practice/* during practice that better facilitates learning. This process involves interpreting and reinterpreting learners' responses to particular experiences, the ways in which learners' constructed meaning in the context of the learning experiences provided, areas in which learners experienced difficulties, and the extent to which the desired learning outcomes were achieved. This interpretation and reinterpretation sometimes evokes immediate changes while engaged in facilitating a learning experience; other times it means rethinking and redesigning learning experiences for the future. This process of constructing and reconstructing *knowledge in practice* by interpreting and reinterpreting learners' responses, and rethinking and redesigning learning experiences increases the likelihood that each new encounter with the same learners will elevate the quality of the learning experiences.

In your teaching you will make decisions about how to frame and present specific subject matter and skills, as well as the pedagogical approach that will best facilitate learning for particular learners. In making decisions about subject matter and skills you need to keep in your mind the big picture of what students need to know and be able to do with the knowledge they construct. For example, after a social studies unit, will the students have greater insights into social and political issues of the past and how they were solved as a way to interpret and solve social problems today? Will students be able to apply mathematics concepts in designing a building, or interpreting city building codes, or reading utility meters? Will students be able to use knowledge of science to determine the composition and level of risk in everyday household cleaning products? My point here is that students need to learn subject matter and skills at a level of understanding that enables application in new and novel situations.

Additionally, subject matter and skills need to be contextualized in the situations where they are regularly used. For example, in facilitating learning to interpret and generate scholarly text for a group of doctoral-level students, I begin the process by analyzing the structure of examples of the types of writing they are to produce. We begin by carefully examining a research report, giving particular attention to the abstract, noting how the big idea is communicated and how the statement of the problem is presented. This is not done as a lecture, but rather as a discussion where students work in small groups with their peers to identify the distinguishing features of specific parts of the particular research report. Initially, we look carefully at word usage and sentence structure. This encourages students to develop a rubric for judging their own scholarly writing. This makes an immediate difference in the writing of many of my students especially those who have been practitioners for a while and have not engaged in academic writing. This approach to contextualizing subject matter and skills works for elementary and secondary students as well.

Of course, there are other dimensions of contextualizing subject matter including making connections with what learners already know and have experienced, and making connections with their social identity and cultural heritage. Making connections between the familiar and the unfamiliar, and what is valued by the learner facilitates the learning process.

The way we frame subject matter, the learning experiences we provide, and the personal messages we convey to our students are grounded in our vision of how they will participate in the larger society. In teaching students at an urban junior high school I envisioned that some might choose to become professional historians; thus, I was careful in teaching skills of historical inquiry, using original sources to verify historical accounts of events and situations, visiting museums to view historical artifacts, and introducing the students to people in this profession. I envisioned that others of my students would be attracted to policy making at various levels of government; thus, I gave particular attention to how policies were developed and implemented and to the impact on different groups in the society. My students talked with policy makers and visited the courts and the legislature. This way of framing subject matter and learning experiences is grounded in a sociocultural perspective on learning and an ideology of democracy and social justice in a society where diversity is valued and where there is fair and equitable treatment of all citizens.

However, in my research on low-performing urban schools I learned the impact of an ideology grounded in deficit thinking and teaching in the absence of a sound theoretical perspective. In these schools, many teachers believed that the best of instructional practices would make little difference in their students' academic progress because they lacked appropriate skills and experiences and their parents did not provide adequate guidance and supervision. The vision these teachers held for their students included dropping out of high school, minimum wage jobs, low-income housing, and the inability to actively contribute to the society or to provide for their own families. These teachers had not taken the time to get to know their students, to learn with their students, or to think deeply about their own classroom practices. When these teachers engaged in dialogue with their colleagues, discussing the approaches that worked in their classrooms and challenges they had yet to resolve, they began to see the relationship between instructional practices, students' characteristics, and learning outcomes. Over time, these teachers were better able to facilitate learning for their students and were pleased with their students' performance. They came to better understand their students, and they began to craft a theory of learning that explained their instruction and their students' responses to it. Their vision for their students' future became more positive—they embraced a new ideology framed by hope and prosperity for their students and grounded in democracy and social justice.

Through observation and interaction with my students I have come to realize how much teachers influence the development, even transformation, of their students as persons. Many of my students have been influenced through our interaction to take on my profession both as a classroom teacher and as a university professor—they have been influenced by my beliefs and practices. Many have felt supported and validated. Others have felt challenged, and a few graduate students have even felt disturbed by my strong advocacy for social justice. The curriculum, pedagogy, and the social context in classrooms are powerful forces in identity formation, in influencing students' personal and social development, and in determining the place each finds for himself or herself in the society. When a teacher is able to create a social context in the classroom in which each student feels accepted, appreciated and valued, students develop self-confidence and a sense of belonging as a member of the group. This encourages students to take risks that enable them to grow academically and intellectually and to develop the social networks that support finding a place for themselves in the larger society. However, it is important to remember that where students are allowed to fall behind their peers academically or where they have peculiarities that the teacher allows to engender rejection and ridicule from peers, self-protection strategies may develop that can lead to school resistance and participation in a school counter-culture such as gangs.

So, what does it mean to think deeply about classroom practice? It means, for example, seeking an increasingly complex understanding of the procedure for a particular instructional approach, questioning and understanding when a particular approach is appropriate, and being able to articulate a theoretical explanation for why the particular approach is appropriate in a given situation based on a deep knowledge of the subject matter, learning process, and of specific learners. This requires knowledge of a wide range of instructional approaches and strategies from which to choose, how these approaches and strategies are related to teaching particular subject matter and skills, and knowledge of the learners' experiences, preferences, and skills. The integration and application of this knowledge is at the heart of productive teaching, meaningful learning, and achieving the expected learning outcomes for students whatever their background experiences or life conditions.

In sum, teaching is a wonderful opportunity to contribute to the growth and development of whole persons and groups. It is a way to make a very important contribution to the well-being of all people in our society and to enhance the quality of life on the planet. Teaching has been a wonderful journey for me. It has kept me energized, continuously learning, and feeling a sense of responsibility and commitment to academic excellence. I feel proud to have served my students and my professional community to the very best of my ability. I wish you all the best on your journey as a teacher—stay focused and keep the faith.

Sincerely,

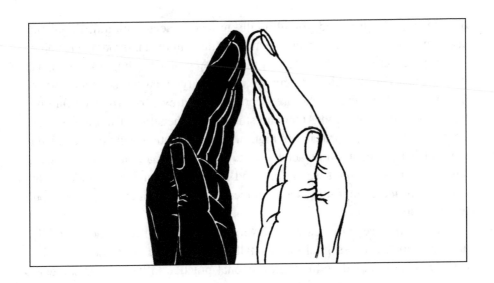

Chapter 20

Dispositions for Good Teaching

Gary Howard

Dear Teacher Colleagues,

Thank you for the work you do in service to our children and for the sake of our shared future. Our vocation is perhaps the most important work there is and among the most difficult. I am particularly grateful for your commitment to serve the diverse cultures, identities, and needs of our nation's children and youth. It is important that we bring the best of ourselves to this work, and to that end I am sharing here what I feel are the core dispositions for good teaching in our pluralistic world.

The focus of my work over the past 30 years has been to struggle with two overarching and related questions. First, what qualities should adults in our classrooms embody to be worthy of teaching our diverse students? And second, how do we best prepare ourselves and our colleagues for this work? In this letter I reflect on the first of these questions[1] from the viewpoint that any discussion of "teacher dispositions" is best engaged from the perspective of students. Children and young adults reflect a racial, cultural, linguistic, economic, religious, and sexual spectrum. Adults in the classroom determine, in large measure, both the tone and the outcome of schooling. On one hand we have teachers working effectively in diversity-enhanced schools, and on the other we have those who are unprepared and even destructive. One urban, low-income, African-American student who benefited from the former, upon receiving an award at her high school graduation, acknowledged the work of her principal and teachers by saying, "You made us think we were smarter than we thought we were." And a Jamaican immigrant student who suffered from the latter said in a town meeting that I facilitated, "Some of our teachers steal our hope."

Between these extremes lies a diverse range of teacher attitudes, beliefs, and behaviors. It is essential that we talk about who we are as educators because our personhood and our professional practice influence our students' experiences. In diverse educational settings, the question for us professionals is one of cultural competence: "Can I teach my students in an authentic, effective way?" From my observations across the country, I have identified four dispositions that characterize good teachers in pluralistic schools.

A Disposition for Difference

I often tell a story about a White male teacher in an urban high school who said to me after one of my speeches, "I have no Black students." I was curious how that could be true since over half the students in his school were Black.

When I inquired about this, he said, "I don't see race, so all my kids are the same to me."

I replied, "You may not want to acknowledge the reality of race in your classroom, but I can guarantee you that all of your Black students know you're White." I then shared my belief that race does not have to get in the way of our teaching, but when it is denied, it probably is in the way.

Since ninety percent of our nation's teachers are White, achieving greater equity and excellence in public education is in large part a process of transforming the beliefs and behaviors of White educators. The three stages of White Identity Orientation that I have identified in my writing (Howard, 2006) provide one conceptual framework for discussing teacher dispositions. Whites in the *Fundamentalist* stage, like the teacher mentioned above, are predisposed to avoid, deny, or rationalize racial differences, thus distancing themselves from any need for self-examination regarding the meaning or impact of their own racial being. Whites in the *Integrationist* orientation are more open. They acknowledge that differences are real and even worthy of celebration, but often tend to approach their teaching from a missionary mentality of "serving the less fortunate." Like their Fundamentalist colleagues, they resist any serious interrogation of privilege, power, or their own potential complicity in the dynamics underlying racial inequities in school outcomes. Whites in the *Transformationist* stage, on the other hand, bring difference into their lives because this engagement challenges them to grow personally and professionally. They are sophisticated in their analysis of racism and vigorous in their efforts to undo the legacy of White privilege. At the same time, they are not apologetic about their Whiteness and can engage with students of color in authentic ways.

The point is that our dispositions toward difference make a difference to our students. It is not *whether* I am White, but rather my *disposition toward* race and Whiteness that matters. For example, Transformationist White teachers in the many schools I have observed issue fewer discipline referrals to students of color, not because they are afraid to discipline (that is an Integrationist behavior), but because they have the capacity and skills to prevent most cross-race confrontations. And this is not just an issue for White educators. Similar dynamics are at play with, for example, a religiously conservative, Black, heterosexual male teacher in his interactions with gay and lesbian White students. Or with a middle-class Latina teacher in her work with a wealthy, Muslim, immigrant, male student. Culturally competent teachers who can negotiate across these multiple dimensions of difference are simply better educators.

A Disposition for Dialogue

Dialogue is where differences become meaningful. Through dialogue we discover how we are similar or different from others and how to build bridges of understanding. Over many years of conducting professional development workshops, I have found that the thing teachers most often mention as the highlight of these experiences is "the opportunity for open and honest conversation with my colleagues."

Teacher-to-teacher dialogue is the essence of professional learning and a key component of school improvement. Professional dialogue is powerful because it provides a reality check across our different perspectives. Such exchange opens the possibility of growth. Unfortunately, I encounter too many educators who are predisposed *not* to engage in reflective conversation. For example, as I was inviting the faculty in a large urban high school to begin a dialogue on differences, a White male math teacher proudly announced, "I have good relationships with all of my students, and so I have no more need for personal transformation." Many of his colleagues were aghast at this comment, especially given the existence of a huge gap in math achievement for students of color in their school. Lacking a disposition for personal growth, this teacher was a detriment to his students' success and a hindrance to his faculty's school improvement efforts.

Teacher-to-student dialogue is equally important. In a dialogic process of teaching, with its flow of conversation between teachers and students, everyone has an opportunity to learn, including the teacher. Visiting recently in a high school special education classroom populated by "behaviorally disturbed" Black and Hispanic male students and one White male teacher, I was able to observe the power of authentic dialogue. As part of his unit on the Constitution, the teacher was discussing the intricacies of *habeas corpus*, a topic of interest to the students, given their familiarity with the juvenile justice system. At one point the teacher made an inaccurate statement about the interpretation of a legal procedure, and one of the Hispanic students turned away from the computer on which he had been searching for a used car (I had been wondering if the teacher was going to confront him about this) and interrupted the teacher: "Excuse me, sir, but that's not how it works in our state." He then explained the correct legalities. Rather than becoming defensive or chastising the student for apparently not paying attention earlier, the teacher merely remarked, "Thank you for that. You're exactly right; my mistake."

This exchange illustrates several elements of good teaching, but I was particularly impressed by the power of the teacher's humility, honesty, and professionalism in engaging only those elements of student behavior that continued the dialogue, rather than extinguishing it. The classroom was infused with a palpable sense of respect for the students' knowledge and for their lived experiences. Working with students for whom schools were not safe or successful places, this teacher navigated across differences so that everyone, the teacher included, could find safe harbor.

This disposition for meaningful dialogue has implications not only for our classrooms, but also for our world. I was inspired recently to learn about a group of former Israeli and Palestinian fighters who have come together under the banner of "Combatants for Peace" (www.combatantsforpeace.org). The members of this group have committed acts of violence in the names of their conflicting truths, in some cases even having injured or killed members of each other's families. In what must be painful conversations, they confess their actions to one another and reinforce their common commitment to give up their ways of hatred and violence. Having met initially in secret, they have now publicly declared that dialogue rather than death is the only way to peace.

In another example of dialogue across differences, a Jewish rabbi, a Christian minister, and a Muslim imam, all U. S. citizens from the Seattle area, have been meeting since 9/11 for "vigorous discussions," and have traveled together to the Middle East in search of healing responses there as well as at home. Says Jamal Rahman, the Muslim member of this delegation, "Interfaith [dialogue] is not about conversion, it's about completion. I'm becoming a more complete Muslim, a more complete human being" (van Gelder, 2007, p. 13).

This human capacity to converse rather than wage war is a skill we want our children to acquire and that we teachers must embody. The disposition for dialogue is a feature of what it means to be educated. Imagine how our post-9/11 world would be different today if those in power in our country had acquired this capacity from their teachers.

A Disposition for Disillusionment

Authentic dialogue across differences is powerful because it allows us to see beyond the barriers of our own culturally conditioned realities. Whatever mind-spaces we may have been socialized into, as teachers we are called to transcend our particular truths and come to a place of greater breadth. We do this because our work requires it. As teachers we must be flexible, genuine, and effective with students, demonstrating empathy and respect for their many realities. We want to share our worlds with them too, but first we must respectfully enter theirs and insure that our world is one in which they feel welcomed.

In 1862, a time of violent collision in our nation, Abraham Lincoln said in an address to Congress, "We must disenthrall ourselves" because "the dogmas of the quiet past are inadequate to the stormy present." With these words Lincoln called himself and other leaders to a reckoning with their own illusions, challenging his fellow citizens to break through old hostilities to claim a higher path. Likewise for us as teachers, we are called to disillusion ourselves from our own race-, class-, gender-, and religion-based assumptions about what is good, true, worthy, and right. This is a positive form of disillusionment, not one of despair or disappointment, but one of strength and reckoning. In Parker Palmer's terms, we are challenged to see truth as "an eternal conversation" across differences (2004, p. 127), rather than as a set of fixed and final conclusions. This kind of proactive disillusionment moves us from a smaller reality to a larger one, from a circumscribed world to a more open, complex, diverse, and ever-changing environment. Such are the environments of our schools.

My wife uses a cultural immersion assignment to invite her preservice undergraduates to experience disillusionment. The students choose opportunities to enter cultural contexts different from their own, contexts that place them in the minority. One young White woman chose to attend an African-American church in Central Seattle. She went alone, and was "the only White face in the congregation." The traditional time came for guests to introduce themselves, but as her turn approached, the student became distraught. She had never been in a Black cultural context; she had never been the only one like her. In her anxiety she lost her capacity to speak and walked out of the church before the minister came to her.

One would hope that our teachers come to us with more cultural competence than this young woman exhibited, but we know that she is more the rule than the exception. In the end, the meltdown experience was positive for her. Debriefing her cultural immersion with my wife and her fellow students, she came face-to-face with her own limitations and in a preliminary way began the process of disillusionment from her racial and cultural naïveté. After this lesson in awareness and humility, her subsequent work on issues of cultural competence and culturally responsive teaching was much more reality based. Fortunately she became disillusioned in her university classroom rather than after she entered the profession, which would have required that her students pay the price for her. This is often the case.

Disillusionment is not a single event or even a stage we go through; it is a life-long process that is tied to our dispositions. From over forty years of friendships and dialogue with people of color, and now with a family of multiracial children and grandchildren, I have become disillusioned of my assumptions about race, privilege, and Whiteness. Likewise, through my forty-year marriage and in dialogue and friendship with female friends and colleagues, I have become distanced from my former paradigms of maleness, gender, and sexism. Similarly, through my conversations with the gay and lesbian friends that my children brought home in high school, and now through my own network of gay friends and colleagues, I have become disillusioned of my narrow images of relationship, sexuality, marriage, and intimacy. In addition, through my immersion in spiritual contexts around the world, I have become distanced from the single-dimensional truth and narrow assumptions that I held as an 18-year-old Christian fundamentalist. Echoing the sentiments expressed by Jamal Rahman in the above discussion of interfaith dialogue, I feel that the ongoing erosion of my dogmatic Christian belief structures has only brought me closer to the true meaning of Jesus' teachings. Happily, none of these personal transformations has reached an end point, and I look forward to a lifetime of continuing disenthrallment.

Kwame Anthony Appiah (2006) has a wonderful way of talking about the people we can become through exercising our dispositions for difference, dialogue, and disillusionment. He describes the qualities of personhood that lead to "cosmopolitanism." The cosmopolitan maintains his/her own cultural identity but is not limited by it. The cosmopolitan seeks out differences, is energized by the exchange of realities, and is always open to learn more, to see the world through different eyes. The cosmopolitan expects and even welcomes disagreement yet values community over conflict, and mutuality over dominance. These are the capacities we want our students to embody as they mature, so we as teachers are called to become cosmopolitans ourselves. With this in mind, we can welcome our ongoing disillusionments, knowing that behind each veil lies a greater truth and a better way of teaching.

A Disposition for Democracy

Good teachers know we are preparing our students for something much more interesting, valuable, and profound than standardized tests. Citizenship in a pluralistic world requires a complex skill set that looks very much like the three dispositions we have discussed so far. The strength of character to bridge differences, the power of critical thinking to sustain dialogue, and the self-reflective capacity to be disillusioned from our narrow certainties; these are the lifeblood of democratic citizenship. Good teaching and good democracy flow from the same heart-space of passion for both the *Pluribus* and the *Unum* of our shared humanity.

Also embedded in teaching and democracy is a passion for justice. Good teachers work their hearts out to give their students a chance of success. My Australian colleagues call this "the right to a fair go," a core value that drives democracy and teaching there as well as here. In contrast, the dynamics of social dominance that underlie school inequities work in the opposite direction. I define social dominance as "systems of privilege and preference, reinforced by the consolidation of power, and favoring the advantaged few over the marginalized many." In contrast, social justice is characterized by "systems of equity and inclusion, reinforced by the sharing of power, and favoring the good of the many over the greed of the few."

In this context, school reform can be understood as a movement from social dominance to social justice, as a process of undoing those educational systems that have favored only the few and replacing them with institutional practices that will more effectively serve the many. This is the original meaning and visionary intent of Marian Wright Edelman's passionate plea to "leave no child behind." It is both a vision for democracy and a vision for social justice.

When we acknowledge who is caught in the achievement gap—the same racial, cultural, and economic groups that have been marginalized by the larger societal dynamics of dominance—it becomes clear that "education for all" and "justice for all" are synonymous goals. The work of transforming public education in the service of equity for all of our children is social justice work. It cannot be carried out without the transformation of all other social, political, and economic systems. For example, with the correlation between poverty and school failure it is clear that ending or reducing poverty would be one of the most effective ways to eliminate achievement gaps. It is tragically ironic, however, that the same administration that created the NCLB mandates also put into place economic policies that have exacerbated poverty.

This is how social dominance works: those who have the power to hold educators accountable for raising test scores, also have the power to ensure that they themselves remain unaccountable for alleviating the very inequities that render those test scores so resistant to change. Challenging this dynamic of dominance is the work of social justice, which is perhaps the reason some politicians and academics have worked so hard to decouple the education conversation from the justice conversation. Surely, the legitimate and productive question is not whether we can say "social justice" in educational settings, but rather, how we might transform those and other social settings to actually achieve it.

Teaching for a New Humanity

Speaking recently about social justice with a class in the MIT program at Seattle University, I was intrigued by a question raised by one of the students: "Isn't all of your talk about social justice really running counter to human nature? Aren't we predisposed as a species to seek power over others?" This was an insightful query. Our history has been a story of revolving dominance, with one group establishing hegemony only to be replaced by a more powerful group.

Acknowledging this, I suggested that we are perhaps moving into a new time in our evolution. On a shrinking planet with national and cultural boundaries being erased by both economics and immigration, we are becoming increasingly touched by difference in our daily lives. For the sake of our survival, we can no longer trust our future to laissez-faire social Darwinism, wherein single-dimensional truths continue to compete for power and control. Instead, we need an imperative wherein the survival of the fittest is still in play, but our understanding of fitness favors community over control and dialogue over dominance.

It is true that all U.S. citizens have the First Amendment right to remain imprisoned in their own cultural narrowness. This luxury of ignorance, however, is not available to us as teachers. Ours is a better calling, and for the sake of our students and their world, we must acquire more adaptive human qualities, including the dispositions for difference, dialogue, disillusionment, and democracy. These will enable us to thrive as a species. These render us worthy to teach.

Thank you again for your vision, your commitment, your passion, and your willingness to engage in the life-long journey of becoming a good teacher,

In the spirit of our shared work,

Gary R. Howard

Notes

1. For a discussion of the second question, see my article in the March 2007 issue of *Educational Leadership*, "A Diversity Grows, So Must We."

References

Appiah, K. A. (2006). *Cosmopolitanism: Ethics in a world of strangers*. New York: W. W. Norton.

Howard, G. R. (2006). *We can't teach what we don't know: White teachers in multiracial schools* (2nd ed.). New York: Teachers College Press.

Lincoln, A. (1862). Annual message to Congress—concluding remarks, retrieved from http://showcase.netins.net/web/creative/lincoln/speeches/congress.htm. From R. P. Basler (Ed.; 1953). *Collected works of Abraham Lincoln*. Springfield, IL: The Abraham Lincoln Association.

Palmer, P. J. (2004). *A hidden wholeness: The journey toward an undivided life*. San Francisco: Jossey-Bass.

van Gelder, S. (2007, Winter). Abraham to descendants: "Knock it off!" *Yes!Magazine*. 12–15.

Chapter 21

Red Pedagogy

Sandy Grande

Dear Comrades,

While it may seem hyperbolic to use a quasimilitary term to refer to fellow teachers, I write with a sense that this is a time when teachers, schools and the democratic project itself are under siege from the forces of empire. I am taken by the sheer weight of the years that have passed since 9/11. Like dog years in the life of the nation, it's as if we've endured seven years' worth of trials and tribulations for every one that has passed. Some of the lowlights on the global and national front have been: the U.S. occupation of Iraq, the nonoccupation of Afghanistan, the Patriot Act, Abu Ghraib, the Abramoff scandal, global warming, downsizing, outsourcing, the whole "Brownie"—FEMA—hurricane Katrina affair and Karl Rove, Scooter Libby, the Joanne Miller debacle, the Texas border wall, the energy crisis, mortgage scandal, the AIDS pandemic, and the all-time-high of 1.5 billion people living in extreme poverty.[1]

On the educational front, we've witnessed the escalating assault on Affirmative Action—despite the supposed "win" in the Michigan case—and on public schools—despite the rhetoric of leaving no child behind. With these came the continued undermining of the legitimacy of women (e.g., Larry Summers) and people of color (e.g., Parents Involved in Community Schools vs. Seattle School District; Meredith vs. Jefferson County Board of Education), which work together to reposition the White middle class as the new oppressed. Punctuating it all has been the ongoing corporatization and privatization of education and the growing obsession with profit margins, efficiency, standardization, and empiricism.

All throughout, I've experienced a certain synchronicity—a parallel universe, déjà-vu-all-over-again kind of feeling—because though seemingly disparate, the litany of events appears to be oddly connected. Like the once popular party game "six degrees of separation" illustrates, everything is related. The one important caveat I add to this notion is that not only is everything related, but also all roads lead to Indian Country.

For example, consider the U.S. occupation of Iraq. After terrorists took down the Twin Towers, murdering over 3,000 civilians, an unprecedented fear was unleashed on what we once thought of as an impenetrable empire. In the wake of the nation's mourning, George Bush made his (in)famous declaration that "you're either with us or against us," setting in motion a vengeful zeitgeist that conflated Osama Bin Laden with Saddam Hussein, the Taliban, Iraq, Afghanistan, and for awhile all Muslims, into the "against us" category. The simple message perpetuated by both the left and the right was that "they"—dark-skinned, long-haired, foreign-tongued, non-Judeo-Christian, so-called tribal peoples—threatened *our* freedom, *our* democracy, if not the whole "American" way of life. Sound familiar? Indeed, the parallels between the U.S. occupation of Iraq and Indian Country were so apparent to some Native peoples that they inspired one of the more famous postings ever to travel the American Indian blog circuits. That is, a satiric letter addressed from Native Americans to the Iraqi people, forewarning them of the policies and services they could expect from the new BIA (Bureau of Iraqi Affairs), all detailed in list form, à la David Letterman's Top Ten.

Number 2 reads: "All Iraqi people will apply for a spot on a citizen roll. Citizenship will be open to those people who can prove they are Iraqi back four generations with documents issued by the United States. Christian church records may also be given in support." Number 5, "Each citizen will be allotted one hundred acres of prime Iraqi desert. They will be issued plows, hoes, seed corn, and the King James Bible. All leftover land will be open to settlement by the Israelis." Though wrapped in irony and humor, the posting sheds light on a very serious matter; that is, the pernicious endurance of U.S. colonialism masked as democratic paternalism. So, from 9/11, to the Bush White House, from the Bush White House to policies supporting colonization as democratization, from these policies to Indian Country—three degrees of separation.

Similarly, with Hurricane Katrina, there are three degrees of separation. By all estimates, Katrina was a monstrous natural disaster that exposed an even greater national disgrace: centuries of oppression and indifference toward poor Americans, African Americans, disabled and elderly Americans. The hurricane blew the shroud off *los olvidados*—the forgotten ones—and made their plight visible to the world. Together we witnessed the indelible images of mostly Black bodies under surveillance being corralled and penned in the Superdome and Convention Center. Only after death and disease took their toll did the government commence evacuation—a chaotic and violent process, where already fractured families were forced to disperse to unknown lands with no guarantee of return. Though on an entirely different scale, the last time a whole class of people was rounded up and forced to migrate at the hands of the U.S. military and under order of the president was in 1838. Thousands of Cherokee men, women, and children were taken from their land, herded into makeshift forts with minimal provisions and forced to march a thousand miles. Under indifferent army commanders, the human death toll in the first waves of removal were unforgivable. In the end, nearly 4,000 Cherokee met their death on the journey known as the Trail of Tears or in Cherokee, *Nunna daul Tsuny*, "The Trail Where They Cried." Who could have predicted that over a century and a half later, so many people would cry again? From Hurricane Katrina to the Superdome; from the Superdome to the mass "evacuation" of the unwanted; from the "evacuation" (or was it a removal?) to the Trail of Tears—three degrees of separation.

Among other things, the above exercise demonstrates how current crises reflect the American Indian experience. For over 500 years, to be Indian in America meant being subject to the random and militaristic powers of the federal government, to live under the continual threat of "eminent domain" (A.K.A. detribalization, termination, and/or plenary power), and to be corralled onto reservations of poverty, despair, and dependency. But today, the post-9/11 imperialism of the Bush regime has initiated an *Indian-ization of America*—a historical moment where we are all feeling the effects of *colonization*—a multidimensional force underwritten by Christian fundamentalism, defined by White supremacy, and fueled by global capitalism. Some may question the idea that we *all* pay the price for the colonialist project,[2] rebuffing Memmi's notion that "colonization can only disfigure the colonizer." But in the wake of Katrina I think even the most callous among us are beginning to question whether it's possible to disperse the poor and colonized far and wide enough—to build the walls high and fast enough—to maintain the quixotic comfort zones of the investor class. The truth is that eventually levees break, tyrannies tumble and empires fall.

Under this umbrella, present-day mercenaries plunder and profit by domesticating and undertheorizing democracy, reducing it to a sound-byte politics of empty platitudes and bottom-line assessments. Such rhetoric has assisted the deployment of policies of deregulation, privatization, unrestricted access to consumer markets, downsizing, outsourcing, flexible arrangements of labor, intensified competition among transnational corporations and in the centralization of economic power. The goal from the start has been to dismantle the constellation of existing economic and social structures (read: all that is public and common) with any potential to obstruct the so-called logic of the pure market (read: the gluttony of the private sphere) (Hursh, 2003). Since the ideology of privatization rests squarely on the shoulders of rabid individualism, it is imperative for all of its sentinels to not only embrace the dogma of self-interest but also denigrate anything that speaks to group and community, including race and tribe.

Critical pedagogy

For reasons outlined above, building a curricular program based on the principles of critical pedagogy not only makes sense but also constitutes a pedagogical imperative. In other words, insofar as the project for colonialist education has been deeply informed by the social, economic, and political policies of U.S. imperialism, an education for decolonization must also make no claim to political neutrality and engage analysis and social inquiry that troubles the capitalist, imperialist aims of unfettered competition, accumulation, and exploitation. Toward such aims the principles of critical pedagogy are clearly relevant. In particular, its foregrounding of capitalist relations as the axis of exploitation helps to frame the history of the colonized as one of dispossession and not simply cultural oppression, and its trenchant critique of postmodernism reveals the current obsession with identity politics as a dangerous distraction from the imperatives of social transformation.

That being said, I offer a riff on the tried-and-true principles of critical pedagogy. Specifically, a *Red* critique of critical pedagogy decenters capitalism as the central struggle concept, replacing it with the broader construct of colonization. This fundamental difference shifts the pedagogic goal away from the critique and transformation of capitalist social relations of production (i.e., *democratization*), toward the critique and transformation of colonialist relations of exploitation (i.e., *sovereignty*). This is not to say that the political/pedagogical projects of democratization and sovereignty are mutually exclusive; on the contrary, in this new era of empire, I suggest that sovereignty may offer democracy its only lifeline.

Such is the premise and promise of *Red Pedagogy*. It is an indigenous pedagogy that operates at the crossroads of Western theory and indigenous knowledge. In bridging these knowledge worlds, *Red Pedagogy* asks that as we examine our own communities, policies, and practices, we take seriously the notion that to know ourselves as revolutionary agents is more than an act of understanding who we are. It is an act of reinventing ourselves, of validating our overlapping cultural identifications and bringing them to bear on our social and political lives. As such, *Red Pedagogy* is, by definition, a space of engagement. It is the liminal[3] and intellectual borderlands where indigenous and nonindigenous scholars encounter one another, working to remember, redefine, and reverse the devastation of the original colonialist "encounter." The main imperative before us as citizens is to reject capitalist forms of schooling and to acquire the grammar of empire as just *one* tool for unthinking our colonial roots.

For teachers and students, this means that we must be willing to act as agents of transgression, posing critical questions and engaging dangerous discourse. It means calling into question the hegemonic discourses of unilateralism, monoculturalism, English-only, consumerism, nationalism, and free-market fundamentalism that construct education as a privilege and consider instead the implications of multilateralism, multiculturalism, multilingualism, contingency, and coalition that reasserts education as the right of a people. In the end it also means undertaking a deep examination of the colonialist project and its implications for all of us, understanding that at root is the quest for a reconciliation of the relationship between democracy (the rights of a nation) and sovereignty (the rights of a people). Such is the theory of knowledge that forms the foundation of *Red Pedagogy*. Specifically, it offers the following ways of thinking around and through the challenges facing American education in the twenty-first century, in particular our need to define a pedagogy for decolonization:

- *Red Pedagogy* is primarily a pedagogical project wherein pedagogy is understood as inherently relational, political, cultural, spiritual, intellectual, and perhaps most importantly, place based.
- *Red Pedagogy* is fundamentally rooted in indigenous knowledge and praxis. It is particularly interested in knowledge that furthers understanding and analyses of colonization.
- *Red Pedagogy* searches for ways it can both deepen and be deepened by engagement with critical and revolutionary theories and praxis.
- *Red Pedagogy* promotes an education for decolonization where the root metaphors of relationship, sovereignty, and balance provide the foundation.
- *Red Pedagogy* is a project that interrogates both democracy and indigenous sovereignty, working to define the relationship between them.
- *Red Pedagogy* actively cultivates a praxis of collective agency. That is, *Red Pedagogy* aims to build transcultural, transnational, and intergenerational solidarities among indigenous peoples and others committed to reimagining a sovereign space free of imperialist, colonialist, and capitalist exploitation.
- *Red Pedagogy* is grounded in hope. This is, however, not the future-centered hope of the Western imagination, but rather a hope that lives in contingency with the past—one that trusts the beliefs and understandings of our ancestors, the power of traditional knowledge, and the possibilities of new understandings.

With regard to delineating more specific approaches related to *Red Pedagogy* and its use in classrooms, like other critical theories, *Red Pedagogy* is not a methodology but rather a consciousness and way of being in/reading the world. As such, it is not a something that can be "done" by teachers or "to" students, nor is it a technique that can be lifted, decontextualized, and applied. It is rather a way of thinking about knowledge and the

processes of teaching and learning as it emerges within and through relationships—between students, teachers, communities, and places.

I would argue that these principles of *Red Pedagogy* have relevance to
other colonized communities knowledgeable of their own histories and connections to place through language and relationship, whether those communities are in the Ninth Ward of New Orleans, the South Bronx, or Tucson,
Arizona. Because, in the end, a *Red Pedagogy* is about engaging the development of "community-based power" in the interest of "a responsible political, economic, and spiritual society." That is, the power to live out "active
presences and *survivances* rather than an illusionary democracy." Vizenor's
notion of survivance signifies a state of being beyond "survival, endurance,
or a mere response to colonization," and toward "an active presence...an active repudiation of dominance, tragedy and victimry." In the wake of such
tragedies as 9/11 and Hurricane Katrina, I find the notion of survivance to be
both humbling and poignant. These events speak passionately to our collective need to decolonize our minds, bodies, and souls, to push back against
empire and reclaim what it means to be a people of sovereign mind and body
that also ultimately respects the sovereignty of the Earth of Pachamama and
all her beings.

Even more recently, the world witnessed yet another tragedy at the Kentucky Derby with the horrifying death of the filly Eight Belles. As onlookers
grieved they seemed to miss the larger tragedy that *is* the Kentucky Derby:
the rushed capitalist production of horses for maximum profit, the breeding
of beautiful but disposable beasts manufactured to survive for only short
bursts of speed. They personify the valorization of the genetic mutant understood as purity and repudiation of "mongrelization" despite the proven and
inherent resiliency and strength of hybridity. Today, everything from animals
and food to athletes and candidates are being mass produced for short bursts
of excellence, not stamina, for the moment, not the long run. There will
likely never be another Seabiscuit—89 races and his "win of the century" at
Pimlico, all after a lifetime of dedicated and earnest performance.

All this is made possible by the opiate of the masses—technology and
the religion of change as progress and progress as change. Iron Man and
Speed Racer are the films of the day. We are in a time when we contemplate
and choose daily the drug of short-term profit over long term investment.
The record-high gas prices and housing crisis reveals how many were des-
perate for the quick fix, for their chance at the brass ring, for the promise of

profit over life. It seems that you can fool most of the people most of the time.

Like Cesar Milan, we need a pack leader, a people whisperer to rescue us from our own devices. Milan, otherwise known as the Dog Whisperer, turns supposedly out-of-control dogs into calm and balanced creatures. He does so, not by training the dogs but by educating the people—the "owners"—transforming their often anxious and frenetic dispositions into calm and assertive energy. He helps them to understand that it is not about discipline or behavior in one moment, rather it's about building a life-long relationship that exists well beyond its ebbs and flows. We need to learn from this and reject the valorization of the moment, of sound-byte politics and pedagogies obsessed with measuring accountability, measured on one day, by one test, through one means. Instead, we need to choose to embrace the long haul, the legacy, the big picture, the mountain, the generations, the ancestors, the whisper.

What I am beginning to discern from all of this is that the Indigenous project is not about justice as much as it is about the pursuit of balance. The resistance of the new, fast, and sleek in favor of the smooth, traditional, and quiet. It's the replacement of "To each his own," and "May the best man win," with "We are all related," and "All for one and one for all." The lesson for all of us is to continue to resist the colonization—that is the commodification, deracialization, and dispiriting—of our minds, bodies and souls. To embrace the Indigenous project, or what I call a Red Pedagogy, is not only anticapitalist and decolonialist but also profoundly spiritual.

The hope is that we will shape schools and processes of learning around a decolonial imaginary where Indigenous and non-Indigenous peoples work in solidarity to build transcultural and transnational coalitions to construct a nation free of imperialist, colonialist, and capitalist exploitation. When I think of this kind of coalition building I think of the poignancy embodied in the Mexican soldiers (many of them Indigenous) who marched north to San Antonio, the site of the Alamo, carrying food and water for families displaced by hurricane Katrina. It was the first time a Mexican army crossed into the United States since the U.S.–Mexican War of 1846–1848. Surely, the ironies here can't be lost on everyone, not even Tom Horne.

If we can all just commit to the insurgency inherent to this kind of border crossing and coalition building, I know we can define a strong and poetic vision for education. The stories of the peoples of the Ninth Ward, the World

Trade Center, West Tucson and other colonized communities serve as a reminder to all of us that, just as the specter of colonialism haunts the collective soul of America, so too does the more hopeful spirit of Indigeneity.

Please remember: Each One Teach One.
Yuspagrasunki. Muchas Gracias. Thank You.

Notes

1. According to economist Jeffrey D. Sachs (2006), *extreme poverty* refers to households where individuals are unable to meet basic needs for survival. "They are chronically hungry, unable to access health care, lack the amenities of safe drinking water and sanitation, cannot afford education for some or all of (their) children, and perhaps lack rudimentary shelter...and basic articles of clothing such as shoes" (p. 20).

2. I have defined the colonialist project elsewhere (Grande, 2004) as being underwritten by Christian fundamentalism, defined by White supremacy and fueled by global capitalism.

3. Victor Turner (1974) introduced the concept of liminal space as being representative of a period of ambiguity, openness, and indeterminacy.

References

Hursh, D. (2003). Neo-liberalism, markets and accountability: Transforming education and undermining democracy in the United States and England. *Policy Futures in Education*, *3*(1), 3–15.

Sachs, J. D. (2006). The end of poverty: Economic possibilities of our time. New York: Penguin.

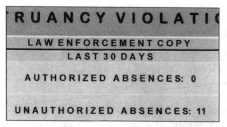 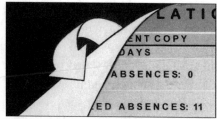

 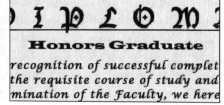

Chapter 22

Teaching Boldly:
A Principal Who Has Touched the Future

Úrsula Casanova

Dear Fellow Educators,

Surely I'm not alone when I say that helping to plan and open a brand new school was once my dream. I thought it had to be easier than trying to change a place with a long history and established traditions. That, I knew, was a very difficult task that tended to dead-end against: "...but that's the way we always did it..." So I had always wondered what it would be like to open a new school. Then a few years ago, while I was researching the problems of high school completion, I was able to learn how one administrator used such an opportunity to realize not only his dreams but those of his staff and students.

So, what does happen when an assistant principal is chosen to open a brand new school and also given the time and financial support necessary to plan and hire the administrative team, faculty, and staff? Well, surely it depends on the principal. In the case of Jon W. that opportunity was: "...a chance to start something brand new, from scratch…it's a great gift." So he set out to develop with a group of teachers the philosophy for a school where: "…we would make a difference…we would help kids be success-ful…we believed it, stated it, put it in writing…posted our mission statement all over the school, and it's still there."

When I visited that school sixteen years after its opening in 1988 I found the mission statement, as Jon had said, posted all over the school. There it was, in big gold letters against a dark background: "Cibola High is commit-ted to success…challenging students and staff to achieve their highest poten-tial." I also knew, from previous research that Cibola students were, in fact, outperforming other state high schools with similar demographics. Further-more, all those who are still around gave the credit for this achievement to Jon W., the principal who "opened" the school.

One would be hard-pressed to describe Cibola's soft-spoken founding principal as bold; yet his resoluteness, his readiness to venture into uncharted territory and, his confidence in going against the grain speaks to boldness with a quiet voice born out of frustration: "…seeing so much frustration in schools, so much student frustration about…not achieving. Seeing a lot of faculty frustration where you could see the faculty real unhappy…because they didn't believe they could make a difference. They had lost hope in themselves and in the kids." That frustration gave him the hope and determi-nation to plan for a new high school where all students would be expected to succeed.

But it takes more than hope and determination to create a new school and to ensure student success. Jon was also blessed with an unerring instinct for selecting the right people to accompany him on the journey toward excel-lence. Among them, everyone tells me that Jim Sullivan turned out to be es-sential to Cibola's success. Sullivan, or "Sully" as everyone still calls him, understood that students' expectations were framed within the limits of the possibilities they saw for themselves. He believed that his role as a counselor was to open up windows into alternative futures and then provide students the support to realize them. Thus the office of guidance and counseling be-came "the heart of the school." And at Cibola a high school diploma was no longer the goal; it was only a stepping-stone to a more distant but wholly achievable future. The guidance counselors were, in turn, responsible for applying their collective energy to ensuring the realization of their students' loftier aspirations.

During the last four years I have spent many hours at Cibola High School speaking with people at all levels of involvement at the school regularly interviewing a number of students and observing the rhythm of life on campus. Throughout that time I have come to learn the power of a shared goal to influence a school's environment when that goal is deeply held, backed up by enabling policies, and consistently implemented by people who not only believe in the goal but also in their power to realize it.

One of the things I noticed very quickly at Cibola High School was the peacefulness of the campus, even during class changes or in the cafeteria. You don't hear angry voices or brash language although there is plenty of the kind of noise that arises anywhere hundreds of teens are gathered together. This is not happenstance. It has come about as a result of hard work to establish high standards of behavior from everyone. It was all set up at the beginning when everyone knew that opposing gangs would be sharing the new school.

Cibola's attendance area reached across two different and distinctive parts of town. One was home mainly to farming families of Mexican origin and was considered the poorest part of the city; the other a mix of Mexican- and European-Americans from the west side of town. Neither group had ever attended an integrated school. Preparations for that first encounter and for Cibola's high expectations began early in the previous year with visits to the sending schools, meetings with parents and other community outreach. In spite of their foresight, the first few days were not easy.

Gangs on both sides had to be contained for the first few months because the bus was dropping off students 40 minutes before the first bell due to a scheduling error. Jon's strategy was simple. It required, says one of his original assistant principals, "everybody to get to know their students…and the students' family, as well as possible, and for all of us to treat kids with respect and let kids know that we cared about them, that we had high expectations for them, that we would help them meet those high expectations." So, at first, the whole faculty welcomed the students every morning. Once the bus schedule was corrected, all the administrators were out there. It worked. After the first two years the school settled down to a steady and comfortable rhythm that continues to this day. It is not perfect. Incidents happen and rule-breakers are disciplined, but through the many hours I have spent at the school I have heard many laughs but never have I heard or seen adults or students speaking to each other disrespectfully.

That was the beginning but it takes more than respect and good intentions to make a good school and Cibola has to be measured against its own goals. Has the school succeeded in raising their students' expectations? How can its effect be measured?

Cibola High School served 800 students in freshman and sophomore classes when it opened in 1988. Today the school's enrollment hovers around 2,500 students that typically break down into 75% Latinos, 20% White, with African American, Asian, and Native American students making up the remaining 5%, proportions that have held steady for several years. Over 50% of the students are entitled to free or reduced-price lunch and about 25% are English-language learners (ELLs). Many schools cite similar demographics to justify low student achievement and high dropout rates. That is not the case at Cibola High School. Indeed, over 80% of their graduates continue on to 2- or 4-year institutions, and another 10% go on to trade schools or join the military. These outcomes have been consistent for many years.

Cibola's success owes much to Jon W.'s leadership but his guidance was about more than inspiration. It was also about, as some may say, perspiration. Jon W. and everyone on the staff modeled behaviors that continue to this day. The principal and vice-principals are very visible around the school, especially before and after school and during period changes, and some of their time is set aside for classroom visits throughout the year. They are very accessible to the students, and they dress as they might for a corporate office. Two mentors are released from two of their classes so they can regularly visit new teachers during their first two years to observe, give advice and support but *not* to evaluate them.

The Guidance Office continues to be described as "the heart of the school and is a place to 'hang out' for many students. Some of them are "Teaching Assistants" (TA) who help out in that office during certain periods. Others may be waiting to see their counselors who address them by their first names and kid around with them. Others can be seen searching the files that hold applications for scholarships or financial assistance. As one of the counselor's commented, "...our students feel at home here." So much that they may even bring a guitar to play softly while they wait.

But that relaxed façade hides the intensive work they do for their counselees. Cibola's counselors were assigned a lot of responsibility from the very beginning. As principal and head of guidance, respectively, Jon W. and

Sullivan saw the counselors as key to the achievement of their expectations, so their role was designed to be broader and deeper than their counterparts at other schools: at Cibola counselors visit the sending schools several times during the year prior to the arrival of the freshman class to encourage incoming students and their families to plan for high school and beyond. Those pre-freshman meetings are the first of the many times students will hear of Cibola's high expectations for them. Counselors also play a major role in constructing (with the academic VP) the class schedule that begins not with the registrar's plan but with students' needs and choices for electives.

Cibola's counselors are continually involved with their students. Twice a year they meet with their charges to conduct a "credit check" to make adjustments and ensure every student's progress. Since most of Cibola's students fall below the poverty line, one counselor's time is solely devoted to seeking scholarships and other financial resources necessary for students to realize their plans. Besides helping with the search and application for scholarship money, the scholarship counselor is charged with ensuring the completion of required college entrance and state-mandated tests. Another counselor is assigned to work solely with students with special needs to ensure they also reach beyond what others might expect from them. Thus the policies put in place at the very beginning continue to enable students to meet the founders' expectations.

Department chairs, including the head of Grounds Management, also play a larger role at Cibola than at other high schools. They are responsible for developing the department's budget requests, for observing and evaluating their teachers or staff, for planning two annual peer-tutoring sessions for the benefit of the total faculty and, most importantly, they are held responsible for their department's effectiveness. They meet regularly with the principal to help make decisions, solve problems, consider new ideas, and listen to each other. They do this, in the current principal's words, "to carry out Cibola's responsibility to do the best for their students." That is a recurrent refrain at Cibola High School where everyone is expected to be a teacher.

Getting everyone into further education is not something that comes easily at most U.S. high schools, especially when the majority of the students are poor and many of those are also English learners. Cibola is an example of the productive high school defined by Hodges (2000) as a school that educates all its children well, has a clear vision of its teaching and learning goals, and takes action on those goals. This is what Cibola has managed to do better than most high schools with similar demographic profiles and, as it happens, it's what they had planned. The distance between the planning and the doing, however, can be large and may get larger as the years pass and the institutional memories fade.

The uniqueness of Cibola, and of Jon W.'s legacy, is the school's continuous striving to solve the problems that arise along the way in order to reach the intended goal. It is a learning organization, a school where decisions are based on evidence from existing sources or on gathered data measured against the clear mission of the school and staff. It is a school with high leadership capacity and broad-based participation. At Cibola the work of leadership and learning is assumed by the school community as a collective responsibility (Silins & Mulford, 2002). The interventions designed to solve problems as the school developed stand as evidence: unacceptably high freshman dropouts, difficulties encountered by English learners, students falling too far behind, absences due to athletic competition were all problems to be solved. They led, respectively, to the creation of the freshman teams, of an intense, integrated, layered, Structured English Immersion program (SEI); to the development of Vista Alternative High School; and to the creation of an athletic league of neighboring districts to avoid long-distance travel. Each of those interventions was discussed, tested and found to be effective before full implementation.

Jon W.'s influence has also extended to the total school district. One way for leaders to leave a lasting legacy is to ensure that others share and help develop their vision. Leadership succession, therefore, means more than grooming the next principal. It means distributing leadership throughout the school's professional community so others can carry the torch after the principal has gone (Spillane, Halverson, & Drummond, 2002). Jon W. was such a leader. He believed in letting people take charge of the solution to a problem. The "Problems Committee" in which those who brought up a problem had to participate in its solution, was evidence of his leadership style. The development of leadership among his staff was a beneficial side effect of both his trust and his willingness to share responsibilities. This approach has brought many of Cibola's original staff to leadership positions in the school district's offices. Jon W. went from the principal's office at Cibola to the district office, first as assistant superintendent then as superintendent. That tradition has continued. For the last few years the three assistant superintendents at the Yuma Union High School District were members of the original

Cibola faculty, and one of them was recently appointed superintendent. The current principal at Cibola and the principal of the most recently opened district high schools were also part of the original Cibola team.

We can't all be founders of schools, but there is much to be learned from Jon W. While it is true that he was given, as he said, "a gift" when he was asked to take charge for planning and staffing the brand new school, gifts can be misused. Jon had the courage of his convictions and the determination to follow through on them. He traveled to learn all he could about effective high schools, and he sought out the best people he could find to staff the school, first within the district and then far beyond the district's boundaries. Sixteen of the original staff remain there and those who left have often gone on to leadership positions in the district and beyond.

It took a great deal of courage to announce to the world: "all our students will graduate," or to tell a parent to whom life has not been kind that "your child will go to college." It took a lot of hard work to realize those lofty goals that were at first ridiculed by the less ambitious in the town and district. That ridicule has turned to respect and admiration as the school continues to strive to do the best it can for its students. May we all have the same kind of belief in our students and steadfastness about our own goals as we strive to overcome new challenges; may we all boldly touch the future.

Sincerely,

References

Hodges, A. (2000, April). Web of support for a personalized academic foundation. Paper presented at the annual meeting of the American Educational Research Association, New Orleans, LA.

Silins, H. & Mulford, B. (2002). Schools as learning organizations: The case for system, teacher, and student learning. *Journal of Educational Administration, 40*(5), 425–446.

Spillane, J. P., Halverson, R., & Drummond, J. V. (2002). Investigating leadership practice: A distributed perspective. *Educational Researcher, 30*(3), 23–28.

Chapter 23

Letter to My Daughter, a Teacher

Sonia Nieto

Dear Alicia,

The day you decided to become a teacher was one of the proudest days of my life.

For years you had been adamant about not wanting to teach. Growing up, you had seen firsthand what it meant to be a teacher: your father, a middle and high school teacher, and me, a teacher educator, were always busy planning lessons, reading and correcting papers, speaking with parents or students on the phone, agonizing about the latest central district directive or university policy, jubilant when students did well, or worried when they didn't. This was a life, you said, that you did not want.

Even after college, you didn't really know *what* you wanted to do. The only thing you were sure about was your desire to return to France after graduation. You had lived in southern France during your junior year, and this time you had Paris in your sights. With that in mind, you made plans to

live at home and work that autumn after graduation to earn enough money
for your trip.

It was 1992. That November, on the night you turned 22, before we went
to dinner to celebrate the occasion, I asked you to go with me to hear Jona-
than Kozol speak. He was in town to launch his latest book, *Savage Inequalities,* and I didn't want to miss it. I remember the evening so well. I saw how
seriously you listened to Kozol's talk, how quiet you were throughout the
evening as you pondered what he had to say about the tremendous injustices
in our schools. You were aware of these things, of course, but to hear about
the harsh realities of inequality in such vivid terms was deeply troubling. As
we were making our way out of the auditorium, you said, "Mami, I have to
teach! There's nothing that's more important... Maybe I shouldn't go to
France after all; maybe I should stay here and teach." I convinced you—I'm
so glad!—that the problems of education would be here when you returned,
and that you needed to take the opportunity—perhaps the last one you would
have before adult responsibilities took over—to take advantage of your youth
and energy and go to France.

I was thrilled when you said you wanted to teach. You would be entering
a field that I loved, one that I have always believed is the most important
profession there is. How could I not burst with pride? I also knew that it
would not be easy, that you would have difficult days and sleepless nights,
that you would worry about your students and your competence, that you
would be angered by the bureaucracy and the injustice, and that you would
be tired, yes, mostly tired. But here you were, making that important decision, one that filled your father and me with pride.

When you returned to the States, you moved to New York City and you
became a teacher of sorts. Because you hadn't taken any education courses in
college—why would you, after all, since you had never planned on being a
teacher?—you couldn't get a teaching license. So you got a job as director of
an after school program for high school kids in the Bronx, where all your
students were Latinos and African Americans who had been "left behind' by
the school system and our society. Most had never considered higher education, and many were close to dropping out of school. You cared deeply for
your students and you took their work, and their lives, seriously. You made a
difference in their lives.

Because you didn't have certification, the only job you could get was in
a private school. Your first job was as a French teacher in a prestigious pri-

vate school for girls. I often tell people about the day you went to interview for that job. Besides the regular interview, you also had to teach a class. You called us the night before and your father, who had taught Spanish for many years, gave you lots of ideas for the lesson. The next night, you called to let us know how it had gone. Your lesson had gone well, you said, but mostly, you were astonished at the multitude of resources at the school, at the small classes, and at the support for students and teachers alike. You said something then that has stayed with me all these years because it captures perfectly how the context can define whether students succeed or fail: "You know, Mami, my kids in the Bronx would be *geniuses* in this school," you said, underscoring the fact that resources, support, and attention can make a greater difference than genes, zip codes, and even social class.

The context can also define whether a teacher succeeds or fails. That school gave you tremendous support: you had two mentors and a budget for materials, and you were encouraged to attend many conferences and workshops. You were also expected to take on leadership positions, and you were given the resources to do so. As any new teacher, especially one with no formal training in the field, you had some difficult times, it's true, but through it all, you also had tremendous encouragement and help. All of this helped you become a more confident and stronger person, and a wonderful teacher. It was at that school that you learned to teach because, sadly, well-endowed private schools can generally give new teachers more attention and support than most of our public schools.

You have been a teacher for 13 years now. Happily, for us, you made the decision to move back to our town with your husband and our three beautiful grandchildren, and you now teach Spanish and French in our local middle school. It is a good school system, widely recognized for its quality teachers and innovative curriculum. It is also one of the most multicultural school systems I've ever seen, with a good mix of students of various racial, ethnic, social class, and linguistic backgrounds. You often comment on how fortunate you feel to teach here. You respect your peers and you love your students. You've chosen to teach middle school students, by all accounts the most difficult. "Call me crazy," you once said to me years ago, "but I *like* this age!" And as you've become known in the community, I too have gained a new identity: in some quarters, I am now known as "Ms. López's mother." This became most vivid to me a couple of years ago when four young women shouted to me from across the way at our local ice cream shop, "Are you Ms. López's mother? Oh, my God! We *love* her *so* much!" How could I not be proud?

And yet, these are hard times for education, and teachers and students feel it more than anybody. Even good schools experience standardization pressures and the move toward privatization. Rather than a focus on the joy of learning, there's been a shift to scores on standardized tests, as if they measured anything but skills. Rather than viewing education as preparation for life, it's now viewed more and more as preparation for a job. On top of all this, teachers' autonomy is stripped away when they're forced to follow a scripted curriculum, and their effectiveness is compromised when the size of their classes rise, as yours did last year when for a brief time you had 31 students in a Spanish class, a sure recipe for ineffectiveness. Even in good schools, the steady stream of supplies and other material support is diminishing, the result of local, state, and national tax cuts based on politicians' sense that people are tired of paying for education. And who suffers? The most vulnerable, of course, and you see signs of this every day in your work. Even in our school system, which is well resourced and highly supported by its mostly middle-class community, you see how differences in race, class, and language unfairly jeopardize some students over others.

Teaching, of course, has always been hard. Running from class to class, with no time even to go to the bathroom, teachers' days are a whirl of activity, ending in exhaustion when they go home to tend to their own families, caring for children, going to doctors' and dentists' appointments, doing laundry, preparing dinner, and putting the children to bed after three stories each ("Just one more, Mamá, please!") And then preparation for the next day begins, trying to come up with activities that are meaningful and that will engage students, correcting papers, and trying to keep your eyes open beyond 9 p.m.

You're in your fifteenth year of this crazy life of teaching, and we are so proud of you. You teach four classes a day, but beyond that, you spend countless hours on the "extras" not covered in your contract: you help organize cultural events and you cook Latino treats to bring to your students. You stay after school to meet with colleagues. You try to keep abreast of the field by attending conferences and getting ideas that you can try out in your classes. You organized a trip to Spanish Harlem in New York City so that your students would understand that learning Spanish is more than learning how to say *"hola, ¿qué tal?"* but that it means learning about and valuing the cultures of the millions of people around the globe who speak the language. You made the decision to take them to New York – you certainly didn't need anything else on your plate!—because you want your students to learn about and appreciate the great cultural resources of the Puerto Rican/Latino community there. You had to plan numerous fund-raising activities so that all those students who wanted to go would be able to do so because you're all too aware of the disparities in income among your students. And you co-chair an inquiry group at your school on the important topic of the "achievement gap," (as you know, a term I dislike because it implies that the "gap" is a result of students' lack of motivation rather than of structural inequalities that help create the gap) because even in good schools, the kids of the privileged do better than the kids of the poor. And you come home tired every day.

More than ever, Alicia, our nation needs teachers like you, teachers who advocate for their students and for what's right because they understand that their profession is more than a job. Immersed in the daily challenges of teaching and given all the obstacles to doing your job well, I know you must sometimes wonder if you make a difference. You do. You may not see it every day; sometimes you won't see it for years. But the work that you do is precious. You are a mentor not only for Latino kids, but for all kids. The many hours you spend planning, the tremendous patience you have with your students, the care you've shown in working with their families—these things all make a difference, an enormous difference, in the lives of your (our) students.

Thank you for being a teacher, for teaching with love and with empathy, and for keeping not only our family legacy of teaching alive, but also for epitomizing our nation's ideal of public education as the foundation of a strong and vibrant democracy for all its people.

Love,

mami

Afterword

Dear Dennis, Mary, Writers, and Readers,

It would be impossible to not celebrate the words and emotions in *Teach Boldly!* And as I celebrate, I am brought back to the reality that this book is a mandate for socially committed work, which needs to both begin and continue. We have been held deeply under the water of de-professionalization. Teachers have come to be regarded as space occupiers in broken-down rooms without resources, mentorship, or political initiative. This book is an inspiring call for those of us who teach to empower ourselves with the knowledge and cultural capital needed to change our schools.

In 1997, Joe Kincheloe and I edited Paulo Freire's final book, *Teachers as Cultural Workers: Letters to Those Who Dare Teach.* Paulo spoke to schoolteachers about their positions within schools. He insisted that teachers must develop a literacy of power. These ideas are echoed on the pages of *Teach Boldly!* Ironically, schools are one of the last places we go to understand power despite the fact that, as cultural workers, teachers can have enormous impact on the socio/cultural contexts in which they teach. Awareness of the dimensions of power within a school enables teachers to understand how those who hold that power shape the behavior within the school. *Teach Boldly!* guides us in how to apply a critical pedagogical read to schools and then reposition power in socially just ways.

To take such a critical position is to teach boldly, with a spirit of adventure, and with risk. This doesn't imply teaching irresponsibly; in fact, to teach boldly requires responsibility. Teaching with creative risk and intellectual commitment empowers us to employ our curricular expertise, our culturally responsive awareness of students' needs, and our ability to subvert power in order to reform dysfunctional schools, rewrite ill-conceived curricula, and re-educate ineffective leaders. The writers of *Teach Boldly!* confirm that adventurous teaching requires:

- Appreciating the possibility embedded in individuals who have critical consciousness
- Thinking critically and analytically
- Cultivating our intellects
- Understanding the world as it is in relation to what it could be

- Understanding the invisible forces at work in the culture of power
- Lifelong commitments to be global citizens and cultural workers
- A humility that allows us to be good teachers, leaders, and members of our communities
- Teaching ourselves what is important to know, including rigorous familiarization with standards, expectations, and goals of school administrators and boards
- Re-conceptualizing the role of "good citizen" to mean one who speaks and acts with awareness of how power oppresses
- Avoiding the stereotypes of gender, race, sex, class, and ability
- Employing our aesthetic abilities

Actually the list is endless, and *Teach Boldly!* contributes profoundly to it. We have just had the privilege of reading letters from superb educators who dare to live up to the book's title. They have opened our eyes to dreams and possibilities, rekindled our hearts with joy and hope, and empowered us to transform our schools and give our students the knowledge they so deserve.

Shirley R. Steinberg

Commentary on the Chapter Illustrations

Dennis Earl Fehr drew all of the chapter illustrations. Occasionally, Mary Cain Fehr contributed conceptual and visual ideas, as described below. Dennis' commentary describes his creative process and the meaning of each drawing.

Chapter 1 - Christine Sleeter

My drawing for Christine's letter expresses her insight that the curriculum should relate to students' lives and that teachers should include students in its development. The book in the drawing symbolizes passive traditional curricula. Note the stiff figures to the left. As we move to the right, we see the children coming to life by engaging with a curriculum they find more exciting.

Chapter 2 - Mary Frances Agnello

Mary Frances's letter challenges us to see the world of teaching through new lenses. She grounds her letter with nine "E" words: experience, existentialism, excitement, energy, exploration, environment, ecology, economics, and ethics. Mary Fehr suggested the eye chart. It works perfectly.

Chapter 3 - Pixie Holbrook

This drawing depicts plants struggling in polluted soil. The soil is a standardized test answer sheet in which every item is nonsensically numbered 09 (inspired by Yoko Ono's track repeating the phrase "number 9" on the Beatles' *White Album*). The plants represent the joylessness of learning in high-stakes testing climates.

Chapter 4 - Patty Bode, Nora Elton, and Rachel I. Shuman

Patty, Nora, and Rachel's letter is in part about Nora's decision to introduce her students to the work of Keith Haring, an important artist who emerged in the 1980s. Homophobia from school personnel impeded Nora's efforts to teach about this gay artist, so I borrowed Keith's drawing style to depict the tension between people who hold pinched views and those who do not. I enjoyed drawing in Keith's style and used it for Chapter 16 as well.

Chapter 5 - Geneva Gay

Geneva refers to the metaphor of thinking outside the box, so I have drawn a teacher not only thinking outside it, but stepping out of it. As she does, she casts aside the box's contents, the canned curriculum (an idea contributed by Mary, who also suggested labeling the box "teacher proof").

Chapter 6 - Barbara Morgan-Fleming

Barbara's theme is the necessity of teaching against popular currents if they obstruct learning. One rower is moving in a direction opposite that of the others. Barbara's letter inspires us to follow this rower's lead. (One fish is also going against the current. Five minutes' longer recess if you can find it.)

Chapter 7 - Paul Chamness Reece-Miller

Paul's letter vividly recounts the horrors that gay students often suffer in homophobic schools. He speaks of curricula that ignore an issue that accounts for a significant number of teen suicides. The elephant in the room represents the denial of this issue. Neither the students nor the teacher acknowledges that in the back sits an elephant—an obviously perplexed one. I had fun inventing the teacher despite the seriousness of the topic.

Chapter 8 - Angela Valenzuela

Angela's candid description of an act of prejudice she committed in childhood, and what it taught her, resulted in an image expressing the power of cruel words to explode in the psyche of the receiver. As you probably know, Angela went on to become one of the field's most effective advocates of antibias teaching.

Chapter 9 - Mary Cain Fehr

Mary conceptualized this drawing. It refers to the quilt that is an important element in her letter, and to her "water-wearing-away-rock" approach to facilitating change and teaching social theory. Texas Tech University, where we teach, has a beautiful satellite campus in a town called Junction. Through the campus runs a river, the South Llano, that is filled with rounded limestone rocks in which holes have been worn by water current. They are affectionately known in Junction as holey rocks. These rocks appear in the drawing.

Chapter 10 - Sheng Kuan Chung

Using graffiti art, including that of the British artist Banksy (whose image of two bobbies kissing I use in this illustration), Sheng Kuan's intense letter offers a curricular unit designed to raise the consciousness of homophobic future teachers. The irate censors attempting to cover Banksy's figures remind us that the foremost civil rights struggle of our time is yet to be won.

Chapter 11 - George Wood

This drawing represents the heartbreaking story of Tina in George's letter. The background figures symbolize the sinister characters in Tina's life and death. The white strokes in front of them represent her spirit. The page break represents the abrupt, violent, and premature end of her life.

Chapter 12 - Carolyn Erler and Susan L. Allen

The message of Carolyn's and Susan's letter that we must teach children nonviolence evolved in my mind as a row of machine guns planted in the ground, transformed from killing machines into flower vessels.

Chapter 13 - Linda Darling-Hammond

Linda's powerful argument for placing our best teachers in our toughest schools stayed with me, and the image took on a literal form. This drawing is what came out. The kids were fun to create.

Chapter 14 - Linda McSpadden McNeil

Linda movingly portrays her early days as a teacher in a systemically prejudiced environment. Her letter calls for the courage to disobey the system when morality requires it. I chose a badge, perhaps the ultimate authority symbol, to represent her message. A badge image by Shepard Fairey, the creator of the now-iconic red and blue Barack Obama image, was my starting point for this drawing.

Chapter 15 - Donalyn Heise

As I read Donalyn's letter I was struck by how well it crystallizes her theme: Good teaching starts with good caring. As a boy I learned about Native American art from a magazine called *Arizona Highways*. The drawing I envisioned, rooted in this rich tradition, represents Donalyn's theme. Although she does not mention Native Americans, her letter reminded me that caring for our young is humanity's most universal duty and thus transcends not only artistic styles but also cultures in the grand sense.

Chapter 16 - Kara Mitchell

Kara's letter reminded me of the harm that ill-informed good intentions can cause. The teacher in this drawing might mean well but obviously is not doing well. This scene is repeated over and over across the U.S., causing English-language learners to fall further and further behind.

Chapter 17 - Hidehiro Endo

Based on Hidehiro's anecdote about the Japanese child's experience in the school cafeteria, Mary suggested the idea of a peanut butter and jelly sandwich inserted into a traditional Japanese place setting. This represents a displacement of a culinary cultural tradition. Mary and I collaborated on the visual elements for this illustration. All I had to do was draw them.

Chapter 18 - Dennis Earl Fehr

This drawing is based on a photo taken by a keen-eyed teaching assistant of mine, Yen-an Chen, at Project Intercept, an alternative school for students who have been suspended from their original schools for disciplinary reasons. My drawing expresses the view that although this population is perhaps the ultimate Other to our teachers, it contains great talent and potential.

Chapter 19 - Etta Hollins

Etta's letter demonstrates the wisdom of a student-centered approach to teaching. By building relationships with students and making content relevant to them, teachers can direct their chaotic energy into gradually more coherent and productive forms. Inspired initially by a drawing from the artist Frank Billingsley, I expressed Etta's idea in this visual way.

Chapter 20 - Gary Howard

Gary's story, like mine, is of a White boy who grew up in a segregated religious environment. The scene in his letter describing his White student's experience in a Black church brought back memories of my own awakening to prejudice. I chose to represent it with these two hands.

Chapter 21 - Sandy Grande

Sandy's letter draws our attention to the still damaging role of the European invasion of this continent, not only to its Indigenous peoples but to all of us. I visualized her point by drawing a European crown jabbing into the North American landmass.

Chapter 22 - Úrsula Casanova

Úrsula describes a new high school in which a visionary principal and a dynamic school counselor guided a population of struggling students toward graduation and college enrollment. Mary contributed the metaphor of transformation through the art of origami, representing the transformation of these students' lives through outstanding school leadership.

Chapter 23 - Sonia Nieto

Contrasting with Pixie Holbrook's chapter illustration depicting the undesirable product that emerges from the soil of high-stakes testing, Sonia's touching letter to her daughter, a young teacher, inspired this image of beautiful flowers emerging from strong, healthy soil.

Contributors

Mary Frances Agnello is Associate Professor of Secondary Education in the College of Education at Texas Tech University. She pursued French as an undergraduate at the University of Texas at Austin and received her masters and doctoral degrees in curriculum and instruction at Texas A & M University. Emphasizing language, literacy, and culture, she focuses her research on critical pedagogy, diversity studies, and environmental sustainability. She is the author of *A Postmodern Literacy Policy Analysis.*

Susan L. Allen is the Director of Nonviolence Education at Kansas State University. Susan holds a doctorate in media anthropology and published the first textbook in this field, combining anthropology and journalism. Previously, she was director of the KSU Women's Center, research intern at the East-West Center in Honolulu, Senate staffer in Washington, D.C., researcher in Japan, and writer/editor of an alternative newspaper. Currently she is developing a form of nonviolence based on systems and sustainability called "Every Day Nonviolence."

Patty Bode is the Director of Art Education for Tufts University in affiliation with the School of the Museum of Fine Arts, Boston. Her research interests include multicultural theory and practice in teacher preparation, the arts in urban education, and the role of visual culture in the expression of student knowledge and political action. Years of experience as an activist public school teacher and teacher educator inform her art making, research, and teaching.

Úrsula Casanova is Associate Professor Emerita in the College of Education at Arizona State University. She holds a B.A. in Art, an M.S. in Educational Administration, and a Ph.D. in the Social and Philosophical Foundations of Education. Her awards include an Educational Policy Fellowship from the Institute of Educational Leadership, a fellowship from the Inter-University Program for Latino Research of the Social Science Research Council to Stanford University, and the American Educational Research Award for Interpretive Scholarship.

Sheng Kuan Chung is Associate Professor and Graduate Program Director of Art Education and Affiliated Professor of Art History at the University of Houston. He holds a B.Ed. from National Hsinchu Teachers College in Taiwan, an M.A. from New York University, and a doctorate from the University of Illinois, Urbana-Champaign. His research interests include social reconstructionist art education, multiculturalism, visual/media culture, social issues, and Asian aesthetics.

Linda Darling-Hammond is Charles E. Ducommun Professor of Education at Stanford University where she has launched the Stanford Center for Opportunity Policy in Education and the School Redesign Network. Her research, teaching, and policy work focus on school restructuring, teacher quality, and educational equity. In 2006, Darling-Hammond was named one of the nation's ten most influential people affecting educational policy over the previous decade. She recently served as the leader of President Barack Obama's education-policy transition team.

Nora Elton teaches art in Wilmington, MA, public schools, at the Museum of Fine Arts, Boston, and at the Danforth Museum. As this book goes to press, she will begin teaching at a charter school in Brooklyn, NY. In addition to her work in U.S. urban schools, she also taught photography with children and teens in Guatemala. Through implementing relevant multicultural and social justice curricula, Nora strives to empower her students to see themselves as bright, capable, and imaginative future leaders.

Hidehiro Endo is a doctoral candidate in the department of Curriculum and Instruction at Purdue University. His primary research interest is the educational experiences of immigrant/international students. Hiro is also interested in pre-/in-service teachers' experiences, critical race theory, and GLBTQ issues in education.

Carolyn Erler is Assistant Professor of Visual Studies in the School of Art at Texas Tech University. Her research focuses on grassroots political movements, corporate violence, and tactical usages of visual media within networked capitalist culture. Erler has a Ph.D. in Art Education from Florida State University.

Dennis Earl Fehr taught English, reading, and art in the public schools for ten years prior to entering the University of Illinois' doctoral program in art education. After three years in graduate school he accepted a position at the University of Houston, where he taught for ten more years. This led to an offer from Texas Tech University, where he has been art faculty for eleven years. He directs the National Education Taskforce, a nonprofit organization that advocates for children in public schools (www.natedtaskforce.org). Several contributors to this book belong to the NET as well. Two of Dennis' children, Shenoa and Shannon (and their husbands) have entered the teaching profession.

Mary Cain Fehr is Assistant Professor of Curriculum and Instruction at Texas Tech University. She is a former elementary and middle level classroom teacher, art teacher, and instructional technology coordinator. Mary holds a B.S. in Elementary Education, an M.Ed. in Instructional Technology, and a Ph.D. in Curriculum and Instruction. Her research interests include culture and diversity, culturally responsive teaching, teaching and learning in online environments, and creativity in the curriculum.

Geneva Gay is Professor of Education at the University of Washington, Seattle where she teaches Multicultural Education and Curriculum Theory. Her areas of scholarship and research are the intersection of race, culture, ethnicity, and education; teacher preparation for and practice of culturally responsive teaching; multicultural curriculum design; and educational equity and closing the achievement gap for students of color in urban settings. She is a frequent national and international consultant on these issues.

Sandy Grande (Quechua) is Associate Professor and Chair of the Education Department at Connecticut College. She is currently working on developing a Native American think tank, with a home location in New York City. Her research and teaching are profoundly inter- and cross-disciplinary, and they interface critical, feminist, Indigenous, and Marxist theories of education with the concerns of Indigenous education. Her book, *Red Pedagogy: Native American Social and Political Thought* (Rowman and Littlefield, 2004) has been met with critical acclaim. She has also written several articles on critical theory as it relates to American Indian identity, intellectualism, and power.

Donalyn Heise is Associate Professor and Art Education Program Coordinator at the University of Memphis and PRW Project Education Director, and serves on the Board of the Tennessee Art Education Association. She has taught art at all levels of K-12 and higher education and was Director for the Center for Innovation in Art Education and Art and Technology Coordinator for ConferNet, one of the nation's first virtual art-based academic K-16 conferences. Research interests include teacher preparation, art for underserved populations, resilience and art, and art and technology integration.

Pixie J. Holbrook is a National Board Certified Teacher (Early Childhood Through Young Adulthood-Exceptional Needs) from Conway, MA. She has worked in preschools through college, in urban, suburban, and rural settings. She has been a teacher and consultant in public, private, and charter schools in Massachusetts and Connecticut. She is drawn to political action on many topics, including attempts to enlighten politicians regarding her state's standardized testing program. She is a member of the National Educational Taskforce and has published articles in *Kappan* and *Taking Sides—Controversial Issues in Special Education.*

Etta R. Hollins is Professor and Chair of Teacher Education at the University of Southern California. Her scholarship is focused on the preparation of teachers for diverse and underserved students. She is the author of the award-winning book *Culture in School Learning* (2nd ed., 2007). She is editor of *Transforming Curriculum for a Culturally Diverse Society* and co-editor of *Teaching Diverse Populations and Pathways to Success in School.* Etta has served as a consultant on diversity in teacher education for urban school districts, U.S. state departments of education, and NCATE.

Gary R. Howard has 35 years of experience working with issues of civil rights, social justice, equity, education, and diversity. He is a keynote speaker, writer, and workshop leader who travels extensively throughout the United States and Australia. His most recent book, *We Can't Teach What We Don't Know* (2nd ed., 2006), was published by Columbia University and is considered a groundbreaking work examining issues of privilege, power, and the role of White leaders and educators in a multicultural society.

Linda McSpadden McNeil is Professor of Education and Director of the Center of Education at Rice University. She is the author of *Contradictions* *of School Reform: Educational Costs of Standardized Testing* (Routledge, 2000) and a coauthor of "Avoidable Losses: High Stakes Accountability and the Dropout Crisis," *Educational Policy Analysis Archives* (2008). Her research encompasses factors shaping children's access to knowledge in schools, particularly the intersection of our increasingly diverse student population and standardized schooling.

Kara Mitchell has an M.A. from Stanford University and has taught English-language learners from K-Ph.D. in various locations including Virginia, California, Mexico, China, and Massachusetts. She is currently a doctoral candidate in the Curriculum and Instruction program at Boston College and advocates for bilingual learners/ELLs through her involvement in the Institute for Language and Education Policy, the National Education Task Force, and the Massachusetts Association of Teachers of Speakers of Other Languages (MATSOL).

Barbara Morgan-Fleming is Associate Professor of Curriculum and Instruction at Texas Tech University. Her research interests include classroom performance of curriculum and informal aspects of teachers' knowledge. She has recent publications in *Teaching and Teacher Education, Curriculum Inquiry, International Journal of Social Education, Social Studies, Educational Forum,* and *Journal of Curriculum & Supervision.*

Sonia Nieto, Professor Emerita of Language, Literacy, and Culture, University of Massachusetts, Amherst, has written widely on multicultural education, teacher education, and the education of students of culturally and linguistically diverse backgrounds. She has taught at all levels from elementary school through graduate school, and she has been recognized for her research, advocacy, and service with many awards, including four honorary degrees.

Paul Chamness Reece-Miller received his Ph.D. in 2003 in Foreign Language Education from Purdue University. Dr. Miller is currently Associate Professor and Program Chair of Bilingual Education & Diversity Studies within the Department of Curriculum & Instruction at Texas Tech University. Dr. Miller is interested in various facets of second-language learning, as well as social justice issues with a focus on immigrant adolescents and LGBTQ students and teachers.

Rachel Shuman teaches art in public schools and art museums including the Danforth Museum and the Institute of Contemporary Art, Boston. Her commitment to making students' voices more audible through art has been shaped by her experiences with elementary-aged children as well as with teenagers in the juvenile justice and child welfare systems. Incorporating multicultural education by connecting to the students' everyday lives and backgrounds are central to Rachel's teaching.

Christine E. Sleeter is Professor Emerita in the College of Professional Studies at California State University, Monterey Bay, where she was a founding faculty member. Her research focuses on antiracist multicultural education and multicultural teacher education. She has published over 100 articles in edited books and journals. Her recent books include *Unstandardizing Curriculum* (Teachers College Press), *Facing Accountability in Education* (Teachers College Press), and *Doing Multicultural Education for Achievement and Equity* (with Carl Grant; Routledge). She was recently awarded the American Educational Research Association Social Justice in Education Award and the American Educational Research Association Division K Legacy Award.

Angela Valenzuela is a Professor in both the Cultural Studies in Education Program within the Department of Curriculum & Instruction and the Educational Policy and Planning Program within the Department of Educational Administration at the University of Texas at Austin where she also serves as the director of the University of Texas Center for Education Policy. She currently serves as Associate Vice President for University-School Partnerships at the University of Texas at Austin. Valenzuela's research and teaching interests are in the sociology of education, minority youth in schools, educational policy, and urban education reform.

George Wood is Principal of Federal Hocking Middle and High School in Stewart, Ohio. Federal Hocking is a nationally recognized school and leads in personalizing education and graduation by exhibition. Wood is also the Executive Director of the Forum for Education and Democracy (www.forumforeducation.org), a national think tank devoted to reality-based policy options that support the democratic mission of our public schools. He is married to Marcia Burchby, a kindergarten teacher from whom he gets all his best ideas, and is the father of Michael, John, and foster dad of Ivan.

Index

Studies in the Postmodern Theory of Education

General Editors
Joe L. Kincheloe & Shirley R. Steinberg

Counterpoints publishes the most compelling and imaginative books being written in education today. Grounded on the theoretical advances in criticalism, feminism, and postmodernism in the last two decades of the twentieth century, Counterpoints engages the meaning of these innovations in various forms of educational expression. Committed to the proposition that theoretical literature should be accessible to a variety of audiences, the series insists that its authors avoid esoteric and jargonistic languages that transform educational scholarship into an elite discourse for the initiated. Scholarly work matters only to the degree it affects consciousness and practice at multiple sites. Counterpoints' editorial policy is based on these principles and the ability of scholars to break new ground, to open new conversations, to go where educators have never gone before.

For additional information about this series or for the submission of manuscripts, please contact:

Joe L. Kincheloe & Shirley R. Steinberg
c/o Peter Lang Publishing, Inc.
29 Broadway, 18th floor
New York, New York 10006

To order other books in this series, please contact our Customer Service Department:

(800) 770-LANG (within the U.S.)
(212) 647-7706 (outside the U.S.)
(212) 647-7707 FAX

Or browse online by series:
www.peterlang.com